Women Take Issue

Editorial Group

Lucy Bland
Charlotte Brunsdon
Martin Culverwell
Rachel Harrison
Dorothy Hobson
Trisha McCabe
Frank Mort
Rebecca O'Rourke
Olivia Smith
Christine Weedon
Janice Winship

Additional help from

Janet Batsleer

Exchange Advertisements

Eve Brooks

Women Take Issue
Aspects of Women's Subordination

Women's Studies Group
Centre for Contemporary Cultural Studies
University of Birmingham

Hutchinson of London
in association with
the Centre for Contemporary Cultural Studies,
University of Birmingham

Hutchinson & Co. (Publishers) Ltd
3 Fitzroy Square, London W1P 6JD

London Melbourne Sydney Auckland
Wellington Johannesburg and agencies
throughout the world

First published 1978
© Women's Studies Group 1978

The paperback edition of this book is sold
subject to the condition that it shall not, by
way of trade or otherwise, be lent, resold,
hired out, or otherwise circulated without the
publisher's prior consent in any form of binding
or cover other than that in which it is published
and without a similar condition including this
condition being imposed on the subsequent purchaser

Set in IBM Press Roman

Printed in Great Britain by The Anchor Press Ltd,
and bound by Wm Brendon & Son Ltd,
both of Tiptree, Essex

ISBN 0 09 133600 7 cased
      0 09 133601 5 paper

Contents

Acknowledgements   6

1 Women's Studies Group: trying to do feminist intellectual work *Editorial Group*   7

2 'It is well known that by nature women are inclined to be rather personal' *Charlotte Brunsdon*   18

3 Women 'inside and outside' the relations of production *Lucy Bland, Charlotte Brunsdon, Dorothy Hobson, Janice Winship*   35

4 Housewives: isolation as oppression *Dorothy Hobson*   79

5 Working class girls and the culture of femininity *Angela McRobbie*   96

6 Psychoanalysis and the cultural acquisition of sexuality and subjectivity *Steve Burniston, Frank Mort, Christine Weedon*   109

7 A Woman's World: *Woman* - an ideology of femininity *Janice Winship*   133

8 Relations of reproduction: approaches through anthropology *Lucy Bland, Rachel Harrison, Frank Mort, Christine Weedon*   155

9 *Shirley:* relations of reproduction and the ideology of romance *Rachel Harrison*   176

Bibliography   197

Index   207

Acknowledgements

We would like to thank all the members of the Centre for Contemporary Cultural Studies who have helped in various stages of the production of this book. Special thanks to those who helped with the typing, running off and reading of drafts, particularly in the last rushed weeks. Thanks also to Claire L'Enfant of Hutchinson. Finally, we would not have been able to produce this book without the support of our various households and friends.

1 Women's Studies Group: trying to do feminist intellectual work

Editorial Group

This book has been produced by a group of nine women and two men, some of whom have previously worked together in the Women's Studies Group (WSG) at the Centre for Contemporary Cultural Studies (CCCS). This is a postgraduate research centre where students and teachers, as well as conducting individual research, work collectively in groups organized around areas of shared interest - for example, education, media, women's studies. This form of work allows groups to define their own area of study without the formal division teacher/taught or the constraint of examinations. There is also usually some continuity in group membership which makes it possible to attempt extended and continuing collective work. This work is annually presented to the whole of the department in the summer term and has formed the basis for issues of the journal, *Working Papers in Cultural Studies*.

When we decided to do this book we thought we were deciding to produce the eleventh issue of *Working Papers in Cultural Studies* (1). Ten issues, with only four articles concerning women - it seemed about time. Women's continuing 'invisibility' in the journal, and in much of the intellectual work done within CCCS (although things are changing), is the result of a complex of factors, which although in their particular combination are specific to our own relatively privileged situation, are not unique to it. We want here to outline some of the problems the Women's Studies Group has faced, in a way which gives this book some sort of history, but also attempts to deal with the more general problems of women's studies and trying to do feminist intellectual work.

Our situation, as a group of research students, may seem very removed from that of women trying to introduce non-sexist teaching materials in schools, running women's studies (WS) courses on a shoe-string or trying to do feminist research alone in an unsympathetic department or at home with kids. We think, however, that the very different problems of each specific academic environment in which we try to work as feminists are informed by broadly the same basic issues and needs. We are all involved in some way in challenging both the existing understanding of society, and the role and construction of sex/gender within this, and the ways in which this understanding is achieved and transmitted. It is through the questions that feminism poses, and the absences it locates, that feminist research and women's studies are constituted as one aspect of the struggle for the transformation of society which would make 'women's studies' unnecessary.

Working as a group in an academic context raises in a particular way the problems of the relationship between intellectual and political practice. Our relationship to the Women's Liberation Movement (WLM) *as a group* has been ambiguous. For some of us the WSG is our closest contact with the WLM. Others are more active in relation to women's liberation outside an academic context. This topic, and our disagreements over what our practice should be, dominated our early discussions about taking the journal on. The questions this raised became the problem of whom to address in our writings: how far could we assume our readers to be Marxists, or feminists, or both, or neither? We also had to try to be self-conscious about the use we made of theoretical concepts to help us to understand women's subordination more precisely; to avoid a general tendency in CCCS towards an *un*self-conscious use of theoretical language which is one element in perpetuating knowledge as the property of a few. We do not think that we were, by any means, always successful in distinguishing these uses.

Women's studies in academic institutions

The difficulty with writing this type of account is partly that our own rather limited experience is only one example of the way feminists have worked together since the beginnings of the WLM in the late 1960s. One thing to arise from the diverse practices and perspectives of the WLM was women organizing together both to share experiences, and work collectively towards a knowledge of them, and to interrogate and appropriate 'knowledge' and skills which exclude or ignore women. This both preceded and continues to accompany the establishment of WS courses in academic institutions.

We concentrate on our own experiences as a group in an academic institution not because we consider it the more important but because it is in this way that we have experienced problems concretely. We would argue that these problems are partly constituted through the contradictions of women's studies as an academic field.

The Manchester Conference on Women's Studies in December 1976 identified two major problems confronting women's studies in Great Britain. One was the division between academic and non-academic women's studies, the other the 'amorphous nature of women's studies'. The organizing collective understood the problem of the 'amorphous nature of WS' as largely determined by

> an underlying academic versus non-academic conflict concerning both the structure and content of the conference and the participants to whom it was directed.

We agree that this can contribute to a problem of definition for WS in general but think that it also relates to the considerable diversity, in aims, methods and contents, between WS courses *within* various academic institutions. What the organizing collective define as WS's 'amorphous nature' has also to do with WS in itself being a potentially subversive non-academic set of practices. The established structures of learning are continually challenged in the attempt to construct objects of knowledge and to devise ways of learning that are radical alternatives to the institutions within which they exist. Women's studies, like black studies, as a subject or discipline, has political not academic roots (2), and is constituted through the recognition of economic, ideological, sexual and political subordination and exploitation of a social group. Its political origins mean that it necessarily exists in many different forms, and that its very appearance within an academic context is both the *result* and the *occasion* of struggles inside and outside that context (3).

We have to learn as women together, in many different ways and on many different fronts, often drawing on the collective knowledge of the WLM in areas ranging from self-help health care, aspects of legal and financial (in)dependence and so on, right through to various 'academic' courses (4). WS courses have to fight for recognition and at the same time guard against the inroads of academic respectability, viability and fashionability which incorporate and politically neuter them. We would argue that there are inherent contradictions between the political origins and objectives of WS in the WLM and the academic space that these WS courses occupy. As Hartnett and Rendel (1975) put it:

In essence the dilemma for WS is one of maintaining its own integrity within an educational system having (certain) characteristics while trying to infiltrate and leaven all knowledge.

Moreover the divisions do not work only at the level of 'content', as the Women's Report Collective (1975) point out:

We should be asking what we want from WS. Is it to raise consciousness – to provide ammunition – to change the education system – to produce feminists – or all of these? or none of these?

We deal with this point partly in relation to our own work but first we make four necessarily interrelated points about WS within academic institutions. Firstly, taking a WS option or course can act as a form of consciousness-raising particularly as it is mainly women who take these courses. The content of WS courses consists of material with a personal relevance for the women involved. The course can therefore provide a forum in which to explore issues about, for example, sexuality, as they relate to individuals, and enables the participants both to dispel the neurosis-producing 'it-only-happens-to-me' complex, and to situate personal experience and their subjectively registered responses to them in a sociological and historical context. Secondly, WS courses take a different starting point in specific disciplines – that of women. This takes the form either of the discovery of new empirical material or the privileging of already existing material. It takes women's sphere of activity, previously marginalized, and places it centrally. Thirdly, WS provides a critique of sexism and chauvinism in existing theories, texts and courses. This often arises as part of, and along with, the previous two aspects. This is because working from the point of view of women reveals that there is a systematic absence of this viewpoint, and the *presence* of whole sets of assumptions about women (and, usually, their place in the family). It is thus necessary to begin to formulate an explanatory theory which rests on some notion of women's *structural* subordination.

This in turn leads to the need to develop conceptual tools for feminist analysis. This may mean using already existing, but neglected or taken-for-granted concepts like the 'sexual division of labour'. It may also mean the separation of concepts like 'sex' from 'gender' as Oakley (1972) does, and the development of new concepts with specific meanings – for example the usage of relations of reproduction in Article 8 in this book. These concepts are developed and explored in the attempt to understand the material processes which constitute a social formation structured into division and conflict on the grounds of gender as well as class. The struggle for new ways of understanding the social formation (5) means that a 'feminist perspective' in existing disciplines cannot consist of just a token acknowledgement, somewhere, of women. We would argue that society has to be understood as constituted through the *articulation* of both sex/gender and class antagonisms, although some feminists would accord primacy to sexual division in their analyses.

In relation to our own work, one of our main intellectual and political difficulties has been making effective interventions in work that was going on in CCCS. *How* does WS or feminist research transform existing research and knowledge? Where should we start in the attempt to analyse a social formation as structured through *both* class antagonisms and sex/gender? How do we carry out our work without being sucked into the intellectual field as already constituted, i.e. gaining legitimation at the expense of our feminism, losing sight of the informing politics of our work?

To intervene effectively as feminists in other group areas of interest it seems we would have to conquer the whole of cultural studies, in itself multi-disciplinary, and *then* make a feminist critique of it. Or, the alternative we tended to adopt, we could concentrate on what we saw as the central areas of research *within* the *WSG*, and thus risk our concerns remaining gender-specific – our own concerns: the 'woman question' claimed by, and relegated to, the women. Sporadic attempts to argue against the 'hiving off' of the woman question from this seemingly snug corner were viewed as double-binding other CCCS members – either we had something to say and we should say it, or else we didn't, and so we should stop making everyone feel guilty.

The problems will be familiar to feminists. It is only *if* the problem of women's subordination is recognized, politically, that questions about, for example, sex-differentiation, the invisibility of women, the consideration of gender at a structural level, the sexual division of labour, the role of the family arise at a theoretical and intellectual level. However, these questions do not follow automatically from this political recognition, particularly when the focus of study is the general area of, say, 'Education' and not 'Women and . . .' or 'Women in . . .'. The political/theoretical recognition that women have always already been 'left out' (that the field of study will have been constituted through the taken-for-grantedness, and hence, invisibility, of women's subordination) is only the pre-condition for a feminist critique, and subsequently for feminist research. Thus even if a group consciously make a decision, as the media group did, to move into an area of study more obviously related to feminist concerns — in this case from the study of 'hard' current affairs television to a family programme within the same spectrum, BBC's *Nationwide* — there is no guarantee that the resulting work will be 'feminist'. In this case, the research material *reproduced* traditional biases, with some updating. Thus, for example, the gender of interviewers in relation to the type of interview had not been routinely recorded, except in the case of *obviously* sexist items. Our work always confronts the disparity between the sophistication of analyses of the social formation in terms of class, and the relative underdevelopment of work on the structures of sex/gender. We have tended as a group to address ourselves to the problem of the articulation of these two areas at a theoretical level, and are thus constantly undermined by the lack of specificity in our work. It is this necessity — to do concrete, historically specific research from a feminist perspective — which could be described as the most important thing that we have learnt from our last few years.

Establishing the group

The group started in October 1974. Until that time we had been just two or three individual women amongst about twenty men at CCCS. We had worked in various sub-groups, none of which had a serious concern for women as a focus of study, and found ourselves in isolation interrogating text after text for this major absence. The structured absence of women from most theoretical and academic texts poses acute problems when trying to work with this material through insights from the WLM, and alongside material from the WLM, some of which is in many ways antagonistic to theoretical/academic work *per se*. We were constantly trying to understand the *experience* of the absence of women, at a theoretical level (there must be more to this than meets the eye . . .) — to see how gender structures and is itself structured. Although in some areas, at one level, it is a question of the *absence* of empirical material — for example, there is more data available about *boys* at school than about girls — this absence is always already structured. We can't just say 'what about women?' when the answer to this question involves thinking differently about the whole field or object of study. Because women's lives are structured through their subordination, absent data about women cannot simply be filled in — you cannot just add girls' experience of school to boys' experience of school, because the determinants of this experience are *different,* and have to be understood as such before even the question about girls' experience at school can be asked (see Article 5). However, at this stage, we didn't even raise the question of 'what about women?'. We found it extremely difficult to participate in CCCS groups and felt, without being able to articulate it, that it was a case of the masculine domination of both intellectual work and the environment in which it was being carried out. Intellectually, our questions were still about 'absences'. Socially, but inseparable from our intellectual presence, as one woman put it at the time, we could either strive for a sort of 'de-sexualized' intellectual role, or retain 'femininity' either through keeping quiet, or in an uneasy combination with being 'one of the lads'. These problems could only be seriously discussed in a small women's group, a solution which came directly from the WLM. In part, however, it was the influx in 1974 of several more women intending to work on women that finally precipitated the move to set up a WSG — originally only two of us had a thesis topic on women. When it was set up, the WSG was open to both women and men. This is necessarily the case with most WS courses inside academic institutions. However, it was not until the second term of 1975 that one man joined us. The group was, until then, as self-selective in terms of sex-origin as most WS courses.

Unlike other CCCS groups, the WSG had a supportive function for us as women, analogous to consciousness-raising groups in the WLM, and this to some extent gave it an ambiguous function and status in the CCCS. Again in common with many WS courses we were both a *woman's group* and a *women's studies group.* But this political aspect can create problems (which are perhaps more apparent in a research group with a fairly constant membership than, for example, one-year courses) both in terms of our work, i.e. a support group carrying on academic work and, related to this, in the *way* we carried it on. As women, we are inevitably the subject and object of our study. This creates a tension which at one level delivers the political power of our own work, and at another delivers a particular kind of humour, mode of working and an understanding of the uncertainties we all encounter in our work as women. It is based on the recognition of our common experiences of *femininity*. These considerations and their implications resulted in us being split over the question of whether the group should be *explicitly* closed (to men) in the same way that WLM small groups are. We consequently gave out rather contradictory messages to the rest of the CCCS.

It was in an attempt to deal directly with some of these problems that we proposed, in June 1976, to set up a women's forum (WF), a closed women's group, open to all women at CCCS. We hoped in this way to allow the WSG to continue its intellectual project, while discussion of more general feminist issues at CCCS would take place in the larger group. We also saw the WF as fulfilling wider supportive functions for women at and around CCCS. This group was to be the one through which we could organize as women in a more direct relation to the WLM. The proposal provoked lengthy discussion in a meeting at which it originally seemed that no one opposed it. We would now see this in many ways as the beginnings of a more open discussion of the implications of feminism for the CCCS as a whole.

Work in the Women's Studies Group

In the first term the WSG undertook the task of examining 'Images of Women in the Media' for a BSA Women and the Media Conference in December 1974 (see Butcher, Coward *et al.* 1974). The project not only began to spell out for us the complexities of femininity that underlie any simple use of the descriptive noun 'woman' — what kind of woman (mother, career woman, virgin, etc.), what bit of woman (her face, her hair, her body, etc.) — but plunged us as a group into both the difficulties of collective work and the problem of who to address in our writings. The problem of who to address is still with us, and we have had lengthy debates over it in the production of this book.

These problems have increased since the 'Images' paper, as our work has subsequently been more theoretical. Nevertheless coming together as a group was exciting as well as difficult. Meeting other people in different parts of the country over the 'Images' paper was an enjoyable and useful learning process. The paper wasn't collective because of the time limit on the project and our unfamiliarity with working in this way. But, more importantly, it was probably our different understandings of what we were studying that worked decisively against the possibility of such collective work. Our work in this project was informed in an unrecognized way by different theoretical positions. The 'Images' paper, whilst essentially descriptive, relied implicitly on a theoretical understanding of women's position while not actually being grounded in any such analysis. Then, as now, there was a tendency to either collapse political, intellectual and theoretical differences into emotionally loaded personal differences or to not acknowledge them.

The shift to the 'domestic labour debate' in our next term was a response to what we understood as the lack of 'theory' in the 'Images' paper, and followed the attention given to the debate at the 1974 Women and Socialism Conference in Birmingham. More particularly, this shift was seen as an attempt to consider the relation between class and women's subordination at a theoretical level. But in some senses it was a direct next step from the 'Images' paper. Alongside woman as sex object, it was woman as mother and housewife who we had found to be the primary and determining image of the media. More generally this work represented an educative engagement with the difficult economic categories of Marxism. It also marked the beginnings of our group's attempt to develop a marxist-feminist analysis of women's subordination (see WPCS no. 9).

However, the analysis of women's work in the home seemed incomplete. We wanted to understand how the ideological construction of femininity articulated with the analysis of women's labour in the home. In response to this, we turned to Juliet Mitchell's *Psychoanalysis and Feminism* (1975), but were left in the impasse of the dualism Mitchell's work poses between patriarchy and capitalism (see Article 6). Thus our continuing problem was how to attempt the articulation of sex/gender with class, and the relevance of this for political struggle. Our work on particular texts of feminist theory had noted how the existing separation between sexuality and class was reproduced. For example, the analysis of domestic labour had to some extent been incorporated within existing theories of 'orthodox' Marxism with the continuing exclusion of the specificities of sex and gender. It was precisely because of that separation within theory that we next tried to understand the contradictions of femininity as 'lived' (at the same time holding to class specificity) through a study of the particular historical conjuncture which saw the emergence of the Women's Liberation Movement.

However this proposed project on the sixties eventually collapsed. The reasons for this were complicated, and we do not really agree as a group about their relative importance. We look here at two aspects: the relations within the group, and the relations of the group to CCCS as a whole – because these have become foci of our intellectual and political differences. Firstly, our need for solidarity in relation to CCCS became confused with a supposed collective feminist intellectual position which individuals felt they could not argue against because it was 'individualistic' or anti-feminist. It was difficult both to argue among ourselves inside the group, and, as individual feminists, to articulate different positions in the wider context.

Secondly, the setting up of the Women's Forum in this year (1976-7) meant that the WSG was no longer 'the women's group'. The increasing attention generally – under feminist pressure – to areas where women are central, e.g. the family and the welfare state, led to a large mixed group in 1976-7. This caused a superficial return to the 'neutrality' of intellectual groups in which detached discussion of the *object* of study takes place. New problems emerged, which we would now trace to our failure to recognize the very different ideas we had about what the group should be doing. We were not self-conscious, in a way that could be discussed, about the different attitudes we had to women's studies, both as women and men, but also as women who had had differing contact with the WLM. Instead, we assumed an illusory shared feminist position, which gave us little purchase *as a group* on new work, and meant the atmosphere was rather tense, although still much easier for women to work in than other CCCS groups. All of the men, and some of the women, left the group. It was the residue of this group which returned to early feminist texts, in particular Rowbotham (1973) and Mitchell (1971), in order to establish some common ground from which to work. We soon shifted to what emerged as an underdeveloped theoretical concern for us – the understanding of women's subordination at 'the economic level', i.e. women's position in relation to the processes of capitalist accumulation. Without work in that area the sixties' project, and any other conjunctural/empirical analysis, would be likely to flounder. This area of study was pertinent to us in terms of individual thesis work – outside the group in the local Feminist Research Workshop to which most of us belonged – as well as of interest to some sections of the WLM. But it was also important in terms of arguments we were having at CCCS. It was a level of theoretical engagement which, in using marxist economic concepts to understand women's subordination – even if not straightforwardly slotting women into an already worked-out framework – appeared to engage more directly with other work in CCCS. This became particularly clear when we 'presented' the work to CCCS as a whole at the end of the year.

It was during this period that discussion about this book, in which we had to argue our case in CCCS to write and edit it, began. Over this issue the WSG and some of the Women's Forum came together to form the basis of the editorial group. What finally made the CCCS let us do this book was not just that we had 'proved' ourselves in relation to our theoretical work on the economic level in our presentation (see Article 3 which was written up from that work); it also had to do with playing the tapes of women speaking about their lives as housewives (see

Article 4), a forceful demonstration of women's oppression, and of the political object of our intellectual work. What had started off that year as a disparate group uncertain of its aims had, during these struggles within CCCS, developed a solidarity and purpose which has continued to be worked at during the production of this book.

Conclusion

The difficulties we have found in writing this article emerged most clearly when we came to writing its conclusion. There is a real sense in which this book has been produced by, and written out of the contradictions we have tried to locate in this article. We are a group of women and men who came together to produce this book with differing understandings of what feminist intellectual work is, and should be. This depends partly on how we understand both 'feminism' and 'intellectual work' as political practices and their relation. We all think that feminist intellectual work is both an intellectual and *political* engagement within intellectual work. But we differ on whether this is in itself an adequate political practice, *and* whether political adequacy is a relevant criterion in a direct way for intellectual work. We have different approaches to the relationship between Marxism and feminism in terms of political practice. We differ over what feminism *is* in terms of whether *men* can *be* feminists. Further we differ on whether we should be *primarily* addressing women or men, and whether it is possible to address both simultaneously, in the same terms. We find that we have obscured many of these differences in an attempt to produce an account of where this book came from. This means that we disagree, differently, with the emphases of this article.

We have found producing this book to be a process of political and intellectual education both for ourselves and for some other CCCS members. Our initial reason for wanting to produce the book was fundamental: the continued absence from CCCS of a visible concern with feminist issues. The process of the book's production has involved other members of CCCS in the areas of study and interest we have been working on and has contributed towards making feminism more 'acceptable' within the department. It remains a responsibility for us to ensure that feminism's developing presence as an area of debate and discussion retains and increases its political force. Editorial work has been a unique politicizing experience for us. The hours we have spent together, and the extent to which our consciousness of each other, as women, as feminists, and as men working with women on a feminist project, has been increased, would have seemed impossible this time last year. Having completed the book we do not think that the problems of the group's internal or external relations (to CCCS and the WLM) have been solved in any way.

We can only return to what we see as the central issues. One of the things we want from WS is work which contributes to a feminist analysis of 'how things are' - critiques of existing understandings, the discovery of new material and new questions, and the development of a theoretical understanding of women's subordination under capitalism. It is towards this that we have worked in this book, although we understand the struggle to conduct this work differently, and relate differently to the WLM. We also perceive differently the nature of the contradictions in gaining recognition for the validity of feminist intellectual work, within an academic context, and the terms in which this recognition is granted. These political differences make it impossible for us to agree on a conclusion.

Notes and references

1 *Working Papers in Cultural Studies* was published by CCCS. This book, along with future collections of CCCS work, is being published by CCCS in association with Hutchinson.

2 To our knowledge, there are as yet no *courses* in academic institutions which take the oppression of gay people as their starting point. The oppression of gays features in some WS courses and, for example, courses concerned with, broadly, 'sex, gender and society'. The seminars held at the National Film Theatre in London in the summer of 1977, in conjunction with the 'Gays in Cinema' season could be seen as one of the beginnings of such a focus on gay oppression.

3 The early composition of the WLM, with its tendency to attract young white middle-class women, can be seen as having a direct effect on the establishment of WS courses, and on feminist critiques of existing courses. As many of these women were already involved in education, either as students or teachers, the institutions they were already within presented themselves as obvious sites for the political and ideological struggle that the establishment of women's studies courses represent. These struggles continue, and can be related to the introduction, and attempts to introduce, some form of women's studies or at least non-sexist practice and materials, in junior, primary and secondary schools.

4 Hartnett and Rendell (1975) survey existing WS courses, as do Beardon and Stevenson (1974), who also comment on WS as a field of study. The 1976 Manchester Conference on Women's Studies has produced a report on the discussions at the conference. There is now a WEA Women's Studies Newsletter, available from Croft Cottage, 176 Hagley Road, Stourbridge DY8 2JN. Discussion articles on WS include: 'Should Women Study W-S', *Women's Report* Vol. 4, no. 2, and 'W-8', *Catcall* no. 4 (Sept/Oct 1976). The Women's Research and Resources Centre, 27 Clerkenwell Close, London EC1, keeps an index of feminist research.

5 We are here dependent on Althusser's use of the concept 'social formation', first developed in *For Marx* (1969). Broadly, this conceptualizes 'society' as complexly and contradictorily structured through class divisions at specific levels (economic, political and ideological), each of which possess their own particular history, their own internal laws and dynamics. In that reading, the economic is seen as *determinate* within every social formation, but not always as *dominant*. (In the capitalist social formation the economic level is both

determinate and dominant.) It is precisely the difficulty of using Marxist concepts in the analysis of *women's* subordination that we would see this journal as being partly concerned with.

2 'It is well known that by nature women are inclined to be rather personal'

Charlotte Brunsdon

Judge Ewart James, summing up the case against Corporal Reginald Booth at Winchester Crown Court, said that although women had won 'greater equality' with men in terms of jobs, money and government, the law still gives them their protection in sexual matters. *'It is well known that by nature women are inclined to be rather personal.* They attach themselves to persons. They become fond of people and they are inclined to follow them, and they may follow them to their detriment because they are fond of them,' he said. [my italics]

Guardian, 29 October 1977 (1)

This is not in any way a history of the current British Women's Liberation Movement (WLM). I don't mention most of the things women did, and I particularly don't look at any particular campaigns or struggles. There are groups of women at present trying to put together this history (2). I am just writing one way of understanding some of the characteristics of the early WLM. One of these characteristics is the distinctively personal nature of much WLM writing and practice. I suggest here, as have many feminists, that the personal experience of the *recognition* of a common oppression has been a formative feature of the WLM. The implications of this view have had a rather contradictory effect on the article. I have tried to quote from other women as much as possible, but do so in the context of my own argument, which means that at times the quotations carry the weight of that argument (3).

I am using the sentence, 'It is well known that by nature women are inclined to be rather personal,' to focus this article for two reasons. Firstly, it occurs in a statement that 'manages' the contradiction between women's 'greater equality' and their continuing subordination through reference to what is presented as an innate feminine characteristic. Framing the sentence, we have the judge's confidence that he draws on conventional wisdom. This truth is such that it is depersonalized: 'It is well known. . . .' Secondly, the argument he makes - that 'women are inclined to be rather personal' - has been given a double edge by the WLM, summarized in the slogan 'the personal is political'. I examine some aspects of this association of women with 'the personal' in the second part of the article. Here, I want to briefly look at the causal element in his argument: 'by nature'. In this sentence it is ambiguous: both 'women have rather personal natures' and 'women are naturally rather personal'. This ambiguity focuses on *nature*, as meaning both (or either) human personality (which is seen as being sex-differentiated) and a type of originating cause.

The subordination of oppressed groups, and discrimination against them, is frequently legitimated through reference to 'nature' (4). It is usually a case for inferior natural characteristics or against unnatural practices (5). My concentration here on the particular resonance of arguments 'from nature' about women is not in any way to claim that women are the only group affected by this type of argument.

The specificity of the argument from nature in relation to women has several threads, which I present very schematically. Biological and anatomical difference is central to all of them, and I would suggest that it is the *reality* of this difference which gives these arguments their force. I am thus suggesting that arguments from nature have an ideological centrality in the subordination of women, precisely because their reference point is always biological and anatomical – natural – difference. It is these arguments which feminists meet in every area of our practice, and it is possible to see the beginnings of the WLM as the start of a self-conscious organization against them.

I concentrate on the ideological level in this article for two reasons. Firstly, I would argue that one of the central features of the WLM is 'a breakthrough in consciousness'. This is not to suggest that femininity is 'false consciousness', and feminism somehow a transcendence of, or 'outside', ideology. It is to try and recognize that the beginnings of the WLM was perceived by many of the women involved as a break from the traditional leftist practice of organizing around the point of production and economic exploitation, into the uncharted implications of organizing round a 'sense' (Rowbotham) or 'instinct' (Mitchell) of oppression (6). That is, organization that started *from* consciousness – that partly engaged *first* with the ideological level – by challenging the 'naturalness' of our condition.

Our window on the world is looked through with our hands in the sink and we've begun to *hate that sink and all it implies – so begins our consciousness.*
Williams, Twort, Bachelli (1970, p. 31)

Secondly, ideology remains central to an understanding of women's continuing subordination in days when 'women have won greater equality with men', and discrimination on grounds of sex is now meant to be illegal. We still do not really understand the particular relations in the historical articulation of economic, political and ideological factors which produce the 'intimate oppression' of femininity as lived (7).

Women by nature

Juliet Mitchell points to one 'argument from nature' about women in the approach to a discussion of the consequences for women of the possible transformation of the 'mode of reproduction' through readily available contraception:

The biological function of maternity is a universal atemporal fact, and as such has seemed to escape the categories of Marxist historical analysis. However, from it is made to follow the so-called stability and omnipresence of the family, if in very different forms. Once this is accepted, women's social subordination – however emphasised as an honourable but different role . . . can be seen to follow inevitably as an insurmountable bio-historical fact. The causal chain then goes: maternity, family, absence from production and public life, sexual inequality.

Mitchell (1971, p. 106)

Mitchell here traces an 'argument from nature' which finds women's subordination natural by understanding 'the family' as natural through women's natural procreative ability. She goes on to deconstruct this argument by differentiating the structures of sexuality, reproduction and socialization of children, pointing to their historical, rather than necessary, combination in the modern family.

Leonore Davidoff (1976, p. 125) points to another type of 'argument from nature', which makes a woman *closer* to nature than men.

Since women are for a longer period of time more involved with physiological processes (menstruation, childbirth, lactation) they are seen as closer to nature than men. . . . Men are seen as people, but women are ambiguous simply by the fact of being also conscious beings who are not men but who do take some part in the culture of society. Yet women are active beings in their performance as a 'mediating agency' between nature and culture: the raw and the cooked.

Sheila Rowbotham (1973, p. 7) makes a related point about the cultural construction of feminity in the 1950s: '. . . social science contributed towards a notion of feminity in which baby-doll became a new natural-savage substitute'. Here we have elements of an argument which finds women *more* natural than men - somehow, outside history, and both central to, and absent in, culture. As Trevor Millum (1975, p. 166), commenting on the connotations of exterior settings in advertising in women's magazines, puts it:

It is the woman who maintains this connection, who is in touch with the pastoral past, who guards the health of the community by her adherence to the old stable values, by her functions of childbearing, nursing and rearing, and of cooking and ministering, and the assertion of common sense drawn from the wisdom of the earth: age old tasks which never change. . . .

Perhaps the most important 'argument from nature' for women is that which reads gender difference as the natural expression, rather than the cultural constitution of sexual difference (Mead 1960, Oakley 1972). The centrality of this argument, which underlies and reinforces others, is in the way it permeates every aspect of our understanding of sexual difference. 'Just like a girl' - 'big boys don't cry': we live in a culture of *real* men and *true* women.

We can thus outline, very crudely, the main elements in the ideological matrix which finds women's subordination 'natural'. Naturally different to men through their procreative ability, women are understood as closer to nature than men, more natural; and feminity, as culturally constituted, is seen as the natural expression of these differences, finding its natural fulfilment in the family. It was partly to this matrix of 'naturalness' and its contradictory manifestations that much early WLM practice can be seen as directed. I look briefly here, in a very *general* way at some elements of this practice (8).

At one level it involved the attempt to separate woman from her definition through her procreative ability and her sexual attractiveness to men – *a definition through her body.* Of the Miss World contestants it was written:

> Their condition is the condition of all women, *born to be defined by their physical attributes, born to give birth,* or, if pretty, born lucky, a condition which makes it possible and acceptable within the bourgeois ethic for girls to parade, silent and smiling to be judged on the merits of their figures and faces. [my italics]
> Women's Liberation Workshop, London (1970)

'Born to give birth' – in the period when:

> For the first time there is the possibility that maternity will become an *option* for all women, rather than a vocation they are trained for.
> Delmar (1972)

But when there still remained what Lee Comer (1971) called:

> ... this one central assumption that underlies everything that pertains to women, that a woman's true purpose in life and the pinnacle of her fulfilment is motherhood.

This contradiction has several aspects which have been approached differently. Firstly, what became the fourth demand of the WLM (9), 'free contraception and abortion on demand', the demand for control over our reproductive capacity (10), to choose whether or not to have babies:

> We demand that women have control over their bodies. We believe this is denied us until we can decide whether to have children or not and when we have them. This requires free and available contraception and free abortion on demand.
> *Shrew,* February 1971

Secondly, there was an attempt to break down 'the total identification of women with child-care' (*Shrew,* March 1971): the double-bind which meant women were often either isolated at home with young children, or feeling guilty if their children were cared for in nurseries. The result was both the demand for state provision of twenty-four nurseries, and attempts to demystify the relationship between mothers and their children (Comer 1971, 1974). This often meant trying to find new *forms* of child-care, the active involvement of men; and the endeavour to create a new *content* of child-care, which did not reproduce stereotypical feminine and masculine roles (11).

But women are also 'born to be defined by their physical attributes' in a different sense. The ephemeral phrase 'sex object' was used to condense a whole set of recognitions about this definition through our bodies. Women are reduced to our sexuality, which is at the same time, not *our* sexuality but a sexuality defined in relation to men – both passive and a commodity: a sexuality used to sell men cars, cigars and liquor, and women the commodities to allow us to achieve the ideal which sells us the stuff (12).

No longer the aloof expressionless clothes peg of the '50s the model is required to be 'natural' – however this so called 'naturalness' of the latterday model girl is not allowed to obtrude on the product being sold, rather as Chrissy [the model being interviewed] pointed out 'the model and the product merge' – indeed they are both goods for sale.

Elyse and Bridget (1971)

The commercial exploitation involved in, and the inherent contradiction in the publicity of the make-up, deodorants, bras, girdles, fashions, hair cosmetics which would make us *naturally* just how we were *meant* to look, smell and feel, provided an immediate focus for both discussion and action (13). One example is 'Some thoughts on the successful "think women stink" advertising campaign, or why one woman feels it's worthwhile getting uptight about vaginal deodorants':

It seems pretty obvious that the advertisers' copy equates the natural odours of a woman's body with dirt, the word clean/cleanliness occurs over and over again. The other obvious drift is the use of terms associated with medicine, e.g. gynaecologist, hospitals, etc., as if women have an illness that only vaginal deodorants could cure.

R. Johnson (1969)

The attempt to separate woman from her definition through her procreative ability revealed a major contradiction. We might be defined through our bodies, but our bodies were at the same time unknown to us. We might know, through the years of 'problem pages', to avoid chips and 'all greasy foods' if we didn't want to get fat or spotty, that we should regularly apply grease to our faces if we wanted to keep our complexions (always take care not to pull or rub the sensitive skin round the eyes), but many of us didn't know what the doctor saw when we had an internal examination, or what a clitoris was. Sheila Rowbotham (1973):

Think for example how we learn even our psychology and physiology from our oppressers. We substitute our own experience of our genitals, our menstruation, our orgasm, our menopause, for an experience determined by men. We are continually translating our own immediate fragmented sense of what we feel into a framework which is constructed by men.

The attempt to separate our selves from a definition through our bodies at the same time manifested itself in the determination to reclaim them, through learning about them ourselves:

We think that the first self-examination should be about getting to know what your vaginas and cervices look like rather than establish the presence or absence of an infection. In the women's movement we demand the control of our own bodies –

self-examination is about understanding our potential for health, while most doctors are taught to concern themselves only with disease.

'Notes by a women's health group,' *Spare Rib* 21

We began to try and understand our own sexuality, rather than our sexuality defined in relation to men.

From our own position of growing awareness and consciousness of our selves, we have no further needs of male definitions of our sexuality; they are obsolete. From now on women want to hear from each other, to construct a body of knowledge which corresponds to reality.

P. Whiting (1972)

This had very different implications for different women. Perhaps a choice for celibacy, perhaps struggling for change in heterosexual relationships, perhaps 'coming out' as lesbians (14): 'For the first time in my life I was not ashamed of being a woman and a lesbian' (Bruley 1976).

... inclined to be rather personal

The WLM has shown that we have to understand women's relationship to 'the personal' in several different ways: in terms of women's structural position within the 'production and reproduction of material life' (see Article 3), how this is understood and represented politically, and ideologically, and how women live their lives within and through these terms (see Articles 4, 5 and 7). It is in the interrelation of these different levels that we find some of the elements which contribute to the particular power and, eventually, if remaining within these terms, limitations, of much of the experiential writing of the early WLM.

We attempt to outline some aspects of women's structural position in the next article in this book. Here I want to concentrate on the way that the WLM began to challenge and transform some of the definitions and representations of women's situation in our society which underlie our inclination to be 'rather personal'. I argue that this involved a *personal* engagement, at the level of consciousness that has been a precondition for analyses of women's situation which attempt to grasp the elements that structure this consciousness. Thus, I argue that the discovery of the politics of the personal is *central* in understanding women's subordination, but that remaining within the politics of personal experience will not fundamentally transform this subordination.

Defined primarily through our destinies as wives and mothers - to be somebody else's private life - women are principally placed, politically, ideologically and economically, in 'the personal sphere' of the family.

The 'family', as it is experienced, is the woman and the children *in* the house, the flat or the room and the man who comes and goes.

Williams, Twort, Bachelli (1970)

The Red Collective (1971) argued:

> The domestic unit is the institutionalised expression of the dissociation of emotional and work life, and, it is within the domestic unit that women live. Women therefore live their lives concretely more within one side of the capitalist fragmentation of work and emotionality, in the sphere of the exclusively private and personal, the primarily emotional.

This sphere is understood as radically apolitical, both *outside* 'politics' and as natural, undetermined by the mode of production (Brunsdon and Morley 1978). Through this women have a political status which is either *exceptional,* and involves a precarious juggling with their femininity (Butcher 1977; *Images of Women* 1974) - compare the press treatment of Margaret Thatcher and Golda Meir - or, alternatively, an apolitical status as housewives (consumers). The implications of this apolitical status when women take political action as housewives is sometimes that it can be represented and understood as non-political. Thus Michele Mattelaut (1975), discussing the role of militant action by women in the downfall of the Popular Unity government in Chile (15); argues:

> Paradoxically, the peculiar element which the Right was counting on, and which it used with impunity, arose precisely from a sacred part of the dominant ideology - the division between women and politics. This separation, once unconsciously present in every individual . . . allowed the bourgeoisie to present the women's new activity as devoid of political content and to have it accepted as such. Traditional symbols and values which unequivocally defined the meaning of women's behaviour were relied upon to legitimise these demonstrations. Demonstrations were seen as the spontaneous reaction of the most apolitical sector of public opinion, brought together and activated by a natural survival instinct.

Sue Sharpe (1972) summarized this 'division between women and politics' in terms of cultural meaning: 'Women mean love and the home, while men stand for work and the external world.'

It has been argued that a large part of the unrecognized work that women perform in this personal sphere is *emotional* work; the emotional centre for both men and children:

> Women provide the intimate personal relationships which are not sanctioned in the work organization, although the system itself is dependent on the maintenance of this emotional outlet. Women are made synonymous with softness and tenderness, love and care, something you are glad to come home from work to.
> Sharpe (1972)

That is, although women generally carry the responsibility for the day-to-day running of the home at a material level (shopping, cooking, cleaning, etc.), they are also responsible for keeping it running *emotionally.*

> A woman needs time alone - after a day of being a public servant to the rest of the family, of giving out all the time, of being open to all demands. . . .
> Williams, Twort, Bachelli (1970)

Part of the social acquisition of femininity is the learning of these *personal* skills (Bellotti 1975; Sharpe 1976; Loftus 1974).

> This woman lore is a delicate art, half imparted by other women, half learned from experience. She attunes herself to him, she picks up the slightest quiver of resentment, nurses his vanity with tenderness, follows the flow of his speech, responds to his rhythm.
>
> Rowbotham (1969)

A necessary learning for survival, and the way to what has been understood as success for a woman: 'getting her man'.

Women's place in this personal world is contradictory. For women, the personal world is constructed as central – to be a woman without the personal fulfilment of fulfilling the personal desires of others, and tending to their needs, is to fail to be a true woman. Further, the values associated with the home are designated *human* values – basic, central and natural; it is the sphere of personal freedom, of love, of familial relations (Davidoff, L'Esperance and Newby 1976; Zaretsky 1976). However, this world and these concerns are largely invisible in the 'real' world of commodity production which is 'a man's world' but which is nevertheless dependent on the home world. Sheila Rowbotham (1973, p. xv) wrote of the radical potential of women's situation:

> Women as a group span both the world of commodity production, and production and reproduction in the home. In their own lives the two coexist painfully. Traditionally, the interior, private work of the home is feminine and thus the integration of women into the public work of work and industry is only partial. The contradiction which appears clearly in capitalism between family and industry, private and public personal and impersonal, is the fissure in women's consciousness through which revolt erupts.

Juliet Mitchell examines, in *Woman's Estate* (1971), the particular political and cultural context of the birth of the WLM in the 1960s (16). Changing black consciousness (Black Power, Black is Beautiful), the anti-Vietnam war movement, an expanding education system and 'the student revolt' were formative in the consciousness of the mainly white middle class women who first began organizing together as *women*. Mitchell finds another element in the 'politics of experience': 'an analysis of society from the perspective of one's self' which she traces directly to R. D. Laing and anti-psychiatry (17):

> In the ideology of capitalist society, *women* have always been the chief repository of feelings. They are thus among the first to gain from the radical 'capture' of emotionality from capitalist ideology for political protest movements.
>
> Mitchell (1971, p. 38)

She thus points to the transformation in the value accorded to personal experience present in the radical movements of the late sixties.

The dependence on direct experience is one of the aspects of our oppression –

the culturally limited representation and exclusion of our experience is one of the conditions of our subordination.

This inability to find ourselves in existing culture as we experience ourselves is true of course for other groups besides women. The working class, black, national minorities within capitalism. . . .

Rowbotham (1973, p. 35)

For a subordinate class or group, thinking only through direct experience and common sense, does not allow the construction of a coherent oppositional world view, although it may provide the basis for limited political action (Gramsci 1971; Nichols and Armstrong 1976; Harris 1968). Rather, it produces an understanding of events as episodic and random, in which personal experience is the strongest continuity, and direct experience exists as the only form of 'proof'. What is experienced may be in contradiction to available explanations, but it is very difficult to work out coherently why or understand how. So despite *the experience* of contradiction, what is often 'proved' is the naturalness of the way things are.

It is partly within these contexts that the distinctively personal character of much WLM writing and practice can be understood. We have to hold not only the background of the sixties - the political upheavals, the availability of the Pill, the increasingly important role of women as consumers, the 'sexual sell' - with women's 'privileged' place in the personal sphere and its particular contradictions, but also the forms of consciousness of oppressed groups and classes - the reliance on direct experience in relation to fragmentary and partial access to coherent ways of thinking about the world which only confirm subordination. The WLM began to piece together a way of understanding the world from *the point of view of women,* which *necessarily* drew on individual experience.

At a very simple level, it could be said that the WLM began to explore what Simone de Beauvoir called woman's 'otherness', Betty Freidan's 'the problem that has no name'. To examine through 'a sense of oppression' the experience of being a woman in class society.

To be born a woman has been to be born, within an allotted and confined space, into the keeping of men.

Berger (1972, p. 46)

The beginnings of the WLM was partly concerned with *recognizing* this space - as 'allotted and confined'.

The present inability of 'she' to speak for more than herself is a representation of reality. . . .

Rowbotham (1973, p. 34)

Everytime a woman describes to a man any experience which is specific to her as a woman she confronts his recognition of his own experience as normal.

Rowbotham (1973, p. 35)

It is 'allotted and confined', not just in terms of the type of jobs we can do or what we get paid for them, the provision of child-care facilities, the availability of contraceptives and abortion, but also in terms of how *we,* as well as men, experience and think of ourselves.

We have been defined negatively in relation to the culture into which we have been born: our experience has tended to be made invisible, and in the face of male definitions we have, until recently, kept quiet.

Dalston Study Group (1976, p. 76)

Society has made us women in a male-defined world. Locked inside heterosexual couples most women never break from the bondage of father or husband. The ideological hold of patriarchy persists to make women feel weak, passive or dependent. Our relationships with each other are usually governed by jealousy and competition.

Bruley (1976, p. 21)

These relatively recent statements draw on the strength of being involved in a movement which is women-only (18). The exclusion of men from the movement has to be understood as an essential element in women learning to speak for and of themselves:

The most common ailment among oppressed women is lack of confidence usually manifested in inarticulateness or incoherence.

R. Larne (1969)

But it was not only a question of confidence; it was also a question of breaking through a primary definition of one's self in relation to men:

But, all in all, they some way felt that they didn't really feel second class in every cell of their bodies, and refused themselves any real feeling of fervour, possibly because in some way it might mean betraying their men. At the next meeting we voted to exclude men, because we knew it would be more difficult without them.

J. Williams (1969)

The exclusion of men was, at this stage, a decision that demanded constant justification:

The next meeting we held we decided not to have men because we wanted to work things out amongst ourselves. One man came in fact to this meeting and kept saying we must have a theoretical reason to exclude him. We said we didn't have one but we were fed up with being told by men what we ought to think about ourselves and them.

Rowbotham (1972, p. 95)

The political and theoretical reasons for a women-only movement began to come clearer through being in women-only meetings:

The separatist politics of Women's Liberation may have come out of one of the chief manifestations of women's oppression: their diffidence, but it certainly debouches straight into its central theory – that it is women as a group who are oppressed, and that, though all oppressed groups should work to a point of solidarity with each other, their own understanding of their own situation comes from their own analysis.

Mitchell (1971, p. 58)

One of the men said that, by coming to our meeting, he was joining the movement. We explained to him that just as whites cannot, by virtue of their colour, join the black liberation movement, so men cannot join the WLM.

Shrew, August 1971

This clarity came from what could in general terms be described as consciousness-raising – the beginnings of the development of a group consciousness. The specific organizational form of consciousness-raising was the small local group, which was usually closed for some period of its existence.

In order to become an effective small group it is necessary to relate and trust one another as a group. To attain this closeness as a group we can talk together at weekly meetings on a personal level. . . . Once this close knit friendship has been attained we should have the basis of an effective group.

Diana (1971)

There have by now been many accounts of consciousness-raising groups, although few circulate outside the WLM (19). It is a practice which has many, many aspects – no two groups ever talk about exactly the same things in the same way, and each woman's experience of the process is different. Its insights have been differently understood in ways which have led to different political, theoretical and anti-theoretical positions and practices. I write here, as a feminist and a socialist, a very partial description of what seem to me important elements in the context of trying to think about the importance of the 'personal' for women.

Much early WLM writing could be described as consciousness-raising, if consciousness-raising is understood, at a very basic level, as a process/practice through which women began to make 'she' speak for more than 'herself' by first learning to speak *for and of herself.* And this often from a situation akin to that Friedan had described, particularly as it was mainly white middle class women who first became involved in Women's Liberation.

They did not lack *things.* On the contrary they often had too many things. But they felt that their lives were empty. They did not know who they were or what they wanted to become. *It was by no means apparent that their situation could be understood politically. How could you organise around a sense of emptiness?* [my italics]

Rowbotham (1973)

The (pre)beginnings of one London group:

On Peckham Rye in South London there is a one o'clock club – financed and run by the GLC parks department – for women and their children under 5. Over a period of 18 months a group of about six women were meeting there in the afternoons with their children, and talking, mainly about their children, their hair, their husbands and their homes. The chatter seemed to have an umbrella over it – an umbrella of depression (misery). This torpor was by no means such a concrete fact that it could be talked about objectively.

J. Williams (1969)

Earlier work had pointed to the contradictions in women's situation (20). For example, Hannah Gavron, in her study of the conflicts of housebound mothers had concluded:

The role of woman today is incredibly ambivalent. There is an air of confusion which hangs over the whole question of women, their functions in society, which seems at times to extend to every aspect of their activities.

Gavron (1966, p. 129)

Henri Lefebvre had *noticed* women's particular situation, but failed to allow it any specificity *from the point of view of woman* in his analysis:

... the misery of *everyday life,* its tedious tasks, humiliations reflected in the lives of the working classes and especially of women, upon whom the conditions of everyday life bear heaviest. . . .

Lefebvre (1971, p. 35)

Lefebvre *recognizes* the effects of women's structural position, but what the WLM began to do was to argue that the construction of femininity through our destinies as wives and mothers, and hence women's responsibility for the day-to-day running of the home, materially and emotionally, whether or not they also did paid work, was both *oppressive* to women and was *necessary* for the continuation of the 'system'. Women were in a position of structural subordination, which was both most hidden and most apparent in the female experience of everyday life; hidden, because the female experience of everyday life is confined to women, while the male experience is generalized, understood as *the* experience: women have a women's *page* while men have a newspaper. Apparent, only when we begin to articulate that experience, organize around it. The WLM has made a sustained assault on an understanding of everyday life constructed in masculine hegemony (21): an understanding which takes women's subordination for granted, just as black movements have exposed the taken-for-granted racism of this (white) culture. And in doing this the WLM questions what the left too has taken for granted: 'The intimate oppression of women forces a re-definition of what is personal and what is political' (Rowbotham 1973: xi). Everyday life is broken open, revealed as structured through domination and subordination at both its most intimate and banal levels. Sheila Rowbotham wrote of *The Feminine Mystique:*

Her book was a revelation to many women because it was so determinedly about everyday matters. And most of our lives are 'everyday'. It includes all those little things which became so important because women encountered them over and over again.

Rowbotham (1973, p. 5)

She has also, through her own experience, tried to trace the changing consciousness of the women on the student left who were most involved in the beginnings of the WLM:

> The Ford's women also helped to make the question of women's specific oppression easier to discuss on the left. At first the men would only admit that working class women had anything to complain about. Very defensively at first, and with no theoretical justification, only our feelings, women on and around the student left began to try and connect those feelings to the Marxism they had accepted only intellectually before.

Rowbotham (1972)

The practice of consciousness-raising is that of becoming conscious of being a woman in a man's world, of how each individual inhabits the structures of femininity. It is a process through which women began to understand our individual experience as being structured by being part of an oppressed group.

Sharing oppressive experiences with other women gives them the understanding that the situations described are not personal but social. The awareness that revealed that problems are common to all the women in the group consequently shifts the attention away from one's own inadequacies towards finding the real causes of these problems and gives a perspective that can lead to action. It also gives strength to go back to those inadequacies and start to change them.

Tufnell Park (1971)

It is the process of discovering the way that personal experience is *at the same time* not only unique and individual but also gender specific. The process through which gender specificity was recognized was precisely one of speaking from and to individual experience. Consciousness-raising developed through the process of putting back the 'WO' in 'MAN', of placing *centrally* the personal experience of 'the 51 per cent minority group'.

However, this process demands its own transformation, the placing of the now 'present' woman within an understanding of class society, in order to understand the particular historical and structural determinants on her previous 'absence'. This attempt is fraught with contradictions and difficulties which exist at different levels (22). The making of a feminist consciousness in the finding of a *common* oppression is a labour which must recognize the *different* oppression of black women, lesbians, of older women, working class women, as well as those women most articulate within the dominant culture, young, straight, white middle class women. The attempt to move beyond 'experience knowing' is complexly caught in its own origins, unless it recognizes *more* than sexism.

Gay Liberation and Women's Liberation have both pointed to the social construction of the sex/gender identity which is lived, with whatever difficulty, by the individual in class society. We have argued that men are masculine and women are feminine in a relation of domination and subordination which is partly sustained through the ideological construction of sexuality as heterosexual genitality - thus tied to reproduction (23). As pointed out earlier, this challenges the 'naturalness' of the images and roles of women in our society. By extension, it also challenges the 'naturalness' of the feelings through which we experience ourselves, particularly those structured through the major sphere of personal life, the family. One of the implications of this argument is that it displaces the individual as the originating and unique 'source' of the feelings through which experience, by pointing to the social constraints of this experience. We see women's 'natural inclination' to be 'rather personal' as specific to women's situation.

One implication of finding the personal political is the recognition that the personal is political in a class society which defines it as apolitical. One of our difficulties becomes how to understand this connection precisely, to make a politics that is more than personal. To avoid interrogating the personal is to miss the specificity of women's oppression as lived, but to remain within this interrogation if to remain where our subordination places us. There is no easy fit between theoretical knowledge and consciousness which does not tend to dismiss or reduce one or the other, or of the relation between the intimate politics of a small group and a wider political activity. We have somehow to hold the necessary articulation of female experience (our oppression lies partly in the invisibility of this experience) with the struggle to understand the determinants on this experience to allow us to change it at a more than individual level (24).

Acknowledgements

I am very grateful to Barbara Carter, Rowena Clayton, Catherine Hall and Janice Winship for struggling through this piece at various draft stages. It's not their fault that it is as it is.

Notes and references

1 Booth, in what became known as the 'Casanova Corporal' case, faced nine charges, including procuring women to have unlawful sexual intercourse and obtaining or attempting to obtain money by deception. He was sentenced to one year's imprisonment.

2 They can be contacted through the Women's Research and Resources Centre in London, 27 Clerkenwell Close, London EC1.

3 This may well mean that I have implicated other women in a position that they would not hold.

4   Not specifically in this context, Williams (1976) examines changes in the use and meanings of 'nature'. Williamson (1978) discusses 'nature as a referent system' in her examination of advertisements.

5   These arguments are widespread in a way which means they cannot really be referenced to particular authors as *sources*. The debate around intelligence testing and innate ability provides one focus. Much writing on 'race' and the justification of discrimination against ethnic groups provide another. The representation of homosexuality as a perversion is a third. What seems important is that 'arguments from nature' are used both at a common sense level: 'it's only human nature', 'it's unnatural', and (consciously and unconsciously) within more theoretically elaborated systems of thought.

6   Rosalind Delmar (1972):

> Another new feature of modern feminism is its analysis of ideology. American feminist groups started to discuss the visible manifestations of women's day-to-day oppression. This led to a critique of 'male chauvinism': the ideology of male domination.

I concentrate here mainly on the British context, between 1969 and 1972. I do not look at the extent of the important American influence.

7   Some of the other articles in this journal examine different theorizations of women's subordination, while some are more concerned with femininity as lived. I am concerned here with what I would see as the precondition of this work: the recognition of women's oppression as it was posed by the WLM.

8   The generality of my argument should not be mistaken for a *general* overview of the WLM in Britain. This piece is very selective – I hardly touch on the politics outside the personal, and this gives a rather misleading impression. The two collections of British WLM writings, Wandor (1972) and Allen, Saunders and Wallis (1974), provide more of a basis for an overview. There is also the consideration that the particular politics of the WLM means that much of its history remains as local and personal knowledge, unwritten, and only partly and fragmentarily accessible in old leaflets, conference papers and publications. My own involvement began in 1971.

9   I do not here consider all of the first four demands on the WLM. The continuing definition of woman through her procreative capacity is sustained by, and sustains, women's differential socialization, education, employment opportunities and pay and trade union activity. The two demands I have not discussed are those for equal pay (see Article 3) and equal education and opportunity. The 1974 conference in Edinburgh added demands for 5) legal and financial independence for women, and 6) an end to discrimination against lesbians and the right to our own self-defined sexuality.

10   Ehrenreich and English (1974), and Oakley (1976), discuss the exclusion of women from control over reproduction.

11   *Out of the Pumpkin Shell* (1975) is one account of running a Women's Liberation playgroup - in Birmingham. The other most accessible accounts are those in Wandor (1972).

12   Anne Koedt's 'The myth of the vaginal orgasm' (1970) was an influential pamphlet on female sexuality.

13   The London Women's Liberation workshop manifesto (1970) had as its second point: 'We are commercially exploited by advertisements, television and press'. There was a demonstration at the 1969 Festival of London Stores where Miss Nelbarden Swimwear was appearing (*Shrew*, July 1969). An early account of the Miss World demonstration (*Shrew*, November/December 1969) appeared in the same issue as a report of a group discussion on wearing make-up.

14   Myers, Mitchell, Kay and Charlton (1976) discuss the changes in their own lives since becoming involved in the WLM. Gay Liberation Front started in 1970, and an adequate account of the recognition of lesbians' oppression would have to chart the struggle within GLF *and* the WLM. Wilson (1974) raises some of the issues of gay politics in the WLM.

15   I know that Chile is Chile, not England, but I think the point still holds. Jo O'Brien (1971) makes a similar point about our historical knowledge of British women:

> It is acceptable for women to act over food prices because this accords with the idea that they are, and always have been, domestic centred. We do not hear of the female trade unionists in that town, the women who formed the large Nottingham Female Political Union in 1838 to support Chartism and the numerous female political associations that were scattered all over the country at the time. Such activity does not agree with common assumptions about the apolitical nature of women.

16   Rowbotham (1972) stresses the importance of the campaign led by Lil Billocca and the fishermen's wives to improve the safety of trawlers in 1968, and the 1968 Ford's machinists' strike, in giving women the sense of the possibility of effective organization.

17   See R. D. Laing (1967) and D. Cooper (1968).

18   The Dalston Study Group's comment is made in an article which suggests that the 1976 Conference on Patriarchy drew on traditionally masculine, rather than feminist, modes of organizing. Sue Bruley's pamphlet explicitly contrasts several years of involvement in a left group with the experience of a consciousness-raising group.

19 The most accessible British accounts are Sue Bruley's (1976), those in Wandor (1972), and sections in Mitchell (1971) and Rowbotham (1973). Roberta Henderson (1976) considers the problem of 'consolidating consciousness'.

20 See Rapaport and Rapaport (1971).

21 See footnote 25, page 74, for the usage of masculine hegemony (sorry).

22 *Conditions of Illusion* collects writings of the WLM between 1972 and 1974 which give some idea of the diversity of developments. This collection does not include much writing from a separatist political position, which is another distinct development. Rowbotham (1977) discusses some of the developments in the WLM.

23 See Articles 3, 6, 8 and 9 for different approaches to theorizing women's subordination in relation to reproduction.

24 The reader is here better directed beyond the confines of this article. As far as reading goes, perhaps to periodicals and magazines like *Red Rag, Gay Left, Spare Rib, Women's Report, Catcall, Scarlet Woman.* Most of these can be obtained through the Publication and Distribution Co-operative, 27 Clerkenwell Close, London EC1R 0AT.

3 Women 'inside and outside' the relations of production

Lucy Bland, Charlotte Brunsdon, Dorothy Hobson, Janice Winship

Introduction

We have attempted here to work on the articulation of sex/gender and class in an understanding of women's subordination. We have tried to hold on to 'the two-fold character' of 'the materialist conception' of the 'production and reproduction of immediate life' which is posed, though inadequately developed, by Engels in his preface to the first edition, 1884, of *The Origin of the Family, Private Property and the State*.

What we have learnt through feminism – particularly in relation to women's position within the patriarchal relations of the family (1), their 'economic' position as wives and mothers, and ideological position within femininity – sits uneasily with what we know of the capitalist accumulation process. For an adequate analysis we have to work simultaneously with class and patriarchal relations. We have to interrogate the concepts of capital from a knowledge and recognition of women's subordination.

Women's relation to capital is most obvious in their role as wage labourers. However, the specificity of their position economically and ideologically within social production is predicated on women's role as reproducers of labourers, in the family. At the same time, it is this role in the family which limits the extent to which we can *understand* women's subordination *only* through the economic relations of capital. We are, therefore, directed 'outside' the relations of capital to the patriarchal relations between women and men which capital 'takes over', and to the particular ideological constitution of femininity that those relations construct.

We work briefly in three main areas:

1 Women's work in the home.
2 The state's contribution to women's subordination.
3 Women's waged work.

We conclude with a piece on the equal pay and sex discrimination legislation, which seems to us to represent a condensation of the contradictions of women's continuing subordination, and which appears to operate through these contradictions.

Women working in the home

So Oliver assures Chloe, when she complains about the burden of the children. And who pays, he asks? Not you, but me. Yes, thinks Chloe, in her heart, but your money is easily earned. I pay with my time and energy, my life itself.

Fay Weldon, *Female Friends*

I have been married for two years this December. My wife is now 19, and I am 20. My problem is that she never does the housework willingly. I have always got to ask her or to tell her to do it, and then she does it with resentment. I have tried many ways to get her to do it, and she still doesn't. I work nights – four out of seven – and my wife works a five-day week, and I always seem to land up doing the housework after a hard night's work.

I don't really mind helping, but she never appreciates it, and never understands how I feel. Our marriage is perfect, apart from this one thing, which we are always quarrelling about.

Letter in the *Sun*, 14 November 1977

Feminists have consistently located the site of what Sheila Rowbotham (1973) calls woman's 'intimate oppression' as her role within the family. As Juliet Mitchell puts it:

> Quite simply, how do we analyse the position of women? What is the woman's concrete situation in contemporary capitalist society? What is the universal or general area which defines her oppression? The family and the psychology of femininity are clearly crucial here. However inegalitarian her situation at work (and it is invariably so) it is within the development of her feminine psyche and ideological and socio-economic role as mother and housekeeper that woman finds the oppression that is hers alone. As this defines her, so any movement for her liberation must analyse and change this position. (1971, p. 14)

She argues that the key structures of women's situation (which combine to form the complex unity which determines her position within society) are production, reproduction (of children), sexuality and the socialization of children (Mitchell 1971, p. 101). We go on to examine women's production outside the home later in this article (1), but are first concerned with Mitchell's other three structures, which in our society intermesh in the family, and woman's 'ideological and socio-economic role as mother and housekeeper'.

The early writings of the current (post-1969) women's movement (2) in this area, following the pioneering work of Friedan (1963) and Gavron (1966), had first concentrated on the articulation of the *experience* of housework (3). The concern was primarily to bring to *visibility* woman's work in the home, and to have it recognized as work, unpaid though it might be, and to challenge the received idea that it was performed easily out of our instinctual desires to nest-make and nurture.

Isolated, the only adult in a private house, the housewife is yet crowded, by emotional and physical demands of her family, by the unseen pressures of society.

But although isolated the housewife is never alone – her domain is the kitchen, the most communal room, and even the possibility of sleeping alone is denied her.
Williams, Twort and Bachelli (1970) (4)

These writings formed the basis for the beginnings of an analysis of women's role in the family from a feminist perspective. Very crudely, these analyses can be differentiated as radical or socialist feminist, depending on the relative determinacy accorded to gender or class (5). We intend to concentrate on the latter (6).

Margaret Benston (1969) set out to establish that women as a group have:

> a unique relation to the means of production. . . . The personal and psychological factors then follow from this special relation to production, and a change in the latter will be a necessary (but not sufficient) condition for changing the former. If this special relation of women to production is accepted, *the analysis of the situation of women fits naturally into a class analysis of society.* [our italics]

While endorsing the necessity of analysing the relationship between women's subordination and the mode of production, we would now argue that to suggest that 'an analysis of the situation of women fits *naturally* into a class analysis' can have a tendency to neglect specific (historically capitalistic, but not *necessarily* capitalistic) determinations of women's situation.

The shift from writing about *being* a housewife/mother developed into an increasing concern with the precise articulation of housework and the capitalist mode of production. As Gardiner, who has been consistently involved in what has become known as the 'domestic labour debate', writes (1975, p. 109):

> The focus of the debate has shifted towards an emphasis on the role of female labour in the family in maintaining and reproducing labour power, since this provides a theoretical link between the family and the capitalist mode of production in which labour power is bought and sold.

This shift in emphasis at a theoretical level was sharpened, within the Women's Movement, by the different political demands that accompanied different analyses. The publication, in October 1972, of *The Power of Women and the Subversion of the Community* by Dalla Costa and James was the first extended argument for the political organization of women in the community, an analysis which later formed the basis for the demand of wages for housework.

There is also the question of the extent to which this shift in emphasis was influenced by the intellectual and political traditions of the British (and American) left. Firstly, in terms of political resistance to the questions raised by Women's Liberation:

> I was just finishing this when my husband came in and asked what I was doing. Writing a paper on housework. Housework? He said. Housework? Oh my God how trivial can you get. A paper on housework.
> Mainardi (1970)

Secondly, and this point is rather assertive in a paper of this length, through the economistic tendencies in marxist and socialist analyses which shaped both women's and men's criteria for 'a materialist analysis of women's oppression' (7). In this case we would argue that this tendency was manifested in a refusal to recognize women's oppression unless it could be grounded in their *exploitation* by capital (8). These factors, we would argue, must be considered as having some determining effect on the particular form and terrain of what developed into the 'domestic labour debate'. Thus Jean Gardiner's statement (1976, p. 109):

> domestic labour did not even exist as a theoretical category before the current feminist movement made it into an area of theoretical and political debate....

can usefully be considered in conjunction with Maureen Mackintosh's retrospective criticism of the limitations of the debate:

> ... the women's movement has generated a great deal of debate upon the same theme; the necessity of the family to the reproduction of the capitalist mode of production. This debate has made clear to many women — the consciousness has yet to filter down to much of the male left — the inadequacy of an analysis of the family which centres attention on the necessity of housework for capitalism while failing to give an adequate characterisation of the social relations generated by the reproductive role of women. Mackintosh (1977, p. 119)

Mackintosh here points to the necessity of an analysis of women's work in the home which addresses levels other than that of the *economic* necessity of housework for capitalism. The implications of this passage are not fully examined in this article, but are considered, in differing ways, in other articles in this journal. Here we look briefly at some of the arguments of the 'domestic labour debate'.

One way of approaching the theoretical background to the debate is to see it as an attempt by socialist feminists (9) to 'open up' the question of the maintenance and reproduction of the labour force, which is one element in the reproduction of the forces of production, necessary to the reproduction of any mode of production (10). Marx:

> The maintenance and reproduction of the working class remains a necessary condition for the reproduction of capital. But the capitalist may safely leave this to the worker's drives for self-preservation and propagation.
> Marx (1976, p. 718)

The Political Economy of Women Group (PEWG):

> In focusing on domestic labour we are reflecting the view, common to almost all writing on this subject, that women's role in the home is crucial to her subordination under capitalism.
> PEWG (1975, p. 3)

The maintenance and reproduction of the working class is a condition of the reproduction of capital because of the particular nature of labour, sold as a commodity, labour power, under capitalism: although it can be bought and sold, it cannot be separated from the individual whose ability it is:

> ... labour power can appear on the market as a commodity only if, and in so far as, its possessor, the individual whose labour power it is, offers it for sale or sells it as a commodity ... the proprietor of labour-power must always sell it for a limited period only, for if he were to sell it in a lump, once and for all, he would be selling himself, converting himself from a free man into a slave. ... In this way he manages both to alienate his labour-power, and to avoid renouncing his rights of ownership over it.
>
> Marx (1976, p. 271)

Thus, while Marx is concerned at a theoretical level with the commodity labour power, the condition of the appearance of this is the day-to-day and generational reproduction of human beings, as Marx makes clear:

> ... in the course of this activity, i.e. labour, a definite quantity of human muscle, nerve, brain, etc. is expended, and these things have to be replaced. ... The owner of labour-power is mortal. If then his appearance in the market is to be continuous, and the continuous transformation of money into capital assumes this, the seller of labour-power must perpetuate himself 'in the way that every living individual perpetuates himself' (sic), by procreation.
>
> Marx (1976, pp. 274-5)

The reproduction and maintenance of the human beings who are the bearers of labour power has been historically accomplished in 'the family', organized through the sexual division of labour, which, under capitalism, takes 'the extreme form of the separation of the general economic process into an industrial and a domestic unit' (Coulson, Magas, Wainwright 1975). The nature of the 'domestic unit', concerned with the reproduction and maintenance of the labour force, which *always* remains a precondition of the reproduction of capital, is partly determined by the absolute separation capital sets up between the worker's individual consumption and her/his productive consumption (11), and the necessity for the worker to sell her/his labour power to obtain the means of subsistence. The historical 'separation out' of the domestic sphere has been accompanied by, and articulated through, developing, and originally class-specific ideologies of domesticity, femininity, and personal life, which have contributed to the representation and understanding of the home as a private sphere, undetermined by the capitalist mode of production (Hall 1974; Davidoff 1973, 1976; Zaretsky 1976).

In our society, the work involved in 'the maintenance and reproduction of the working class' is done mainly by women (12) as unwaged work in the home, regardless of whether they also do waged work (usually of a similar nature) outside the home. The roles of wife and mother, in relation to the reproduction of capital, are centrally those of the reproduction and maintenance of the labour force. We do the shopping, cooking and cleaning, soothe our husbands and look after the children. The determinations on the domestic by the industrial sphere, which contribute to the reproduction of the specific social relations of the sphere (the relations of subordination of women to men) are central to an understanding of women's position in the home. As Sally Alexander observes, writing of women's work in nineteenth century London:

> But a wife's responsibility for the well-being of her husband and children always came before her work in social production, and in a patriarchal culture, this was seen to follow naturally from her role in biological reproduction.
>
> The intervention of capitalism into the sexual division of labour within the patriarchal family confirmed the economic subordination of the wife. By distinguishing between production for use and production for exchange, and by progressively subordinating the former to the latter, by confining production for use to the private world of the home and female labour, and production for exchange increasingly to the workshop outside the home, and male labour, capitalism ensured the economic dependence of women upon their husbands or fathers for a substantial part of their lives.
>
> Alexander (1976, p. 77)

It is thus argued that the reproduction and maintenance of the labour force is, historically conducted through specific relations, the particular capitalist articulation of the sexual division of labour and the nexus of relations which construct and contribute to women's 'ideological and socio-economic role as mother and housekeeper'. This is the hidden, and historically specific content of 'the worker's drives for self-preservation and propagation' – and it is in this context that women's role in the home must be considered.

Engels located woman's role in the home as central to her continuing subordination, but understood capitalism to be progressive in this respect:

> The emancipation of women and their equality with men are impossible and must remain so as long as women are excluded from socially productive work and restricted to housework, which is private. The emancipation of women becomes possible only when women are enabled to take part in production on a large social scale, and when domestic duties require their attention to only a minor degree. And this has become possible only as a result of modern large-scale industry, which not only permits the participation of women in production in large numbers, but actually calls for it, and moreover, strives to convert private domestic work into a more public industry.
>
> Engels (1972, p. 152)

It has seemed clear to feminists (13) that despite 'the participation of women in production in large numbers' (14), increasing (if fluctuating and at present declining) state intervention, and the penetration of the home by commodities, domestic duties do not yet require women's attention 'only to a minor degree'. Coulson, Magas and Wainwright (1975), and later Adamson *et al.* (1976) have argued:

> ... the central feature of women's position under capitalism is not their role simply as domestic workers, but rather the fact that they are *both* domestic and wage labourers.
>
> Coulson, Magas and Wainwright (1975, p. 60)

This has led feminists to try and understand,

> Why have housework and childcare, in modern industrial societies such as Britain, continued to such a great extent to be the responsibility of women, and organised on a private family basis?
>
> Gardiner (1975, p. 47)

Much of the literature has concentrated on the attempt to analyse housework in relation to marxist categories of political economy. There has been extensive interrogation of the adequacy of some marxist concepts to contribute to an understanding of the political economy of women, and the material basis of their subordination. Ann Foreman characterized the main questions that have emerged from this literature as:

> What is the relation of women to the production of labour power? Does the work of women in the home produce value? Is capitalism likely to socialise this work? And what is the significance of the fact that women go out to work as well as working within the home?
>
> Foreman (1977, p. 113)

We now intend first to look briefly at some of the arguments over productive and unproductive labour; the value of labour power; housework in relation to the production of surplus value; then to briefly state how we understand domestic labour, and then to go on to consider the question of the socialization of domestic labour.

The distinction between productive and unproductive labour (15)

Marx uses 'productive' in two senses. Firstly, the more general one of socially useful labour (labour which produces use-values, undertaken in all societies), and secondly, to mean labour that is exchanged against capital rather than revenue (16). Thus, in the latter sense, the same *kind* of labour can be productive or unproductive. You can peel potatoes at home, in a state school kitchen or in a commercial restaurant. Workers employed by capital, in addition to reproducing the value of their own labour power, produce surplus value – they are productive *from the point of view of capital*. Is housework productive only in the general sense – the production of use-values? (Coulson *et al.* 1975; PEWG 1975; Adamson *et al.* 1976) or does it also contribute to the production of surplus value (Harrison 1973; Seccombe 1974; Gardiner 1975, 1976) or is it directly engaged in the production of surplus value (Dalla Costa and James 1972)?

The value of labour power

Marx:

> The value of labour power is determined, as in the case of every other commodity, by the labour time necessary for the production, and consequently also the reproduction, of this special article. In so far as it has value, it represents no more than a definite quantity of the average social labour objectified in it. Labour power exists only as a capacity of the living individual. Its production consequently presupposes his existence. Given the existence of the individual, the production of labour-power consists in his reproduction of himself or his maintenance. For his maintenance he requires a certain quantity of the means of subsistence. Therefore the labour-time necessary for the production of labour-power is the same as that necessary for the production of those means of subsistence; in other words, the value of labour-power is the value of the means of subsistence necessary for the maintenance of its owner.
>
> Marx (1976, p. 274)

All contributors to the domestic labour debate recognize the historical and cultural determinants on the subsistence level of the working class. The problem arises over whether women's labour in the home – peeling and cooking the potatoes after buying them, or just adding water to a packet of 'Smash' – is taken as a given or not. Is it, and should it be, included within an understanding of the 'labour time necessary for the production, and consequently also the reproduction of this special article'? (17) That is, while all the contributors to the debate *recognize* the necessity of the woman's contribution to the 'means of subsistence', the difference lies in the way this contribution is understood theoretically, which depends partly on whether it is thought that the housewife's private labour in the home can/should be understood through Marx's categories for the analysis of labour exchanged on the market. Here it seems important to stress that labour power as a concept (the ability to labour, sold as a commodity under capitalism) is *not* sexed, just as, in the abstract, capital is indifferent not only to the use values of the commodities which are produced, but also to the sex/gender of its domestic and wage labourers. However, concretely, this is not the case, and there are grounds for arguing that, historically, male and female labour powers have different values (Beechey 1977; Foreman 1977).

Surplus value/surplus labour (18)

The domestic labour debate has partly been 'about' whether and how housework contributes to the production of surplus value (see *Distinction between productive and unproductive labour,* above). It has been argued that the housewife produces surplus value directly, because she produces the value-creating commodity, labour power (Dalla Costa and James 1972). Alternatively, that she contributes to the production of surplus value through her surplus labour in the home, which forms part of her husband's consumption, and thus increases the time he spends in the production of surplus value by lowering the necessary labour time (variously, and in different forms: Harrison 1973; Seccombe 1974; Gardiner 1975).

Within the terms of this debate, we think domestic labour can most usefully be characterized as 'the production of use-values under non-wage relations of production, within the capitalist mode of production' (19) and thus not contributing directly to the creation of surplus value; a private, concrete labour, in the main performed by women, which is essential to the reproduction of labour power under capitalism, concerned as it is with the reproduction and maintenance of the bearer of labour power, the labourer. We find this labour neither productive nor unproductive in Marx's more specific sense because:

> [Housework under capitalism] remains a specific labour to which the concept of abstract labour does not apply....
>
> Coulson, Magas and Wainwright (1975)
>
> ... to compare domestic labour with wage labour is not comparing like with like....
>
> PEWG (1975, p. 10)

From this 'orthodox' position (20), the terms of the domestic labour debate as analysis of the relationship between women's continuing subordination and the capitalist mode of production become more explicitly inadequate. For example, Seccombe (1975, p. 89 fn.) argues that he looks at:

> the substantive component of domestic labour, subtracting out the timeless household and child guardian aspects of the housewife's role. This latter aspect is not measurable in terms of labour time or value.

On one hand, we find this 'substantive component' 'not measurable in terms of labour time or value'. On the other, it is the myth of 'the *timeless* household and child guardian aspects of the housewife's role' that much feminist literature has engaged with (Comer 1974; Oakley 1974b, 1972; Hall 1974; Davidoff, L'Esperance, Newby 1976), arguing for cultural, historical and class specificity. It is the 'timelessness' of women's 'immeasurable' role in the home, and its implied 'naturalness' which has provided its major ideological justification. What Seccombe calls 'the substantive component of domestic labour' is a labour of love precisely because it is performed through 'the household and child guardian aspects of the housewife's role' which have to be considered in conjunction with the particular construction of romantic love between men and women under monopoly capitalism (Millet 1971; Firestone 1972; Greer 1970):

> For a woman's labour in the home typically does not only contain the caring work described above [of children, the elderly, the sick], but also the much less obviously necessary tasks of providing services for an adult male, in a relation of personal dependence upon him.
>
> Mackintosh, Himmelweit, Taylor (1977)

We are thus arguing that women's overall responsibility for the maintenance and reproduction of the labour force cannot be adequately 'thought' through the categories of capital alone. Women's role in the home, from the point of view of capital, cannot be understood without attention to the specific historical and ideological articulations of the sexual division of labour, in relation to particular forms of 'the family' through which women's sexuality is organized for reproductive ends, and the effectivity, in the construction of femininity, of the ideologies of domesticity and romantic love (21). From the point of view of women:

Women are trapped into a material dependence upon a man by our lack of access to a decent wage, the absence of services to make full-time waged work and child care compatible, the ideological and social pressures to marry, and the almost complete absence of any alternative to the family as a way of life, a learned sense of inferiority, and the personal effects of isolation and overwork.

Mackintosh, Himmelweit, Taylor (1977)

It is in relation to these points (22) that we want to look at the debate over the socialization of domestic labour. The PEWG (1975) try to 'grasp the fact that the socialisation of domestic labour is necessary in order to permit women to work in wage labour' and argue that there has been a reduction in the time which has to be spent in the home for the production of an acceptable standard of living for the family. That is, although they have rejected the attempt to quantitatively compare domestic labour time with wage labour time, they *are* trying to use some concept of necessary labour time in relation to domestic labour, although they recognize that *actual* labour time varies from home to home:

By the socialisation of domestic labour we do not necessarily mean *a reduction in the time actually spent on housework by full time housewives* ... what we mean is the replacement (and at the same time the transformation) of the work done in the home by goods and services produced for the market or provided by the State: laundries and prepared foods, education and health care. [our italics]

PWEG (1975, p. 13)

They understand the limits of this capitalist and state socialization of domestic labour as lying principally in the sphere of market conditions - although they recognize contradictory political and economic factors - and thus the implication of their analysis seems similar to that of Engels, although only likely to be fulfilled under boom conditions: 'Up to now, capital has been unable to overcome the obstacles to complete socialisation of domestic labour' (PWEG 1975, p. 13). Davidoff, considering the rationalization of housework, points out:

What must be kept in mind is that technical improvements in equipment, such as those exemplified by the use of the small electric motor, are not of the same order as fundamental changes in the organisation or aims of housework.

Davidoff (1976, p. 145)

The problem of 'the substantive component' of women's work in the home thus reappears in this analysis (23), as it does in those analyses which view domestic labour primarily through the necessity under capitalism of individual private consumption (Coulson, Magas, Wainwright 1975; Adamson *et al.* 1976).

The enforced privatised consumption of the family could never become optional under capitalism; consequently a residual portion of the work that accomplishes this consumption is structurally necessary. . . .

Seccombe (1975)

The limits to the socialization of domestic labour, as argued here, are given in the processes of capital accumulation, the separation of labour power from the labourer, productive consumption from individual consumption. However, it cannot be 'deduced' from the logic of *Capital* (Adamson *et al.* 1976) that the work through which the individual private consumption that is necessary for the reproduction and maintenance of the labour force is achieved, will always be performed by *women*. Contradictory demands are being made on women in a period when 44 per cent of the paid work force is female, a period

. . . of the so-called crisis of the family, epitomised by the legalisation of divorce and the appearance of female sexuality no longer organised solely to reproductive ends.

WPCS (no. 9, p. 114)

The possibility of the capitalist organization of individual consumption in forms other than a two-parent family must be considered (however unlikely this may seem for more than minority groups of the population). This question is important because it engages partly with the question of how far certain types of feminism can be considered 'a rationalist exigency of capitalism' (*WPCS*, no. 9, p. 114).

The sexual division of labour is taken for granted in a rather different way in the argument for 'wages for housework', which carries an implicit position on the socialization of domestic labour. The argument here is that wages (the 'sign' of value under capitalism) are *due* to housewives, as they are *already* involved in social production:

. . . the family under capitalism is a center of conditioning, of consumption, and of reserve labour, but a center essentially of social production.

Dalla Costa and James (1972, p. 10)

The family is the 'social factory' where women produce the commodity labour power:

What we meant precisely is that housework as work is productive in the Marxian sense, that is, it is producing surplus value.

Dalla Costa and James (1973, p. 53, fn 12)

Demanding wages for housework on the basis of this analysis, as both recognition of and recompense for social labour, can be seen as a demand for a sort of 'righting' of the 'phenomenal forms' to fit what are argued to be the 'real relations'. A short-cut to a kind of privatized socialization, which still leaves *women* doing the same work in isolation (24).

Ann Foreman more suggestively locates women's continuing, though increasingly contradictory, place in the home as partly a result of successful working class struggle for a 'family wage', particularly at the end of the nineteenth and early twentieth centuries:

> ... the growth in strength of the working class movement was pitted towards defining labour power as a male capacity and demanding accordingly that their wage should reflect this fact.
>
> Foreman (1977, p. 120) (See also Alexander 1976; PEWG 1975)

Here we can begin to see the articulations of the sexual division of labour within the capitalist mode of production as both the historical *outcome* and *site* of struggle. Thus the struggle for a family wage is also the struggle to define women in terms of their reproductive capacity. The benefits to capital of women's role as mother and wife are secured through masculine hegemony (25) which struggles to define women through, and confines them to, these roles. It is through this historically complex and contradictory 'relegation' of women (ideologically, if not always actually) to the 'private sphere' of reproduction - and hence through a recognition of the real divisions within the working class - that the retention of women's work in the home must be considered. 'The family' as the site of women's subordination, and the specificity of women's oppression in her 'ideological and socio-economic role as mother and housekeeper' has to be understood historically through ideological and political determinations which articulate with the benefits to *capital* of the family as an *economic* unit.

The state, reproduction of labour power and the subordination of women

Our concern here is to examine the way in which the state contributes to women's subordination (1). We would argue that the specificity of this contribution lies primarily in the state's concern with the reproduction of labour power. We take those state apparatuses, legislation and ideological practices which are centrally concerned with the reproduction of labour power to designate a working definition of the 'welfare state'. It is clear that what is commonly conceived of as the welfare state, or welfare aspects of the state, involves more than the reproduction of labour power. However, we wish to centre on this one aspect, thereby also denaturalizing the ideological connotations of the concept of 'welfare'.

From capital's viewpoint there are several aspects to the reproduction of labour power:

1. Capital must be supplied with a continuous source of labour power - a new generation of preferably healthy labourers;
2. capital, being in itself a creative and transformative process, requires in its labour continuous changes of skills and aptitudes/motivation;

3   as a lever of capital accumulation, capital needs an industrial reserve army, in a state of serviceability for capital;
4   capital desires an acquiescent work-force, politically and ideologically (2), to ensure its continued existence, though this is never achieved unproblematically.

But this is not to view the welfare state as simply acting in the interests of capital; the welfare state's development must also be seen historically as the outcome of class struggle.

If we are taking the welfare state as both concerned with the reproduction of labour power from the viewpoint of capital *and* labour, we must ask what are the consequent implications for women. Under capitalism, labour power is replenished and replaced in the sphere of private consumption, primarily within the family. The family is the site of biological reproduction, but is also the main site for the regulation of sexuality and the acquisition of sex/gender roles, and other aspects of generational and day-to-day reproduction of the labourer. But in relation to the welfare state's concern with the family, it is crucial to bear in mind that both the welfare state's ability to monitor the reproduction of labour power, and the very form of that reproduction, are predicated on relations of domination and subordination between the sexes, power relations, within the reproductive circuit (the circuit of biological reproduction and reproduction of the labourer). State control of the reproduction of labour power has utilized these existing patriarchal relations, thereby reinforcing their pre-capitalist partiarchal nature.

Thus state concern with the reproduction of labour power has centred on women both as biological reproducers and in their wider role within the family. In fact, it is clear that welfare state legislation has largely defined and reinforced women's role as wives and mothers, reproducers of the present and future labour force.

On the other hand, if we see aspects of welfare legislation as 'won' by the working class, we must note that British working class strength and demands for welfare have evolved with an ideology which also centrally locates women within the family. This can be partly linked to the development of a notion of the 'family wage', the defining of labour power as *male*. As Ann Foreman (1977, p. 119) notes, the organized working class

> developed a tradition of values and expectations. Among them, and in pride of place, was the belief that the wage should be sufficient to maintain the worker's wife at home.

A woman's 'place' also came to involve a view of women as ensuring the sanctity of the home in contrast to the harsh world of labour – the ideology of 'domesticity'. We must remember that:

> ... neither the family nor ideology can be seen as imposed on a passive working class, rather as phenomena it plays a part in forging.
>
> Foreman (1977, p. 130)

We would argue that this ideology of a woman's 'place' became crucially incorporated into the ideology of social democracy, with welfare legislation reinforcing its materiality (3). Again, however, it must be stressed that working class attitudes were and are predicated on relations of domination and subordination between the sexes, which predate capitalism. Thus it is incorrect to see the nature of women's subordination as either determined solely by the economic and political 'needs' of capitalism or the result of class struggle; women's subordination under capitalism lies in the articulation between patriarchal relations and capitalist development.

We shall attempt to show that although the welfare state has encroached on certain functions performed by the family and the neighbourhood, e.g. education, care of the old, disabled, mentally handicapped - developments that appear to have accompanied the shift into machinofacture - in other respects the state has fundamentally shored up the family and women's role as mothers, through various forms of regulated intervention and support.

We shall thus look briefly at three significant historical moments in the development of British welfare legislation:

1. The struggle around the Factory Acts in the mid nineteenth century.
2. The reforms introduced under the Liberal government prior to the 1914-18 war, which created the basic framework of our contemporary 'welfare state' with the introduction of insurance for unemployment, maternity, health, old-age pensions, school meals.
3. The body of ideology and legislation enshrined in the Beveridge Report of 1942, much of which was enacted by the Labour government after the Second World War.

This will be followed by a consideration of women and welfare in the post-war period. It is important to stress that we are not positing a unilinear development of the welfare state. The historical moments delineated are highly specific and represent definite *qualitative* shifts in the nature of welfare, particularly after the Second World War, with the introduction of *universal* provision and the notion of 'social rights' (4).

The Factory Acts

Marx presupposed the existence of the private sphere of the family, lying outside the circuit of capital, but he was unconcerned with how labour power is reproduced: '... the capitalist may safely leave its fulfillment to the labourer's instincts of self-preservation and of propagation' (Marx 1976, p. 718). In fact, even in the heyday of *laissez-faire* in the early nineteenth century in Britain, reproduction was not left to the vagaries of the labourer's instincts of self-preservation: witness the marked moral intervention of the period, the beginnings of state education, state regulation of child welfare, and massive growth of bourgeois philanthropic activities. Marx's comments seem stranger still in the light of his extended account of the struggle around the working day (prior to and during the introduction of the Factory Acts), a struggle which highlighted capital's need for state intervention into the reproduction of labour power.

Until the Factory Acts' restriction on the working day, the main form of exploitation had been the extraction of absolute surplus value: the lengthening of the working day. But capital had used this form to such an extent that it had produced 'the premature exhaustion and death of its labour power', and thus its concern with valorization was ultimately threatening its own existence (5). The state's enactment of the Factory Acts (and also the Public Health Acts in the same period) (6) can thus be seen as directly benefiting the long-term interests of capital, but, we would argue, also representing gains won by the working class. However, it is debatable whether the Factory Acts can be seen unambiguously as a gain for *women* in terms of their potential for economic independence. The first few Factory Acts applied only to adolescent, child, and female labour, and with their hours thus restricted, women became less attractive employees. This could be seen in one respect as a victory for male trade unionists at the expense of women, in that there was now less likelihood of women's unskilled labour being used to aid de-skilling and to undercut male workers. Further, the Factory Acts extended the definition of a minor to include women, thereby reinforcing the notion of women's dependency on men. However, influences shaping the Acts were more complex than this; as Wilson (1977, p. 9) points out, there were also moral debates on female sexuality concerning, for example, the 'indecency' of women working in the mines. Henceforth, the question of women and children working became seen as a *moral* issue.

The limitation by the state of the extraction of absolute surplus value directed capital to the production of relative surplus value; concern with increasing the intensity and productivity of labour. This shift can be seen as a crucial historical moment in that it represents both the state's first major intervention into the reproduction of labour power, and the first example of any working class agitation resulting in the 'winning' of social reforms.

The Liberal reforms

The welfare legislation in the period before the First World War came in the wake of great concern with national and imperial efficiency. On the one hand, there was the problem of alleged physical deterioration: the Boer War had revealed the British worker's physical puniness (50 per cent of those enlisted were unfit). On the other hand, there was also alarm in relation to the declining birth rate. In response, the Interdepartmental Committee on Physical Deterioration was set up in 1903 and many of its recommendations were enacted in the ensuing legislation.

In addition to the National Insurance Act of 1911 (which applied to few women), measures were introduced to promote the health of mothers and children: the legislation to provide free milk for babies, the beginning of health visiting and midwifery, and clauses relating to parental neglect. Not surprisingly, these measures went hand-in-hand with the promotion of motherhood and denouncement of the 'working mother'. As Booth wrote in his popular *In Darkest England and the Way Out* (1890, cited in Wilson 1977, p. 110) (7):

> The home is largely destroyed where the mother follows the father into the factory, and where the hours of labour are so long that they have not time to see their children. . . . It is the home that has been destroyed, and with the home the home-like virtues. It is the dis-homed multitude, nomadic, hungry, that is rearing an undisciplined population, cursed from birth with hereditary weakness of body and hereditary faults of character. . . . Nothing is worth doing . . . that does not Reconstitute the Home.

As Wilson notes (1977, p. 102) a preoccupation with eugenics was widely prevalent, particularly among the Fabians. In the Fabian tract, *The Decline of the Birthrate*, Sidney Webb recommends state action to encourage the wealthier sections of society to reproduce themselves; it was believed that the poor were breeding at a much faster rate than the rest of the population, thus contributing to national degeneration.

The Liberal legislation also reflected concern with what was seen as a vast undermass of dejected labour, the industrial reserve army. Boards were set up in 1909 to fix minimum wages and maximum hours in sweated trades, thus preventing sections of capital exploiting women workers in particular and attempting the destructive consumption of labour power.

The Beveridge Report

The Beveridge Report (1942) can be seen as the first body of proposed legislation which actually introduced the idea of *planned* reproduction of labour power. But the report must also be seen as a response to economic and political mobilizations of the war, and demands for a reversal of conditions of the inter-war period. Yet such demands came primarily from *male* trade unionists (8):

> The major demands were for male full employment, an adequate insurance for male workers, for themselves and their families.
>
> PEWG (1975, p. 28)

Again, women's interests were subsumed to men's, with women relegated to the family as dependants of men.

Wilson sees three basic principles underlying the report: the principles of subsistence income; of insurance; and of the sanctity of the family. A central concern with motherhood was in part a response to (again!) the declining birth rate (9), and Beveridge's proposal for family allowances was meant not only as a form of income redistribution in addition to a social insurance system (an income redistribution *within* the working class, and not between classes) (10) but also as a material inducement for propagation (11). Beveridge's position was transparent: 'In the next 30 years housewives as Mothers have vital work to do in ensuring the adequate continuance of the British race and the British Ideals in the world' (Beveridge 1942, pp. 52-3).

The report throughout stresses the importance of the family as an economic unit, with the need to 'treat man and wife as a team' (p. 49). Beveridge erroneously assumed that once the war ended, most married women would cease to be waged workers and would return to the home: 'the great majority of married women must be regarded as occupied on work which is *vital* though unpaid' (p. 49). 'During marriage most women will not be gainfully employed' (p. 50), he argued, which justified the notion that should a married woman take on paid work, she would neither pay contributions, nor receive benefits. Thus married women were assumed to be economic dependants of their husbands and thus their dependence was reinforced. Although Beveridge removed the anomalies concerning single women (12) who, in terms of benefits, were to get the same as men, their contributions were to be lower on the grounds that a man, unlike a woman, was making contributions on behalf of himself *and* his wife. Here we see the implicit assumption of the 'family wage'.

The Beveridge Report also revealed the state's concern with the yoking of sexuality to the family. There was a definite position against 'immorality'; for example, Beveridge recommended a separate allowance for deserted, separated and divorced wives, *only* on condition that they were not responsible for the breakdown of the marriage. Further, there was no provision in the scheme for unsupported mothers.

We have argued that the state's concern with the reproduction of labour power has crucially involved its shaping and shoring up of the family and the woman's location within the family as mother, wife and dependant of her husband. Before turning to a consideration of the central contradiction facing women in the post-Second World War period, it is useful to delineate the different modes of welfare state intervention into the family. This intervention takes the form of a) regulation, b) 'support', c) supercession:

(a) The attempts to regulate the way in which women service the worker and bring up their children in the home are less 'obvious' than the demands of the assembly line, but are for that very reason all the more insidious and mystifying. As PEWG notes (1975, p. 23): '. . . since the war the ideological pressure on women in the home has increased enormously and a veritable army of social workers has been trained in family case work'. Social work 'control' basically involves intervention into families where reproduction of labour power is threatened. In addition, the state, through family law and legislation on matters of sexual morality plays a central role in monitoring and controlling sexual ideology and its relation to the family. The extent of such regulative intervention is often overlooked, since in bourgeois ideology these matters belong *par excellence* to the intimate or private sphere, but the array of legislation dealing with such areas as divorce, separation, adoption, fostering, abortion and contraception, rape, prostitution, homosexuality, etc., belies this.

(b) In its 'supportive' role, the welfare state maintains a family in existence as a unit. The characteristic methods have been allowances, supplements, free school milk, health care, etc. At the ideological level, the ideal of 'motherhood' dominant in much welfare legislation and the practices of welfare agencies, acts to regulate and support women's role within the family as reproducers. Families are almost always ideologically constituted as families-with-children, or families-with-the-function-of-child-care. Yet most families or most people do not have children – they have either never been there, or have not yet arrived, or have left. A woman's sexuality is invariably defined primarily in relation to her capacity to bear children, not as an integral part of her being over which she has control and the right to define as she chooses.

(c) The welfare state's encroachment on certain 'traditional' functions of the family has already been mentioned. Whether capitalism can or will dispense with the existing form of the family remains an open question.

The post-war period

After the war, with the Labour government's commitment to full employment for *men,* married women became the industrial reserve army (see Beechey 1977) and as Wilson (1977, p. 158) notes:

> This period then saw the development of a contradiction between the need to expand the labour force, and the need to raise the birthrate, and tangling with this were the new anxieties about the emotional well-being of children. Women have been the battle ground of this conflict within capitalist society ever since, for what has been attempted is to retain the mother as, in practice, the individual solely in charge of the day to day care of children and yet at the same time to draw married women, the last remaining pool of reserve labour, into the workforce. These demands are not fully compatible.

It is these two aspects of women's lives, their role in production either as members of the work-force or as part of the permanent reserve army, and their role in reproduction or childbearing and child-care, that constitute a major contradiction both for capitalism and for the state, a contradiction that has to be *managed* (13).

One outcome of this contradiction lies in the predominant post-war definition of a woman's dual role as 'a negative one that sees her mothering function as interfering with her work, and her work function as interfering with her child rearing' (Wilson 1977, p. 151). A 'solution' to this contradiction has been the rise of female part-time work (see *Equal pay* section, pp. 67–71).

However, the welfare state not only attempts to *manage* a contradiction; its provisions have themselves had contradictory outcomes. As the PEWG (1975, p. 26) points out:

> ... those very services designed to support and maintain the family unit have in many instances provided women with sufficient means to break away from it, to

bring up their children independently of their husbands. And the more remedial benefits are introduced, for single parent families, the more parents in unsatisfactory relationships are likely to separate and the weaker men's sense of obligation as breadwinners for their families may become.

Further, through driving away wage-earning children, means-testing has weakened the very family that the state set out to support (see J. Cowley *et al.* 1977).

But it is not simply that welfare policy throws up new contradictions; the ideology implicit in the welfare state is itself in contradiction with structural changes. Most of the patriarchal assumptions enshrined in the Beveridge Report have remained locked into welfare legislation. Yet, although a woman's financial dependence on her husband is still assumed, the reality of the situation is somewhat different. As H. Land (1975, p. 119) points out:

At the very least, one in six of all households, excluding pensioner households, are substantially or completely dependent upon a woman's earnings or benefits and the majority of these households contain either children or adult dependants. Among pensioner households a woman is the chief economic supporter in just over half of the households.

The managed contradiction between woman's role as a waged worker and as a domestic worker and reproducer, and the concomitant rise of female part-time work, has itself accelerated militancy among women. The rise of the WLM itself is partly an outcome of this contradiction, and four of the WLM's six demands are directly concerned with reproduction and the relation between reproduction and the state. The limitations of the two demands which do *not* confront this question, the demands for equal pay and equal education and opportunity, are exemplified in the unsatisfactory outcome of the Equal Pay and Sex Discrimination Acts (see below): neither of these Acts questions in any way women's reproductive role, and neither has led to economic equality for women.

This begs the question of how women are to regard welfare legislation and to assess reforms' progressive potential for them *as women*. As has been indicated, the welfare state is deeply contradictory: it is in certain respects 'won' by the working class, but in others, advantageous to the dominant class interests at a certain historical conjuncture. However, as we have attempted to show, its contradictory nature is at its most apparent in relation to women.

The welfare state has undoubtedly led to a rise in living and health standards, but these material improvements have done little to alter the basic dependence of women, whether on their husbands, or on means-tested benefits. As PEWG notes (1975, p. 29), many people feel that the material advantages of the welfare state have been almost outweighed by the repressive ways in which services have been administered, and the social control exerted through them. Certain welfare legislation has had progressive elements, but it has rarely led to any form of democratic control over the *implementation* of that policy, particularly in the case of control by and/or for women. It is obviously crucial to ask why this is the case.

At the conception of the welfare state, the labour movement never really raised the central question of democratic control. This was due partly no doubt to the ideology of social democratic politics in which gains 'won' from the state in terms of welfare were seen *in themselves* as steps to transforming the state. In addition, as PEWG points out, the left has never placed much emphasis on struggle in the sphere of reproduction, either domestic or socialized, which is in part due, of course, to the dominant sexist ideology of a woman's 'place' being in the home, i.e. reproduction is the work and concern of women.

The six demands of the WLM are all at some level demands of the state. These demands must be seen as neither totally separate nor primarily economic; only their *combination* acts to challenge the underlying roots of women's subordination. The fifth demand, the demand for financial and legal independence, appears to make the most direct attack on the patriarchal nature of the state (the ten demands of the Campaign for Financial and Legal Independence all confront those aspects of welfare policy which most centrally define women's dependence on men). However, it must be stressed that the welfare state's ability to create and reinforce this dependency is predicated on women's subordination as biological reproducers. Further, we must struggle not merely for the realization of these demands, but also for control over their implementation (see *Equal pay* section below).

Women in waged work

I'm a trained machinist, but I can't work during the day because of the kids. I can't afford to have them looked after. I'd rather do day work, but I'd live in poverty if I didn't do night cleaning. People don't do night cleaning for fun.

Wandor (1972, p. 152)

In comparison with other aspects of women's position, women's wage labour most obviously concerns the economic relations of capital. However if, for example, we examine their labour in the post-Second World War period (from which the examples here are drawn) (1), it is impossible to understand the complexities of women's entry and engagement in the labour market through the economic alone, even though it is the processes of capital accumulation that provide the over-reaching umbrella under which women's wage labour takes place (2). Capital accumulation establishes certain 'needs' in relation to the labour force, economic needs which women primarily come to fulfil for *ideological* and *political* as well as economic reasons. These determining factors concern birth control and associated demographic changes in the family (Titmuss 1963) which also relate to a shifting *ideology* of domesticity: 'a woman's place is in the home' or isn't it? (3). They include political changes focusing around trade union policies, particularly the predominantly male trade union struggle for a 'family wage' and full employment (for men) (4) and disparate state policies. Here we would consider immigration policy which in the fifties encourages immigrant labour and then later restricts immigrant entry to create the space in which married female labour can be taken on

(Cohen and Harris 1976); the state's underprovision of child-care facilities (5), and so on (see preceding section on the state).

The specificity of the analysis of female wage labour lies not only in the fact that it is determined by more than the economic. It pertains also to how we conceptualize the economic itself. Female wage labour is always premised on women's position economically and ideologically in the *family*. As we have already argued, it is the patriarchal family in its relations within the processes of capital accumulation which is the site of women's subordination. If we are not to lose the specificity of that subordination in its particular form as wage labour, our analysis must attempt to hold, simultaneously, the family and the labour process, *within* an understanding of the contradictory developments of the capitalist accumulation process. That process has not only at its production 'end' developed new forms of labour in which women have become engaged, but at its consumption 'end' penetrated and altered women's domestic role. That alteration in the post-Second World War period has also been particularly significant for their wage labour.

We can only understand female wage labour then, after we have considered, first, women's patriarchal reproduction of the capitalist commodity, labour power. Second, we must address ourselves to what is, in some of its aspects, integral to that: a woman's involvement at the point of exchange of commodities, i.e. as a buyer of commodities, and her consumption of those commodities, upon which her domestic labour and the family's individual consumption is founded (6). In addition, we must consider the exchange and consumption of commodities which, while ultimately related to women's position in the family, concern femininity more generally. A woman's femininity is visually constructed from and 'aided' by capitalist commodities, which women *themselves* in part produce and chiefly sell *by means of* their own femininity. It is in this whole area of commodity consumption that we are concerned with capitalist expansion/diversification of commodity production as Marx has detailed it. Only third can we look at female wage labour as overdetermined by these two aspects.

This section on wage labour has two parts: one from the point of view of capital; one from the point of view of women's subordination.

CAPITAL ACCUMULATION
Here we want to consider these aspects:

1 Expansion/diversification of consumption of commodities which presupposes production of those commodities and hence, particular forms of labour as well as consumption.
2 Capital's need for cheap labour.
3 Reserve army of labour.

These developments as they affect and include women, i.e. from the *point of view of women's subordination*, not capital, are determined by *patriarchal relations*, within which women are dependent on men: men's dominance as it is structured through what we call the *social relations of reproduction* of the individual sited primarily in the family.

Thus second:

WOMEN'S SUBORDINATION
1 We examine women as a reserve in terms of how, within the capital accumulation process, these social relations of reproduction are determining, and
2 consider how their *sexuality* as structured by those relations of reproduction intervenes in their position as wage labourers.

Capital accumulation

1 *Expansion/diversification of consumption of commodities*
At the most general level there are two contradictory tendencies of capital (7). Capital strives to reproduce itself on a constantly expanded scale through the extraction of *relative surplus value*. This results however in a tendency for the *rate of profit* to fall so that capital also sets up procedures to delay that fall (8). One aspect of capital's expanded reproduction is the tendency for a concentration and accumulation of capital and its tendency for a concentration and accumulation of capital and its tendency towards centralization. Integral to those processes, one of their 'levers' (Marx 1976, p. 779) is *competition* in the production/consumption of commodities to realize the greatest surplus value. Competition and the production of relative surplus value demands widening consumption and circulation, i.e. *more* consumption as well as *different* consumption; hence the *need* to consume in those ways (Marx 1973, p. 93). Corresponding to the production of new commodities, Marx points also to the necessarily increasingly differentiated *division of labour*

> A precondition of production based on capital is therefore *the production of a constantly widening sphere of circulation,* whether the sphere itself is directly expanded or whether *more points within it are created as points of production.*
>
> Marx (1973, p. 407)

> The production of *relative surplus value,* i.e. production of surplus value based on the increase and development of the productive forces, requires the production of new consumption; requires that the consuming circle within circulation expands as did the productive circle previously. Firstly: quantitative expansion of existing consumption; secondly: creation of new needs by propagating existing ones in a wide circle; *thirdly:* production of *new* needs and discovery and creation of new use values. In other words, so that the surplus labour gained does not remain a merely quantitative surplus but rather constantly increases the circle of qualitative differences within labour (hence of surplus labour), makes it more diverse, more internally differentiated.
>
> Marx (1973, p. 408)

This creation of new branches of production, i.e. of qualitatively new surplus time, is not merely the division of labour, but is rather the creation, separate from a given production, of labour with a new use value; the development of a constantly expanding and more comprehensive system of different kinds of labour, different kinds of production, to which a constantly expanding and constantly enriched system of needs corresponds.

Marx (1973, p. 409)

Although it cannot be specified by the accumulation process itself, the 'need', while determined by production, is felt within the family. It is the family which consumes more and differently.

On the one hand the family (always the labourer's family for Marx) 'benefits' from a wider provision of commodities while yet being more bound to the capitalist relation.

Instead of becoming more intensive with the growth of capital, this relation of dependence only becomes more extensive, i.e. the sphere of capital's exploitation and domination merely extends with its own dimensions and the number of people subjected to it. A larger part of the worker's own surplus product, which is always increasing and is continually being transformed into additional capital comes back to them in the shape of the means of payment, so that they can extend the circle of their enjoyments, make additions to their consumption fund of clothes, furniture, etc. and can lay by a small reserve fund of money. But these things no more abolish the exploitation of the wage labourer, and his situation of dependence than do better clothing, food and treatment, and a larger *peculium* in the case of the slave.

Marx (1976, p. 769)

It is within this more extensive relation of dependence that women, particularly as domestic labourers in the home, become enmeshed in capitalist production at the *consumption end* (9). Their production of use values and their service labour, in the process of becoming commodity production and state servicing respectively, are transformed.

First, for example, the fresh peas grown in the garden become the can of peas, not just to be eaten in season but all the year round, i.e. a quantitative increase of peas eaten and more importantly of commodities consumed. Then the peas become frozen or quick-dried - more expensive - therefore women need to engage in paid work to be able to afford them. While then the new branches of production of domestic goods potentially 'free' the housewife from much domestic labour, at the same time hers and the family's 'needs' become different and greater. She must now shop not simply for the curtains she no longer makes but for cushion covers to match, the lampshade to complement, etc. The ideology of domesticity in play here supports the fulfilling of these new 'needs' yet contradictorily they can only be obtained within the working class by women entering wage labour, a move which the new production and new divisions of labour in part make possible.

Second, however, the family itself becomes dependent, sometimes on market relations, but also on the state for services which women originally performed (see *State* section, pp. 46-54). The expansion of the welfare state apparatus has contradictorily reinforced women's entrenchment in the home and also required them as wage workers. While relieved of some of their home responsibilities, women come to perform these tasks publicly for a wage. The health, education and social services expansion has relied heavily on women in part-time and full-time capacities.

A third feature of the expansion/diversification of consumption concerns not only the form of labour in the *production* of commodities, but the diversification of the division of labour within the *circulation* process. Expanded distribution associated with the growth of marketing as an important part of the whole process has involved the steady growth across all industries of clerical work (Ministry of Labour 1968); a considerable increase in the number of retail outlets – more sales personnel, mainly women; as well as an increase and transformation of the advertising apparatus in which women sell their sexuality to themselves and men by selling commodities (10).

We would argue that at least for the post-war period it was principally the production of household commodities – 'labour-saving' devices for the home, together with cheap subsistence commodities previously produced as use values in the home – which contradictorily drew women into social production. It was these 'carrots' which as Wally Seccombe argued, made it economic sense, as well as in capital's interest, for women to take on paid work (11). There is no similar relation in this period between men's wage labour and the *particular commodity production which capital* carries on. To summarize, for women in the post-war period, that relation is significant at several different levels.

(a) Married women are relieved of some of the burden of domestic labour so have time to do paid work, but simultaneously become *more dependent* on commodities, e.g. food, clothes, by going out to work.
(b) Also, in part, they go out to work for those commodities, i.e. labour-saving devices which are just outside the price range of a single wage. (This is not to suggest that most women do not do paid work to provide subsistence necessities.)
(c) They work in those industries manufacturing such commodities: assembling electrical equipment, in light engineering, as well as in food processing.
(d) For some young, single women – particularly those employed as boutique assistants, receptionists, air hostesses – consumption of certain commodities, i.e. make-up and fashion (in which trades it is again women who are primarily the employees), is essential to the sale of their labour power.
(e) This same group plus other women work in the distribution/marketing apparatus which promotes and sells such commodities.

2 *Capital's need for cheap labour*

While the expansion/diversification of commodity production contributes to capital accumulation, the continuing extraction of relative surplus value which this represents 'founders on the tendency for the rate of profit to fall through the changing organic composition of capital' (Beechey 1977, p. 50). It is also those modes capital adopts to delay that fall which seem particularly pertinent to women's history:

(a) *By reducing the allotment made to necessary labour* and by
(b) *still more expanding the quantity of surplus labour with regard to the whole labour employed.* . . . There are moments in the developed movement of capital which delay this movement other than by crises. . . .
(c) *Unproductive waste of a great portion of capital.*
(d) . . . the fall likewise delayed by *creation of new branches of production in which more direct labour in relation to capital is needed, or where the productive power of labour is not yet developed.* [our lettering and italics]

Marx (1973, p. 750)

(a) Leaving to one side for a moment the first and most important mode in relation to women: 'the reduction in the allotment made to necessary labour', we can see that capital has often taken on women wage labourers within this whole framework of economic terms. Thus:

(b) 'Expanding the quantity of surplus labour with regard to the whole labour employed.' When, as in the post-war period, the ratio of working to dependent population is not growing, when there are checks on immigration, then married women are seen as one of the few available sources to check and possibly increase this balance (12). An increase in that ratio - more women entering social production - represents more labourers to be exploited, an increase in the working class. 'Accumulation of capital is therefore multiplication of the proletariat' (Marx 1976, p. 764), and therefore represents the necessary expansion of surplus labour. That surplus labour is even further increased because women are paid below the value of the labour power: the value of labour power is spread over husband and wife.

(c) 'Unproductive waste of a great portion of capital'. In particular here the massive circulation processes which do not produce surplus value but on which productive industry is now dependent, constitute such a waste - again a heavy reliance on female labour.

(d) 'New branches of production in which more direct labour in relation to capital is needed'. Labour-intensive industry of which the rag trade is a familiar example predominantly employs married women, either as home workers or in factories. The clothing industry of the 1950s and 1960s rests not on modernization of the technology of clothes production but on such labour-intensive use of female labour (13).

To return however to capital's attempt to reduce 'the allotment made to necessary labour', i.e. to employ labour as cheaply as possible, it is that tendency which contradictorily catches women whichever way they turn (14). This reduction is partly achieved by cheapening *subsistence* commodities which the competition between capitals brings about.

Capital therefore has an immanent drive, and a constant tendency, towards increasing the productivity of labour, in order to cheapen commodities and, by cheapening commodities, to cheapen the worker himself.

Marx (1976, p. 437)

While such a cheapening may potentially mean less housework for women, as the family can afford to buy commodities which previously she would have made, the continual incorporation in the post-war period of *luxury goods* into the means of subsistence of the working class both accentuates and counteracts this cheapening: the value of labour power is increased rather than reduced. With married women becoming more available for work on a much wider scale difficulties and contradictions are set up for capital.

The value of male labour power is premised on the family unit in which women perform domestic labour (Beechey 1977, p. 51). It is generally convenient for capital to maintain this arrangement. At particular times of crisis, e.g. unemployment, it is possible to pay male labour power below its price on the assumption that women in the home will temporarily work harder (15). Furthermore when women become wage workers the value of their labour power is also premised on the family unit - on them as dependants, receiving part of their means of subsistence from the man's 'family wage'. As Veronica Beechey argues, female wage labour either has lower value than male labour power or is paid at a price below its value. In both cases it represents a depression of the value of society's average labour power (16).

Capital can only retain these advantages of cheap labour power - unpaid labour in relation to the reproduction of male labour power, and cheap female labour power - so long as women continue to labour in, and have prime responsibility for, the home and child-care. The introduction of part-time work for women would seem to be particularly advantageous to capital in this respect. Even if unions are still fighting for a 'family wage', the practice of both husband and wife working is likely to undermine that, while at the same time: first, women in the family continue to bear the labour of reproduction of labour power; and second the position of responsibility there makes it a 'buyer's' market for their labour power. On all these counts the value of society's average labour power is kept down (17).

For capital the general resolution to these contradictions has been to constitute women as a reserve army of labour. For women as wives, however, 'they are situated in a state of permanent transition between the two modes of labouring, the capitalist and the family mode' (see Article 9).

3 *Reserve army of labour*

The creation of a reserve army of labour is one of the features of the contradictory processes of capital accumulation. In general, with technical advances, labourers are 'set free' in greater proportion than they are needed by new production. The growth of the service sector and the welfare state, by providing employment, and trade union activity, in fighting against changes in the labour process which create redundancies, are two ways in which this tendency has been modified. Marx argues that capital needs an industrial reserve army as a lever of capital accumulation: first, as a flexible population entering new branches of production and then being dispensed with as the labour process requires a different labour force; second, to act as a competitive force through 'depressing wage levels or forcing workers to submit to increases in the rate of exploitation and thus increasing the level of surplus value extraction' (Beechey 1977, p. 56).

Women's subordination

1   *Women as a reserve army*

Women do not rest easily within Marx's description, although it is clear that they are *as women* a reserve army for capital.

This conceptualization of women as a reserve army, distinctly demarcated as women, must presuppose a *sexual division of labour*. But the concept 'sexual division of labour' neither explains nor is itself explained by the concept 'reserve army'. We have always to explain what kind of division it is, not to leave it as a 'simple category' (Marx 1973, pp. 102-3) which we know commonsensically (as Marx and Engels both do) to be based on sex difference and which we apply across history and culture. As Marx describes with reference to the category of 'production' and 'property' we must reconstruct that apparently general and simple category as contradictorily composed of more concrete historical relations.

> The concrete is concrete because it is the concentration of many determinations, hence unity of the diverse. It appears in the process of thinking, therefore, as a process of concentration, as a result, not as a point of departure even though it is the point of departure in reality, and hence also the point of departure for observation and conception.
>
> Marx (1973, p. 101)

The sexual division of labour, as we have already indicated, does not arise as a *sexual* division from capital's own structures. Rather capital has built its own divisions on to already existing sexual divisions. The implications of that however are that, in the sexual division which is our starting point, capitalist and patriarchal structures are *inseparable*. The sexual division of labour structured in masculine dominance is 'colonized', 'taken over' by the structures of capital. That is not to say that it has lost its patriarchal determinations, as the Revolutionary Communist Group pamphlet implies (Adamson *et al.* 1976). Within the dominating structures of capital the sexual division of labour 'arises', as they are correct to say, from the separation of labour power from the labourer, i.e. in the relation between the reproduction of capital accumulation and the reproduction of the individual (labourer or capitalist) who is the necessary agent in the first reproduction. It 'arises' too in the separation of 'production' from 'consumption' (productive consumption and individual consumption) even though capital does not itself stipulate that different groups, let alone different sexes, must be involved at the different moments. As we have described it, the first appearance of the sexual division of labour analytically is in the family: women are domestic labourers, concerned with all the functions associated with bringing up children, *dependent* on men who earn the family wage. We cannot describe that dependent relation as capitalist even if it is supported by state and market intervention as well as overdetermined by capitalist ideologies. Sex/gender identity of women and men, primarily constructed in the family and organized around their respective labours as mothers and fathers, underlies the *transformed sexual division* of labour within wage labour.

It is through a consideration of patriarchal and capitalist relations inseparably structuring the sexual division of labour that we must consider women as a reserve. Economically, for capital they are a reserve like any other; from the point of view of women's subordination, the *specific* characteristics of female labour are, as we shall see, *defined by* women's position as a reserve. Thus the *particular* articulation of women's subordination through their position as a reserve is only a *general* economic benefit to capital. Our interest in female labour as a reserve does not then quite place it within the terms in which Marx defines 'reserve army of labour'. Married women at least do not become a reserve because they are thrown *out* of social production, but *become available* for social production with advances in commodity production and hence consumption. We would argue that the 'full employment' of men in the sixties has condemned one part of the working class, namely women, not to enforced idleness, but to their overwork as dual labourers – wage labourers and domestic labourers, in their position as an industrial reserve. Veronica Beechey (1977, p. 57) has suggested an important criterion for who is/is not part of the industrial reserve army:

> The preferred sources of the industrial reserve army from the viewpoint of capital are those categories of labour which are partially dependent upon sources of income other than the wage to meet some of the costs of the reproduction of labour power.

Married women then 'comprise a section of the working class which is not predominantly dependent upon its own wage for the costs of production and reproduction of labour power but which in addition is not heavily dependent on the welfare state' as are other categories (the elderly, for example). As Beechey goes on to say, they are a particularly advantageous source of industrial reserve army since they are excluded from the social security system except as dependants. They are therefore a pool of unprotected labour which 'can disappear' back into the family without usually appearing in unemployment statistics (Beechey 1977, p. 57).

Beechey is uncertain whether all women's work can be understood in terms of this concept. However the particular characteristic which she selects as constituting married women as a reserve suggests that it can, and indeed, that women's work must be described in this way. If we pay attention to the *movement in and out of the labour market* which women make, we can see that all 'women's work' is of this kind, even when it is not 'women's work' as such, and whether or not women are the 'preferred source' of the industrial reserve army. They constitute a reserve of a 'peculiar type', controlled not so much by the relations of capital production but by the *relations of reproduction in the family* - even when they are not married (ideologically it is expected that they will be).

Marx descriptively details different forms of the industrial reserve army which Beechey considers in an earlier draft of her paper and which we would like to re-examine (Marx 1976, pp. 784-9). His categories are unhelpfully named and perhaps historically specific. Still they do enable us to begin to conceptualize women as a reserve army which is internally differentiated, not just one monolithic grouping. Although in all cases they are a reserve first because of their position *as women* - as reproducers within the family - that determination operates differently for various groups of women. In each case their potential movement in and out of the labour market is distinct; their dependence on men and the family is different; the kinds of work for which they are an industrial reserve shifts and hence their position as an industrial reserve in the overall regulation of wages, and in relation to men's and women's wages separately, must also be differentiated.

(a) *Floating.* Here Marx considers the 'attraction' and 'repulsion' of workers into centres of modern industry, for example, boys who are only employed until maturity. In relation to women, some young women - as sales assistants in boutiques, hairdressers, receptionists, some secretaries - leave their employment at the birth of their first child, at the latest, and tend not to take up the same work if they resume when their children are older. In these jobs their sexuality and their age, i.e. their sexual attractiveness, is all important: neither men nor older women are eligible. It is also work in which temporary and part-time work are important features. The advantages of the leaving 'of their own accord', in fact because of the contradiction between their social role in production and their 'private' role within the social relations of reproduction, means not just that capital and the state disclaim all responsibility for their 'unemployment', but also:

1 Their wages remain low since their family of origin and then their husband are held partly responsible for their reproduction costs.
2 They are unorganized because their work is 'temporary'.
3 The patriarchal relation is reproduced at work: men don't do secretarial work; sexual attractiveness continues to be a part of what they are selling when they sell their labour power; men treat them as, and often the work involves them as, 'substitute wives', because there is constantly a further supply of such labour (18).
4 In relation to wages as a whole the existence of a group of young women prepared to sell their labour power at a price below its value probably means that capital wins both ways, i.e. men's and women's wages, within office work say, negotiated separately because they are performing different work, are settled at lower rates than they might be if assessed together.
5 As an industrial reserve they are not competing for men's jobs.

(b) *Latent.* Here Marx considers agricultural workers who are passing over into a manufacturing proletariat, but who are dependent on the agricultural population -

their families (women) – to support them when paid work ceases. This situation is analogous to the position of married women when it is materially and ideologically possible for them to be 'free' from child-rearing for some time, i.e. when it is no longer ideologically taken for granted that they should stay at home to look after their children as their sole occupation, nor economically necessary for them to produce all the family's use values. They become available for paid work when their children are at school, if capital needs them, but can safely be absorbed back into the family if work dries up or the 'dual role' becomes intolerably heavy. These women 'choose' to work and 'choose' to leave. In particular this applies to middle class women whose husbands are more than adequately able to support them and their families. This reserve takes up a variety of jobs – not necessarily 'women's work' – which are united by the tendency to be part-time and of low status within the particular job area, whether professional or other: teaching, nursing, secretarial and factory work. As an industrial reserve it is difficult to generalize about their position. In the present economic crisis part-time teachers and social workers are the first to lose their jobs, while part-time employment in industry is on the increase, though at the expense of full-time women rather than men (19).

(c) *Stagnant*. This is the group Marx characterizes as working extremely irregularly for a maximum time and a minimum wage. Here we can refer to women – mothers married and unmarried, who for economic reasons are forced to work where and when they can. With no provision for child-care and the state's insufficient support for the very poor there is always a supply of such labour for capital. In the case of home work like sewing-machining, not only is the pay extremely low but the availability of such labour also depresses the wage of machinists who actually work on the employers' premises. Black women, West Indian and Asian, substantially make up this category, typically doing night cleaning, canteen work or home work during 'unsocial hours' (20).

(d) *Pauperism*. Although the welfare state ameliorates the excesses of poverty to which Marx was referring, nevertheless the women who make up the stagnant reserve – those women often without 'supportive' men, single, looking after elderly parents, unmarried mothers, divorced women, widows, and prostitutes – are all at times likely to be on the verge of destitution.

2 *Labour power and sexuality: femininity/masculinity*
Conceptualizing women in paid work as a reserve army of labour structured by the social relations of reproduction in the family has already posed a meshing of capital' 'abstract labour' and indifference to gender, with patriarchal relations – in particular femininity. This 'meshing' is invariably contradictory for women. When they enter wage labour there is immediately a contradiction between their position as mothers and wage workers (as well as a contradiction in relation to men). While men are affirmed as men in their double relation as fathers and wage labourers through their role as 'breadwinner' – which is why masculinity as a construct can so often be overlooked (21) – femininity is cast in doubt by such a relation. On the one hand, women's role as mothers is often seen to be in jeopardy; on the other, their

femininity carries over into the type of labour they perform: 'women's work', often regarded with derision both by men and women workers themselves. The determination by femininity on women's wage labour is particularly transparent, because waged work in general (despite internal mental/manual divisions) is seen as masculine. This is not relevant simply to the types of job women do, but also to how they carry them out - their consciousness of themselves as workers and men's consciousness of them too.

In this context we have to consider two aspects of the construction of femininity: while we are mothers who serve our husbands and children, we are also the desirable 'sexual object' for men. Both these aspects have been capitalized on in the post-war period: it is through women as *consumers* of certain commodities that capital has intervened in defining the form of femininity - giving children frozen crinkled-cut chips, not home-cut ones, wearing heavy make-up and platform shoes, etc. However the determination by femininity operates at different levels. Here we attempt briefly to separate out these levels in their complex and contradictory articulations with wage relations of capital.

In so far as we sell our commodity, labour power, for a wage as do men, femininity plays no part. Nevertheless the conditions of that sale differ: we are not able to 'freely' sell our labour power on the market because we are not 'the untrammelled owner of our capacity to labour, i.e. of our person' (Marx 1970, p. 168). As Sheila Rowbotham (1973, pp. 168 and 128) argues: 'Within the family the man appropriates the labour power of the women in the exchange of services'; 'Women are thus seen as economic attachments to men, not quite as free labourers.' The sale of her labour power is, then, mediated through marriage: her dependence on a husband and responsibility for family. We have to leave paid work when we have babies or our husbands and children are ill; when our husbands move their jobs to another area; when our husbands express displeasure at our paid work, and so on.

Even when we have seemingly overcome these obstacles and sell our labour power, we are not free of our gender determination. In 'modern industry', where Marx maintains as a tendency that 'natural' differences of strength should no longer be applicable and therefore that men and women should enter on the same terms, the hierarchy of labour which is established follows a sexual division, in so far as the semi- and unskilled work is usually performed by women (Beechey 1977, p. 51). In this way women's labour can be used in the processes of *de-skilling*. However because of the power of the unions - usually male - to resist these processes and women's usually differential place in the labour market, it is not often that women are in competition with men, their unskilled labour replacing men's skills (22).

In these jobs where women are not doing 'women's work' as such (although it comes to be defined as that) women still, inevitably, live within their femininity at work. It is in the way they are treated by men at work (particular sexist incidents: for flirting with; as strike breakers and/or as workers not to be supported over equal pay strikes); the way they themselves see their work and its role in their lives (secondary to home, its convenience to home in terms of travel, little attention to the interest of the work, temporary, 'nice people,' etc.); their minor participation in union affairs (meetings at times when married women have to be at home 'servicing' the family, or the type of union activity – for better conditions as well as pay – which are gender-determined (23)). As Audrey Wise (1974, p. 282) writes:

Women aren't interested just in wages, equal pay is much more than a wage demand. Equal pay is a demand for self-respect, it's more than a demand for equal money, it's hygiene, safety, cold and things like that.

In other wage labour women take their femininity with them in terms of the *use value* of their labour as 'servers': in the home they serve their families. In paid work they serve 'consumers' in hospitals, canteens, etc. As clerical workers or secretaries they serve men and the company (24). Or it is the use value of other 'feminine' work in the home that they carry over into paid work, e.g. sewing-machining and detailed handiwork. Inversely, as home workers their femininity confines them to the house as they carry out 'women's work' for a wage, which, because of this 'doubly feminine' wage position, is extremely low, i.e. they are further removed from the masculine bargaining power associated with masculine jobs.

In yet other jobs female sexuality as sexuality on display is part of the *use value of the commodity labour power itself* (25). For some secretaries, receptionists, boutique assistants, it is essential to be attractively feminine as well as to serve. This particular group of women workers embody a curious contradiction. As Juliet Mitchell describes it they are in the *most advanced* and the *most primitive* sectors of capital. These women are in effect selling their own sexuality in the same way that advertising uses women's sexuality to sell other products. In this position they are 'the subject of the most advanced ideological utilization made by capitalism; its chief ideological means of creating its markets' (Mitchell 1971, p. 143), while at the same time working in 'backwards' areas of capital in terms of how their labour is exploited.

At the ideological level this contradiction extends to all women workers, and in the sixties was of particular significance to young educated women. This group of women, who experienced an 'equal' education with men, found first that 'equality' was not carried over into the jobs they were able to find (they were expected soon to leave 'as mothers'), but discovered second that they had to live up to both an image of 'equality' with men and of sixties femininity in which skirts rose startlingly higher each week. While some secretaries, for example, may not experience that contradiction – to them their sexual attractiveness may nurture the illusion of a power and equality at work – it was to this group of young educated women that the contradictory patriarchal relations of sexuality, hitherto private, became publicly visible. It was that bringing-to-visibility of patriarchal structures, now invested with the capitalist commodity form, *in contradiction* to what women believed was their social equality, which played an essential part in the development of the Women's Movement at the end of the sixties.

Here they are doing a grand job as teachers, doctors, and barristers, running companies and ministries and banks, just like men and ready for separate tax allowances when suddenly skirts soar up to flash point, somebody opens up Bunny Clubs and the image shatters.

How can you take them seriously after that? Could you ever be sure that inside every bank manager there was not a sex symbol trying to get out?

'Unfair Comment?', George Newman, *The Times* 31 October 1966

Equal pay

There are limitations attached to reforms, but reforms also set up new contradictions and new possibilities for struggle. The question we should, therefore, ask is not whether changes in legislation since the '30s or '40s have improved the position of women. Rather we should ask of any particular reform what new contradictions it sets up for women, how these affect their consciousness and the ability to organise.

PEWG (1975, p. 30)

We want to conclude this article through an understanding of the Equal Pay Act and the Sex Discrimination Act (1) as, in part, a condensation of the contradictions of women's continuing subordination under capitalism, which we have already considered. We briefly examine the legislation, which, though proposed in the sixties, was implemented in the mid-seventies, in terms of its *potential* and *actual* effects on women.

The Equal Pay Act and the Sex Discrimination Act were the legal means by which women should have achieved equal pay by 1976. The Equal Pay Act pertains to women's economic inequality and although it seems to concern the relation of inequality between men and women, it only does so on *capital's* ground of the value of labour power. Whilst in *theory* the Act should herald at least economic equality for women, the contradiction which prevents this from becoming reality is that it does not consider the position of *structural inequality* in which women are placed before they enter the wage market. It cannot challenge women's inequality before they enter the labour market which is premised on their role in the family. The division of labour which keeps women primarily responsible for the home means that women do not have even the right to equal exploitation in capitalism. To really transform the situation of women, the Sex Discrimination Act would have to confront the deeply embedded ideologies of domesticity and femininity which dominate women's lives.

The introduction of the Equal Pay Act and the Sex Discrimination Act

The history of the political struggle which at last resulted in the Equal Pay Act is itself contradictory. The TUC accepted the principle for eighty years, but only when external pressures demanded active response did it pursue the matter further than an annual or biennial resolution (Pinder 1969) (2). The Act finally takes its place within the context of 'progressive' law reform of the sixties as part of the movement towards 'equality of individuals' before the law. It was no coincidence that the Act was finally introduced in 1968 – Human Rights Year, and the fiftieth anniversary of the granting of female suffrage. During this year women's organizations and other bodies reviewed the progress made since 1928 and also catalogued the disadvantages still existing in employment, etc. The government's income policy, though making no reference to sex, did ensure that pay problems would receive more publicity than before. The Race Relations Act (1965 and 1968) was understood by some to reveal a situation which put immigrant males in a more privileged position, in some respects, than indigenous females. The publication of the Government Social Survey on women's employment (Hunt 1968) gave more publicity to the problems of working women. This report had much coverage on radio, TV and in the press, calling for an end to all discriminatory practice.

Two events in June 1968 put the question of women's pay to the forefront of the interest of both the public and the employers of large numbers of women. The first was the strike of the women sewing-machinists at Ford's Dagenham plant which, although initially over grading, was taken up by the engineering union, the AEF, as a matter of equal pay. One of the results of the strike was the formation of a national organization of trade union women to campaign for equal rights (Smith 1974). At the end of June, Barbara Castle, Secretary of State for Employment and Productivity, promised to 'put new life' into discussions that her department was having with the TUC and CBI on equal pay, and indicated that it should not take any longer for introduction into the private sector than it had in the public sector.

The Equal Pay Act was introduced by Barbara Castle and brought in by the Labour Government in 1970, but five years were allowed before it was finally operative. During these five years employers were supposed to make plans for the implementation of equal pay within their own wage structures. This period of leeway, in fact, gave employers the opportunity to restructure and redefine jobs, and circumvent the terms of the Act. Under the Act, the Secretary of State was empowered to make an order for women's rates to be raised to 90 per cent or more of men's, if s/he thought 'orderly progress' was not being made, by 31 December 1973. A report published by the Office of Manpower Economics in August 1972 gave evidence of deliberate circumvention of regrading, the separation of men and women workers with union agreement, general lack of progress, and a widespread attitude among employers that they would wait for the Act to be enforced before doing anything (Trodd 1972).

Effects of the Equal Pay Act

Two years after the implementation of the Act, women still lag behind men in wages. Though young men and women who start work in their teens earn about the same, the difference begins to show very quickly. For the highest paid manual workers between 21 and 24, men will average (1976 figures) £80.8 per week while women will average £54. Among the same group of non-manual workers men will earn £74.6 compared with women's £59.1 (Equal Opportunities Commission 1977).

The Equal Pay Act was never meant to give equality to *all* women workers, and indeed, it is impossible for most women to achieve equal pay even within the limited terms of the Act. The Act says that a woman is entitled to equal pay if

1. She is working 'like work' (i.e. the 'same or broadly similar work') with a man, or
2. her job, although it is not the same or broadly similar to a man's, has been rated as of equivalent value to a man's job under a job evaluation scheme.

If a woman's job falls into either of these two categories, and she is not getting equal pay, then she can apply to an industrial tribunal (Coussins 1977).

The Act leaves a tremendous number of women who can make no claim that they are doing 'like' work with men. In the majority of cases, women's work is in a small range of jobs at the lower end of the job market, e.g. secretarial, clerical, service and catering, and in the retail trade, where there is no male counterpart with whom they can claim equality of work. These women could claim on grounds of their job being of 'equal value' with a man's job, but only if a job evaluation scheme has been conducted. The women working in these jobs are often in situations where they do not belong to a trade union, yet they need strong trade union backing if they are to achieve a satisfactory outcome from any job evaluation scheme (3).

Traditionally women do not do 'like' work with men, and this anomaly is not challenged by the Equal Pay Act. This especially applies to part-time work where women's position is *not* 'equal' to men's because it is premised on their primary responsibility for domestic labour and child-care.

Part-time work – the contradictions

While the Acts appear to provide the opportunity for economic equality, the government has not provided the necessary welfare provisions to enable women to enter the labour market while ensuring that their children are looked after. There has been a decrease in the number of nursery places for the under-fives to a figure less than the 1900 one (Adamson *et al.* 1976). There is no provision for school-age children after school hours and during the holidays, and women with children of school age and under are forced into part-time jobs in order to accommodate their dual role. Part-time work *appears* to and often *does* offer a solution for women in that they can work hours which do not conflict with their domestic role. The increase in part-time work has coincided with the economic crisis for capital, and in this sense part-time work can be seen as a solution for capital.

In such a situation employers are unlikely to risk heavy investment in highly productive capital-intensive techniques of production which would enable them to employ a high-wage labour force. They are more likely to prefer processes requiring a lot of cheap labour and relatively low capital investment. Women workers, and especially part-time workers ... provide a suitable labour force in such circumstances, both because they are relatively cheap in employment and because they are more easily and more cheaply displaced when no longer needed. Gardiner (1975, p. 14)

The Equal Pay Act has revealed the contradictory nature of part-time work as a solution for women. Firstly, the existence of part-time 'paid' work is premised on women's primary role within the family and, therefore, *reinforces* the sexual division of labour which means that women have the prime responsibility for the home and children. Additionally, women suffer if they work for less than sixteen hours a week, as they are not covered by the same terms of employment as full-time workers (Campaign Notes 1975). The existence of part-time jobs can catch women in the double bind of the contradiction which forces them into the jobs in the first place.

Patriarchal attitudes at industrial tribunals

The patriarchal ideology and the division of labour which locates women's role in domestic labour and child-care is reflected in the decisions of some chair*men* at hearings of equal pay cases. In some cases reported by the NCCL, the 'given' nature of and the *low status* accorded to women's roles has been used against women at tribunal hearings. The structural inequality of women as domestic labourers can be used to justify their being paid lower wages than men in the labour market. In one case reported by the NCCL an employer's representative tried to justify the lower pay which a woman toilet cleaner received compared to a male cleaner engaged on the same work. He stated that

a male toilet attendant has to *approach* the job from a labouring point of view and a female toilet attendant approaches it from a housekeeping point of view. [our italics]

Coussins (1977, p. 49)

Here 'housekeeping' is accorded lower status than labouring and used as evidence that the work which the female toilet attendant performs is of less value than that performed by a man. The reasoning used is based on the 'approach' of the worker, thereby suggesting that the 'approach' of the woman based on 'housekeeping' warrants less pay than the 'approach' of a man based on labouring!

A further example of the low value accorded to women's role within the family when it is translated into economic terms is revealed in the case of a woman working as a housemother in a school for handicapped children, who lost her claim for equal pay with the housefather. The chair*man*, Sir Martin Edwards, observed in the written decision:

A housemother is engaged to look after the younger boys and carry out domestic duties. A housefather is engaged to lead the growing boy to a better approach to life and help him in his problems. The roles are largely those of a mother and father in ordinary life; they are both important, but they are different . . . for these reasons, we find that the applicant is not engaged on like work with a man . . . full of admiration as we are for the work which she is doing. . . .

Coussins (1977, p. 47)

The decision reveals the tenacity of the ideology of women's subordination in those on whom women must depend for administration of the anti-discriminatory legislation.

This article has attempted to look at the legislation in terms of the new contradictions which it reveals. The PEWG pamphlet suggests that new contradictions will be revealed, but the Acts also highlight *existing contradictions* which remain untouched by the legislation. The supporters of the Acts believe, as did Engels, that women's entry into the labour market would provide the basis for potential freedom for women. However restricted the powers or aims of the Equal Pay Act, they do offer at least the potential for women's independence and the possibility of seeing women as the main wage earner, able to support a family.

It is within the context of the idea of the family wage that the Act has meant that women have found themselves in opposition to male union wage demands. The possibility of equal pay for women is in contradiction with the idea of the family wage traditionally fought for by male trade unions. The idea of the male as breadwinner is a crucial part of the ideology of masculinity.

The wage packet is the provider of freedom, and independence; the particular prize of masculinity in work. . . . The wage packet as a kind of symbol of machismo dictates the domestic culture and economy and tyrannises both men and women.

Willis (1977, p. 50)

The challenge which equal pay poses has to confront the ideology of masculinity as well as the economic level of the wage. The role of the unions and the need for their support to the claims of women under the Equal Pay Act cannot be overemphasized.

In conclusion, since the terms of reference of the Act do not question the fundamental causes of women's oppression as being located in their reproductive role within the family, the results from these potentially progressive legislations can only be limited. Nevertheless, they do raise women's expectations and self-awareness and thus stimulate pressure for changes which will challenge the ways in which capitalism has exploited women's specific role in production and reproduction. An explanation of women's oppression which addresses the economic level *alone* is too limited, but the contradictions which the Acts reveal point to areas of potential challenge at the economic and ideological level of women's oppression located in their primary responsibility for reproduction.

Acknowledgements

The final draft of this article has been written by only four of us, but it comes out of work started by the Women's Studies Group 1976-7. The original writing group included Rachel Harrison, Val Levin and Roisin McDonough. Our thanks to them for discussing this article with us and particularly to Rachel Harrison who has helped through all the stages of toil.

Notes and references

Introduction
1   See Article 7, footnote 5 (p. 153), and Article 9, footnote 3 (p. 192).

Women working in the home
1   We do not look, in this section, at women's (very underpaid) waged work in the home – as child-minders, home workers, etc.
2   This article mainly draws on British sources, although at points American texts which were central in the debate are used.
3   An early account of housework as *work* can be found in Suzanne Gail (1968). Article 2 examines the concentration on experience in early WLM writing.
4   Their paper, 'Peckham Rye Women's Liberation' was given at the Oxford 1970 Women's Liberation Conference. Now available in M. Wandor (1972).
5   In this distinction, Shulamith Firestone's *The Dialectic of Sex* would be considered 'radical feminist'. See Mitchell (1971, pp. 91-6) for a discussion of this type of distinction.
6   Ann Oakley has substantially developed the sociology of housework. See Oakley (1974a) and with particular relevance to this article the first chapter of Oakley (1974b).
7   Adamson *et al.* (1975), while *recognizing* the importance of the ideological level in an analysis of women's subordination, do not substantially consider this level, and thus underestimate the *reality* of sexual divisions within the working class.
8   Sheila Rowbotham (in Wandor 1972, p. 192): 'The Ford's women also helped to make the question of women's specific oppression easier to discuss on the left. At first the men would only admit that working class women had anything to complain about.'
9   The 1974 Women and Socialism Conference papers have a fairly representative selection of positions, with a clear introduction by Caroline Freeman about the relevance of the debate to feminists.
10 See Marx (1976, pp. 270-80, pp. 709-24, pp. 1060-5); Althusser (1971a).
11 See Marx (1976, p. 717).
12 This article throughout assumes a 'typical' nuclear family. This is not to suggest that (a) we think all women are married, and/or live with men, and/or have children; (b) that women are not the only or main breadwinner in many families; (c) that there are not lots of other exceptions.
13 See Delmar (1976) and Sachs (1974) for feminist critiques of Engels.

14 See Robert Taylor, 'Sex objects: surprise statistics', *Spare Rib,* no. 19, for a summary of 1971 census figures.

15 The following three sections are particularly indebted to the work of the Political Economy of Women Group and to Jean Gardiner's own work.

16 The debate over productive and unproductive labour, and how the distinction is made and used by Marx, is extremely complex. The radical simplification we make, and the limitation of the problem to that of the characterization of housework, is in the context of a summary of, rather than a further contribution to, the debate over domestic labour. In this process, we refer only to elements in individual contributions to the debate, and although we have tried to avoid misrepresentation, this compression may well emerge as that.

17 Thus Seccombe has argued that 'necessary labour time' should be understood to include the wife's domestic labour. Cf. *New Left Review,* No. 83. Gardiner maintained (1975) that 'necessary labour time is not synonymous with the labour embodied in the reproduction and maintenance of labour power once one takes account of domestic labour'.

18 Surplus labour, in any mode of production, is labour performed by the labourer which is in excess of that necessary to ensure his/her survival. In the capitalist mode of production, labour power's unique quality as a commodity is that it creates value. Thus surplus value is the particular form of surplus labour in the capitalist mode of production, and is the basis of capital accumulation.

19 See PEWG (1975) for a summary of the arguments about whether domestic labour should be analysed within the capitalist mode of production, or as a 'client' mode of production articulating with it.

20 See *WPCS* No. 9 for 'orthodox' and 'unorthodox' in terms of the whole debate.

21 Unpublished papers to Birmingham and Coventry Feminist Research Workshop 1976. Catherine Hall, 'The Ideology of Domesticity', and Ray Harrison, 'Romance'.

22 This discussion, inevitably and regrettably through the limitations of our own work, remains at a general level, which is in contradiction with our argument for historical specificity in this area. It is the work of those feminists who have been involved in the domestic labour debate which has made it possible to see its shortcomings.

23 Caroline Freeman (1974) argues: 'We must aim to drive a wedge between the physical tasks of housework and the emotional services wives and mothers are expected to do as *women.*'

24 Freeman (1974) provides an extended criticism of this demand: 'The first defect of this argument is its misrepresentation of the marxist concept of

"productive". The designation of housework as "unproductive" is taken as a slur, instead of as a technical concept allowing us to describe the relation between housework and capital. The productive/unproductive distinction does have implications for the sorts of struggle appropriate for different sorts of workers, but it does not *evaluate* their work.'

25   Masculine hegemony: We introduce Gramsci's concept of hegemony in a very condensed way. Another summary: '... hegemony, for Gramsci includes the ideological but cannot be reduced to that level, ... it refers to the dialectical relation of class forces. Ideological dominance and subordination are not understood in isolation, but always as one, though crucially important, aspects of the relations of the classes and class fractions - economic and political, as well as ideological/cultural' (Hall, Lumley, McLennan 1977, p. 48). This concept is developed by Gramsci in the analysis of *class* relations, and there are obvious problems about 'lifting' it into an understanding of the relations of dominance and subordination between men and women (we are not suggesting that women are a subordinate class). We use the concept for two reasons: it 'includes the ideological but cannot be reduced to that level', which seems to us a central element in the way women live their subordination; it also involves the notion of 'consent' to domination by the subordinate group. Rowbotham (1973, pp. 38-9) discusses the use of the concept *male hegemony* (see also Article 7, footnote 8).

The state, reproduction of labour power and the subordination of women

1   We would like to acknowledge the help of Richard Johnson, and John Clarke and Roisin McDonough's unpublished paper, 'The Family, State and Reproduction' (1977).

2   See Wilson (1977, p. 40), who notes how early welfare legislation's main preoccupation was with the work ethic.

3   See Greenwood and Young (1976) for a discussion of social democratic ideology in relation to the question of abortion.

4   See 'Out of the people: the politics of containment 1935-45' in *WPCS* No. 9.

5   In fact, not only was capital getting through nine generations of its workers in the span of three generations but, as A. Weir (1975) notes, with widespread epidemics, members of the ruling class were also carried off, e.g. Prince Albert died of cholera in 1865.

6   The Public Health Acts of 1848 and 1875 increased the standards of housing, sanitation and planning in the new industrial towns.

7   In fact the suffragettes themselves did not challenge the ideal of motherhood (PEWG 1975, p. 25).

8 A TUC deputation in 1941 pressed the government for a comprehensive review of social insurance.
9 See the article by A. Scott James in the *Picture Post*, 1943.
10 See Kincaid (1973).
11 A survey by Slater & Woodside (1951, p. 189) found public resentment to such inducement: '... they showed indignation that the production of large numbers of children could be expected of them as a duty.'
12 Prior to Beveridge's new legislation, all women, single and married, received lower social insurance and means-tested assistance benefits than men.
13 We are indebted to Roisin McDonough for this point.

Women in waged work

1 For the characteristics of women's employment in this period see: Ministry of Labour (1974); Counter Information Services (1976); and Mackie and Pattullo (1977).

In the latter's introduction they ask, 'What is so special about women's work?'

The answer is that women's work is radically different from that done by men. Women workers are paid less than men, they work in a much smaller range of occupations, they do much more part-time work, and, in manufacturing, they tend to work alongside other women, in a small number of industries. Women are not as skilled as men, for a variety of reasons, and they are neither promoted as much as men nor are they to be found in great numbers in the professions and in management jobs.

And we would add that in the post-war period there has been a gradual increase in the number of women, particularly married women, over the age of thirty-five, working. Their work is predominantly in the service sector. They have become increasingly unionized but much less so than men.

2 Braverman (1976, p. 120) makes the following argument about the attention to the processes of capital accumulation:

... household work, although it has been the special domain of women, is not thereby necessarily so central to the issues of women's liberation as might appear from this fact. On the contrary, it is the breakdown of the traditional household economy which has produced the present-day feminist movement. This movement in its modern form is almost entirely a product of women who have been summoned from the household by the requirements of the capital accumulation process, and subjected to experiences and stresses unknown in the previous thousands of years of household labour under a variety of social arrangements. Thus it is the analysis of their new situation that in my opinion occupies the place of the first importance in the theory of modern feminism.

Let me add at once that none of this is said in order to disparage the need for an understanding of the specific forms and issues of household labour, of the working class family and of sexual divisions and tensions both within and outside the family. . . .

3 See Bowlby (1951), Myrdal and Klein (1956), Gavron (1966), Fogarty, Rapoport and Rapoport (1972) for examples of shifting attitudes towards women's position in the family.

4 For how policy in relation to women's paid work was explicitly premised on male full employment and the 'family wage' and therefore was directed primarily at encouraging part time work, see Young Fabian Pamphlet II (1966) and Manpower Studies No. 1 (1964).

5 See PEWG (1975), Adamson et al. (1976) for arguments and details about the underprovision of child care facilities in this period.

6 See Weinbaum and Bridges (1976, pp. 90-1), who argue that women are 'consumption workers'. While men confront capital in the form of employers,

> . . . in the market for goods and services women confront capital in the form of commodities. . . . The work of consumption, while subject to and structured by capital embodies those needs – material and non-material – most antagonistic to capitalist production; and the contradiction between private production and socially determined needs is embodied in the activities of the housewife.

While they consider the 'contradiction between their work in the market', i.e. their 'work' of buying, and 'their role in the home', using the commodities, they do not take up the contradictions which their position as wage labourers poses.

7 For more adequate accounts of capital's contradictory tendencies, particularly in relation to the labour process, see Braverman (1974), Marx (1976, Chapters 15, 25).

8 Marx's own consideration of women's paid work mainly focuses around an 'earlier' contradiction between the attempt to increase absolute surplus value – which 'founders' on the physical deterioration of the work force and the length of the working day – and the shift to extraction of relative surplus value. See Marx (1976, Chapters 10, 15) and Beechey (1977, p. 50).

9 See also Rowbotham (1973), chapter on 'Imperialism and everyday life'. Also Braverman (1974), particularly Chapter 13, 'The Universal Market', for examination of this whole area.

10 See Braverman (1974), Chapter 15, 'Clerical Workers' and Chapter 16, 'Service Occupations and Retail Trade'. Also Benét (1972) for an account of secretarial work. For general occupational changes see Ministry of Labour (1967), which indicates the importance of women's labour in those changes. On office work, Ministry of Labour (1968).

11 Seccombe (1975).

12 See Manpower Studies No. 1 (1964) and Young Fabian Pamphlet II (1966), which both make such arguments about the need for married women to work in the interest of the economy.

13 A clear indication of the intensive use of women's labour made by the clothes industry providing chain stores is the extent to which home workers are employed. See Hope *et al.* (1976, p. 89).

14 See Beechey (1977, pp. 51-4) to whom we are indebted for much of this argument.

15 See Mackintosh, Himmelweit and Taylor (1977). They discuss both the demand of 'woman's right to work' — the demand for economic independence which means at the same time the right to be exploited, and the work that that ignores: women's work in the home. At times of crises and cuts in services women are vulnerable on *both* fronts, thrown out of jobs *and* forced to do more work in the home.

16 In this context Beechey (1977, p. 53) discusses the relevance to women of the Marxist theory of 'regionalism' of uneven development, i.e. whether married or not, women's position is analogous to that of semi-proletarianized workers on the periphery of capitalist production in the Third World, whose labour power sells at below its value because their wives are engaged in subsistence production on the land.

17 See Anderson *et al.* (1976) for a discussion of how part-time work has become a 'structural necessity' for capital in the post-Second World War period.

18 See Benét (1972), Toynbee (1977), Korda (1974) for accounts of secretarial work which discuss women's sexuality in their work role.

19 See CIS (1976) which discusses part-time/full-time unemployment in relation to the present economic crisis.

20 On home workers who are an ethnically diverse group see Hope *et al.* (1976), *Spare Rib,* no. 33. On black women, West Indian and Asian (the latter often doing homework) see Amos (1977), who describes how West Indian women — mothers who are often supporting families without a man's financial assistance — frequently take on night and early morning work so that they can look after their children during the day. Also Harris (1972).

21 See Willis (1977), who argues for masculinity as a construct which, articulating with class, *differentiates* men along a manual/mental division which working class men live out as a socially superior masculine/socially inferior feminine divide. It is however working class men's recognition of femininity, as it is lived by their wives, which allows that class division to be constructed through sexuality.

22 See the First World War example in munitions and engineering that Beechey gives (1977, p. 55).

23 See Brown (1976), who considers 'Women employees as a problem' which deals generally with these issues. Also Smith (1976) (in same volume – Barber and Allen 1976), who specifically considers the operation of 'masculine supremacy' in Fleet Street, both in terms of how men see women journalists who work alongside them and how women inhabit that masculine culture of work.

24 Baxandall *et al.* (1976, p. 4) discuss how 'executives object when their personal secretaries are removed to typing pools' because they no longer have their every 'whim' catered for, i.e. the 'serving' role which secretaries perform analogous to that of wives, works against the rationalization of the work process: it is resisted by secretaries *and* executives.

25 'Women do literally sell their bodies – if not as prostitutes, then to the publicity industries, modelling and so on – much as men and women sell their labour power' (Mitchell 1971, p. 55).

Equal pay
1 The Equal Pay Act (1970), as amended, now appears as Schedule 1 of the Sex Discrimination Act (1975).
2 For a fuller discussion of the history, and introduction to the Equal Pay Act, see Pinder (1969).
3 Even when they are unionized, women *rarely* get strong union backing to support them. This article does not attempt to argue the importance of the role of trade unions at *all stages of women's* fight for equal pay. For a more comprehensive argument see Coussins (1977).

4 Housewives: isolation as oppression

Dorothy Hobson

DH Do you ever think about yourself and if you do, how would you describe yourself?

AB I'm always looking for something better . . . I can't really . . . I just see myself as the one that has to stop at home . . . (laughs). Sometimes I'm very contented and other times I think 'this ain't fair', you know. I can't really think of myself.

This article is based on current research into the culture of young working class housewives at home with young children (1). The research is conducted by tape-recorded interviews in their homes and covers many aspects of women's personal experience both before they were married and in their present situation (2). The article will concentrate on their present role as housewives and mothers and their understanding of this role in relation to their previous experience as wage labourers. It focuses on the *isolation* of women within the privatized sphere of the home, and attempts to present *isolation* as one of the ways which these women experience oppression and to locate the experience within the structures of capitalism. Although it is recognized that there is no simple way of 'reading' accounts of subjective experience, I would hold that they do point to the sites of structural contradictions, however indirectly. I also think, as is argued by Sheila Rowbotham (1973), that women's subjective experience reveals a 'sense of oppression', and this oppression I would see as having a material basis.

The centrality of women's work in the day-to-day and generational reproduction of the bearers of labour power has been examined in Article 3 of this book and it is on the theoretical position of that article that this analysis is premised.

The capital given in return for labour-power is converted into means of subsistence which have to be consumed to reproduce the muscles, nerves, bones and brains of existing workers, and to bring new workers into existence. Within the limits of what is absolutely necessary, therefore, the individual consumption of the working class is the reconversion of the means of subsistence given by capital in return for labour-power into fresh labour-power which capital is then again able to exploit. It is the production and reproduction of the capitalist's most indispensable means of production: the worker. The individual consumption of the worker, whether it occurs inside or outside the workshop, inside or outside the labour process, remains an aspect of the production and reproduction of capital, just as the cleaning of machinery does, whether it is done during the labour process, or when intervals in that process permit.

Marx (1976, p. 717)

Marx recognized that the production and reproduction of the *worker* is indispensable to capital and that although this takes place outside the labour process it remains 'an aspect of the production and reproduction of capital'. In the same chapter he continues (Marx 1976, p. 718):

> The maintenance and reproduction of the working class remains a necessary condition for the reproduction of capital. But the capitalist may safely leave this to the worker's drives for self-preservation and propagation.

He then writes (p. 719):

> The reproduction of the working class implies at the same time the transmission and accumulation of skills from one generation to another.

It is within this essential region which is outside the labour process that the unwaged work which women perform is located. The work which women perform in this process remains 'invisible' from the point of view of capital, and their oppression also has remained invisible in most analyses of the process of capital accumulation because of its structural absence or 'invisibility'. Likewise, the transmission of skills necessary in generational reproduction, I would locate as performed within the family both before and after the entry of children into the state apparatus of education (Althusser 1971a).

Methodological notes

The method of interviewing in a one-to-one situation requires some comment. I usually feel some apprehension when first arriving at someone's house to interview them, although I am more nervous at the clinic when I initially approach the women. However, the situation in the home is never as tense as an 'interview' may sound because the 'setting' is informal. Young children or babies are usually present, often playing noisily in the room or needing attention, and this eliminates any tendency towards a formal interview. What I find most difficult is to resist commenting in a way which may direct the answers which the women give to my questions. However, when the taped interview ends we usually talk and then the women ask me questions about my life and family. These questions often reflect areas where they have experienced ambivalent feelings in their own replies. For example, one woman who said during the interview that she did not like being married, asked me how long I had been married and if I liked it. When I told her how long I had been married, she said, 'Well, I suppose you get used to it in time, I suppose I will'* (see *Key to transcripts,* p. 95). In fact, the informal talk after the interview often confirms what the women have said during the interview.

It is impossible to tell exactly how the women perceive me but I do not think that they see me as too far removed from themselves. This may partly be because

I have to arrange the interviews when my own son is at school and leave in time to collect him. They may see my life as being more 'exciting' than their own lives but they do not seem to see me as having an 'ideal' life. As one woman put it, 'I bet *even* you have a more interesting life than I do.'* They are certainly always interested in the research and in knowing what other women feel about their own lives.

The methodology and form which I use may tend towards amplification of feelings of isolation and might produce a sensitive reading of the women's lives, which focuses more on their feelings of isolation than on other aspects. I do not think that this invalidates any of the findings, indeed I think it brings into sharper focus my fundamental point. The isolation remains. One woman at the end of her interview when I was leaving, said to me, 'I bet no one ever refuses to let you come to interview them, it's been something to look forward to and I've really enjoyed it.'* The first part of her comment is true: no one has ever refused to let me interview them.

The presentation of tape-recorded material creates problems because much is lost when transferring spoken language to written representation. The particular absences are the inability to represent adequately the significance of intonation and the registration of meaning by non-verbal communication. I am not proposing to examine the significance of non-verbal communication except for the crucial incidences where *laughter* occurs. Sheila Rowbotham (1969) has commented on girls giggling:

> Girls giggle at the moment of taboo. It is a way at once of making a point and avoiding the issue. It precludes criticism and does not give the game away.

In this article the presence of laughter has been identified as a point of theoretical importance in understanding women's oppression. The following comments relating to laughter are based on an analysis of the extract on pages 82-3 below, but the theoretical points about laughter are applicable to the whole analysis. First the woman laughs when she is talking about the jobs she had before she was married. She is conscious that she has had many jobs but never articulates any recognition that it was because the jobs themselves were intolerable that she had so many; rather, she sees the fault as being her own. She describes herself as being 'terrible at jobs' and the laughter indicates that she is aware of this as a fault in her. The second area where laughter occurs is when she discusses the possibility of her going to work instead of her husband. This indicates a recognition that she is mentioning a role reversal which she considers a 'taboo' area, unthinkable unless the boldness and 'scandalous' nature of the proposal is checked, contained and half-denied by laughter. She is aware that the traditional attitude is that the male should work and her suggestion that she would like to take on this role is an area where discussion is to be avoided.

A further point about laughter relates to the quotation at the beginning of this article, taken from a transcript with the same woman: 'I just see myself as the one that has to stay at home . . . (laughs).' Here the woman recognizes her own oppression but accepts the situation, though not without indicating that she realizes that it is unfair. The laughter precludes the necessity for either of us to discuss the matter further; the statement stands but the laughter contains it. It shows a recognition of the contradiction which nevertheless is allowed to stand.

I want to extend what Sheila Rowbotham has written about laughter in relation to my understanding of the significance of laughter in these interviews. In the examples discussed here and in others noted in this article, the laughter occurs at points of contradiction where actual alternatives are possible, if unlikely, or when sites of contradiction are revealed. However, the laughter also establishes an area of *shared understanding* between the women and myself. There is no need for them to explain why they laugh, or indeed why I laugh with them at some points, because the laughter is a form of non-verbal communication which is understood by both of us. It 'works' against the background of *tacit* (consensual) knowledge, of common sense about women, which is constantly evoked in the exchanges, on the basis of which the statements 'make sense'.

Wage labour

The experience which the women have of wage labour has been in the traditional areas of work which are both class and gender specific for working class girls leaving school. They have worked in shops, offices, factories and the lower end of the servicing industries. The following extracts are women talking about the jobs which they had before they were married. I want to concentrate on two aspects of these accounts of working. The nature of the jobs which were performed is self-evident; for the most part they are boring, monotonous labour, and the young women were subject to the occupational hazards associated with such work – they were made redundant and suffered industrial injury (allergic to the plastic). What made the work tolerable and even enjoyable was the company of *other people* at work – someone to talk to. There is then in the accounts a *recognition* that the work which they had to do was boring and that there is a rapid turnover of staff in the jobs but there is no recognition that they and other women workers are being exploited. The faults are identified as personal failings. But what is 'recalled' are the *human compensations* which made intolerable work tolerable.

Anne

DH   When you were at work what sort of job did you do?

AB   I've done all sorts (laughs). I started off in a factory, no, when I was fifteen I had a part-time job on, just Saturdays, while I was at school. Then, I was there for about two years actually.

DH   What was that?

AB   Woolworths. (laughs) And then I left there and I worked in a factory and got made redundant after six months.

DH   What did you do in the factory?

AB   Assembling - record players. And then I went into a factory where they made wire, wire ropes. Very dirty that was. I left that after six months and then I went to Butlins. I'm terrible at jobs I can assure you. (laughs)

DH   What did you do at Butlins?

AB   Two jobs, first I was in a shop, then I went on to waitressing. I liked the waitressing a lot better.

DH   Have you liked the jobs that you've had?

AB   Yes I have. The only one that I didn't like was the dirty one, as I said, the one where they made wire. It was rather, you know, boring, more boring than a lot of factory jobs because it was too noisy to talk. I don't mind working in a factory having boring work if you've got somebody to talk to next to you. But . . . this place you couldn't really talk.

DH   Did you make a lot of friends at work?

AB   Yes.

DH   You don't work now, would you like to go to work?

AB   I'd love to. (laughs) I would, I said to Richard this morning, I said, 'Can I go to work and you have the baby?' I would love to. You know if it wasn't for the fact that he literally will not change his nappies, that is it's a fact, he won't touch them, I'd let him stay at home and I'd go out to work. 'Cause I could get a job easily really, 'cause I do hand-press, power-press and them sort of jobs are, you know, people leave them quick.

Linda

LW   First I went into a shop - Lewis's. I was there for six months and then I left because the hours was too long. I was getting home late and I couldn't go out, and then I went to work in a factory that done garden sprays and I had to leave there 'cause I was allergic to the plastic. And then I went to work at the same place as me mom, in a factory, doing drilling and milling.

DH   Yes, and did you like that?

LW   Yes, I loved it.

DH   Was it the work you liked or . .

LW   I liked the work 'cause you had a different job every day and I liked the people, there was a nice lot of people there.

Betty

BW Well, when I first left school I worked in town in a shop, British Home Stores, and I didn't like it very much and I went to a smaller wool shop afterwards and I used to like it. But then during the summer it went very quiet and I was bored stiff, you know, just ((Mm)) sort of sitting around doing nothing. There was only me and the manageress and sometimes she'd have to go over to the other shop, or if in the dinner-hour she had to go out, or a holiday, and I'd just be left to sort of manage the shop on me own, and it was very lonely with nobody coming in ((Yes)) you know, I tidied up in the morning and you'd sort of wait and keep on waiting all day. ((Yes))

Betty talking about other jobs:

BW Well, there was a nice lot of girls in the office and one fortnight was very quiet and towards the end of that week you could more or less relax but the girls were all right and you could talk to them and that, ((Mm)) to pass your time. But the one fortnight was really busy when the agents were coming in with the books. (. . .) There was a lot of industrial policies and when they was coming in you used to have to check through the files to see if they'd had any other policies out on them and send them up to Head Office. And you'd do the surrenders if somebody wanted to surrender a policy and that. It was interesting.

DH I mean, was it important to you to be among friends at work as much as being at work for what you were doing?

BW Oh yes. I liked to like the people I worked with 'cause I worked at one job, I only stayed there three weeks, the people there were ever so horrible. They didn't speak to you, they sort of kept looking at you funny and you sort of didn't feel as if you belonged; you felt as if you shouldn't be there. They didn't want you there. Well I only stayed there three weeks, I didn't like that job.

These accounts again share the recognition that most of the jobs were unsatisfactory and in many cases boring. In the first extract Anne has no illusions about the nature of the work which she performed. Factory work is identified as being 'boring' and when it was 'too noisy to talk', i.e. not compensated for in the *culture* of work, it became intolerable. However, the fact that she left after six months is expressed almost as a personal failure, confirmed by the laughter discussed earlier in this article. Significantly, while recognizing that factory work is boring, she still wishes to return to it. At another point in the interview she said, 'I'd like to go back to a factory.' In fact, after expressing dissatisfaction with shop work, Linda eventually found a job which she liked in a factory, drilling and milling, and she said that she enjoyed the *work* because of the variation; but the *people* were also important to her. At a later point in the interview she said, 'I miss the money and I miss the lads that I used to work with, you know, like if I went back to that place now it wouldn't be the same because they're not there.'

By far the most common reason which the women gave for having enjoyed their time at work was the company of other workers, women and men, and the opportunity the job provided for talk with other people. Betty explains the loneliness of working in the wool shop when she was left alone. The jobs that she found satisfactory were the ones where as well as providing interesting and varied work to do, she could talk to the other girls in the office. When she was not accepted into the work group at the job mentioned in the last extract, she left the firm solely for that reason.

These accounts all privilege the company of other workers as being an important element in the satisfaction the women experienced while engaged in wage labour. It is not suggested that women only worked for 'company' and have no instrumental orientation to wage labour. What I think this concentration on the social elements of their previous work does reveal is as much a reflection of their present *isolated* situation as compared with their earlier working lives. They see work as an escape from isolation at home – an unconscious expression of an absence in their lives. It is through the concept of *isolation* that the rest of this article attempts to understand women's oppression.

Isolation

The separation of the sphere of work from the privatized sphere of the home under the capitalist mode of production, and the designation of those realms to men and women respectively, has meant that women are at one stage primarily located within the home performing domestic labour and child-care. It is the *isolation* of women within the home and the privatized nature of the work which they perform which some women have articulated as being a site of oppression for them.

> Industrialisation has had these lasting consequences (sic) the separation of the man from the intimate daily routines of domestic life; the economic dependence of women and children on men; the isolation of housework and childcare from other work. Hence, through the allocation to women of housework and childcare; through modern definitions of the role of housewife and the role of mother industrialisation has meant the restriction of the woman-housewife to the home. The restriction is psychological more than physical. . .
>
> Oakley (1974, p. 59)

Oakley sees the restriction as more psychological than physical but the experience of working class women is often one of actual physical restriction in their home with their children (3).

Anne   I said to him, you'll have to teach me to drive and then I can go out. I wouldn't mind so much then, it's just, up here the only connection you have with the outside world is the radio and the tele, and you can't really get much off the tele.

Television and radio is *seen* by the woman as the only relationship which she has with the 'outside world' and this, of course, is experienced as a passive relationship on her part. Television and radio are not, of course, the only relationship which she has with the world. She has relationships with her husband, family and some friends but obviously to *her* these do not constitute the 'outside' world; they are part of her 'family world'. The media is what *she* sees as her connection with the 'outside' world (4).

The following extract gives a further depressing picture of the isolation which young married women experience. The woman speaking, Betty, lives on the ninth floor of a multi-storey block of council flats; she has two children, aged five and two and has been married for eight years. Her husband works, two weeks on day shift and two weeks on night shift, on the assembly line at British Leyland. She has lived in the present flat for five years.

DH Do you know many people in the block?

BW I s'pose I know a few to say 'hello' to, y'know. When I see them I speak to them ((Mm)) I speak to a few of them ((Mm)) but I don't really *know* them to sort of like, to ask them in ((No)) or to go and visit them. I just say 'hello' to them.

DH Have you got any other, erm, friends?

BW Ooh no, they was my friends when I was at work and I lost contact with the one girl I used to work with at Patrick Motors. She gave me mom her telephone number a couple of years ago and I was going to 'phone her up and I never got round to it and then I lost it.

DH What do you do in your spare time, that you have?

BW I don't have too much really, you know, just sit down and watch the little one playing ((Yes)). I do that a lot really.

DH You don't, erm, and it's usually on your own is it?

BW Yes, usually on me own, not like when me husband's here weekends, ((Yes)) but I usually just sit on me own. It's not very often anyone ever comes y'know. ((No)) It's very rare anybody comes. ((Yes))

DH Is your husband on nights very often or. .

BW He does a fortnight about. (. . .) Well he goes to bed about half past nine [a.m.] and gets up about half past five [p.m.].

DH Oh, so you're still on your own really?

BW On my own mostly, yes.

DH And then I s'pose, then you're on your own at night as well?

BW Yes, 'cause he goes out at eight o'clock so I'm on me own all night then, but I got used to it. Y'know at first I was very frightened of being on me own in the night ((Mm)) but you get used to it after a bit. ((Yes)) I didn't feel so

bad, we had a cat at first and I used to feel safe with the cat, which is
ridiculous ((Yes)) and then we had to get rid of it 'cause the neighbours kept
moaning about him all the time ((Mm)) (. . .) Andrew shush cause Daddy's
in bed. When I had Shane he was good company y'know, me first baby. He
was quite a lot of company and I just used to talk to him from when he was
very tiny. ((Yes)) I used to think he understood but I don't suppose he did
(laughs) but he was just like a bit of company, somebody to talk to. (. . .)
Before I had him I used to talk to the cat (laughs) and I'm sure that cat used
to understand. (laughs)

These extracts, although perhaps presenting an extreme example of isolation in terms of actual *length* of time spent alone (because the woman's husband works on a night shift for two weeks out of every four), nevertheless do present an accurate representation of the isolated existence of many women (5). Betty does not know many women in the block of flats where she lives and only knows a few 'to say hello to'. This expression is used to indicate a passing acquaintance with people who are sometimes seen around the district; it does not suggest any form of friendship or real point of contact. It is a phrase which recurs in all my interviews; many women express that they do not really 'know' someone, just 'know them to say hello to'. Like many women after they marry, Betty has lost contact with friends from work and school and the ability to make new friends appears to be difficult. Since girls often have one 'best friend' (see Article 5 in this book), they do not always have a group of 'mates' as boys do, and they often lose their best friend after marriage. I do not want to suggest that women do not *ever* have friends, but simply to suggest that the amount of time which *some* women spend with *any other people* is minimal. When Betty says, 'I usually sit on me own. It's not very often anyone ever comes y'know. It's very rare anybody comes,' it is an accurate reflection on her own state. The lack of contact with other people coupled with the almost non-existence of a social life or leisure activities participated in by women outside the home, presents a depressing picture of the lives of many women (6). Another woman tells of how often she looks out of the window of her flat and counts the cars which go by on the road, nine storeys below her - 'just for something to do'.* To count cars, to talk to a cat for company, indicates that the isolation to which the woman is subjected is an insidious form of oppression.

Domestic labour: endless toil with no leisure

No group experienced the subjective isolation of personal life so deeply as women, trapped as they were within the family, blamed for its egregarious faults, or forced to negotiate the limbo between it and the world of wage labour. As housewives and particularly as mothers, women became a focus of the modern aspiration for personal happiness. The newly emerged areas of personal life were the housewife's responsibility - in particular childhood but also sexuality, emotional expression and the family's pattern of consumption. Far from being a refuge for women the family was a workplace.

Zaretsky (1976, p. 113)

The location of women's domestic labour and reproduction of the agents of labour power, within the privatized sphere of the home, has meant that for women there is neither a physical nor an emotional separation of the sphere of work and leisure. The privatized nature of housework which necessitates the isolation of the individual woman in the home is one of the most recognizable sites of her oppression. The male wage labourer returns to the private sphere of his home to be 'reproduced' in a fit state for work the next day. This period away from work can be seen as the time when the wage labourer has leisure time. However, there is no space for leisure for women at the same time. The woman works in the home during the day when the man is at work but when he returns from work, she still has to work.

DH So you think there's more of a separation between men's work and their spare time than there is for a woman.

BW Yes, I think men have got more spare time 'cause their work they have to go to and so when they come out of it they're away from their work so what they do then really it's up to them. I mean if they don't want to help the wife, I mean nobody can force them to and they can then just sit down all night if they want to and do what they like. ((Yes)) Whereas with a woman they've got to keep on working and they don't clock out at five o'clock, they've still got to cook the tea and do anything else that needs doing. Like if one of the children make a horrible mess of the room or something, or throw a bottle of milk on the floor or tip something on the floor, then they can't say, 'Oh, it's gone five o'clock it'll stop, it'll stop there now till nine o'clock tomorrow morning.' They've got to clean it up.

DH But why do you think women have got, more to do it than men, why do you think women can't say, 'I've finished now it's five o'clock'?

BW Well, there's nobody else to do it (laughs) y'know, you have to do it else it would get left, but I think a man can more or less ignore any mess really, they sort of shut their eyes to it, whereas a woman would, like it's Shane mostly who tips the stuff out, like sometimes he just tips sugar on the floor. Well, I can't sit and look at it, it would worry me to death all night ((Yes)) and I'd have to get up even if I was determined not to. I'd have to get and clean it up 'cause I wouldn't be able to sit still with it there ((Yes) y'know, I wouldn't be able to relax all night till I'd done it. (laughs)

This extract poses the distinction between the working life of men and that of women. As Betty says, men have to go to their work and they leave work behind when they leave the site of production. Men have a choice of what they do because there is a distinct non-working period in their working day. There is no official working time for women. Recent figures reported the length of the working week for housewives as being an average of seventy-seven hours (Oakley 1974). However, women are not forced to work such long hours, but their own self-compulsion drives them on even when they feel that they should be at leisure. This compulsion to work must come in part from the absence of boundaries and from the structurelessness of housework; there are no boundaries between work and leisure and no notion of how much housework is 'enough'. Betty expresses the compulsion she feels in this extract. She recognizes that she is not able to control her own wishes. One reason for this inability of women to stop themselves from working would appear to be connected with their having no place to escape to. It is easier to leave unfinished work if you are not confronted with it continually, but almost impossible if you can see it and know you will have to finish it the next day anyway. Housework is endless toil rather than a series of work tasks to be accomplished, and this has resulted in women internalizing the endless nature of their work. Here is the same woman talking about housework:

DH Do you find it monotonous?

BW It is a bit really, 'cause it's the same thing over and over again. ((Yes)) There's no difference in it all. There's nothing where you can sort of occupy your mind like, I mean just sort of cleaning and putting the vacuum round the floor and dusting and anybody can do it. You're not using any brains to thinking like, how to do it. ((No)) It's just boring really.

DH Do you enjoy housework and if you do, y'know, why do you?

BW Usually, it depends on what mood I'm in. If I'm in a good mood I don't mind doing it and I enjoy it then, but if I feel a bit tired or fed up, I don't 'cause I think, 'Well, I'm doing this and I've got to do it all over again tomorrow. And if I don't do it today, who's going to notice anyway.' And then I sit down and think, 'I won't do it.' But then I look at the floor and think, 'Oh, I can't sit and look at this, I'll have to do it.' Y'know, and then I get fed up of doing it day after day and it seems pointless you know, it don't matter how often I do it I still got to do it and I'm just getting nowhere. ((Yes)) I get a bit fed up.

These extracts reveal the recognition of the repetitive and compulsive nature of housework. The repetitiveness of housework intensifies the compulsion which women experience in managing it. Nothing is really achieved even when the task is finished because it still remains to be repeated the next day. Yet for women there is no escape from housework. It is ever-present, cyclic and infinite.

In the next extract Anne talks about the different nature of her husband's waged work compared to her work in the home.

DH Do you think your husband has an easier or a harder life than you do?

AB Easier (laughs) because he can just walk out of the flat in the morning and forget all about it. I don't know, he just gets out and forgets it but I can't, I'm here constantly. I mean, it's not actual hard, hard work as you put it. I suppose it's hard on your mind really, more than anything. I mean when you're working, he knows his job so well he could almost do it with his eyes shut, he can be thinking of other things and he can get completely away but I've just got to sit here. Hard in a different way, you know what I mean, hard to think, 'What shall I do next?'

It is not the physical nature of housework which Anne finds hard. She says, 'It's not actual hard work as you put it. I suppose it's *hard on your mind* really, more than anything.' It is hard because she has to completely discipline all her own actions, yet the very nature of domestic labour makes this difficult. It is hard to discipline yourself to do something which you know you will have to repeat tomorrow. Housework is in effect boring and monotonous, like factory work, yet in the privatized sphere of the home the woman has no companion to talk to to relieve this boredom. In this extract the woman mis-identifies the home as somewhere from which her husband would wish to escape, when she says that he is free to walk out of the flat and 'forget all about it'. Yet the home is the place where men *escape to,* from the site of production. In fact, men can also escape *from* the home to male leisure activities. Although the women interviewed did not go out independently of their husbands, the husbands did go out to the pub, football matches, with their 'mates', etc., and the women accepted that men had a 'right' to do this.

The home, then, is the site of the 'reproduction of the capitalist's most indispensable means of production: the worker' (Marx 1976) and it is also the woman's work-place. Women, however, cannot escape from the home. 'The woman pays in persona' (Adamson *et al.* 1976). It is the combination of *isolation* within the home and the impossibility of escaping from their place of work to a privatized sphere that structures the oppression which these women experience under capitalism.

Generational reproduction

Women's role in generational reproduction is both the site of their oppression and of the pleasure they experience in 'motherhood'. This is often the most enjoyable aspect of the women's lives, despite the restrictions which motherhood imposes on their freedom. Women may be reproducing the future generation of *workers* but this is not how they experience and internalize motherhood. It is rather, an experience of bringing up and teaching skills to an *individual* and looking forward to the child's future which they express as being enjoyable. There is, then, a marked distinction between short-term or day-to-day reproduction and long-term or generational reproduction. Housework may be boring but child-care is more pleasurable. Yet the role of bringing up children is a site of contradiction for women. The women that I have talked to often express ambivalent feelings in negotiating this role with their wish to return to work.

DH Did you prefer working to being a housewife?

AB Yes and no. I mean I preferred working but I wouldn't give him up [the baby]. You know what I mean, if I've got the choice now of going back to work and just leaving him with somebody, I'd rather stay at home with him. So yes I preferred work but I couldn't leave him with somebody to go to work. It's not that bad.

DH What do you see yourself doing in the next few years, or have you got hopes for yourself for the future?

AB Well I want to have more children and get over the business of having a family and get them, well the youngest to the age of five, school age, and then I'd like to take up another job, part-time at first until I can take on full-time, you know, until they're really settled in school and they know what they're doing and know how to cross the roads . . . you know, then build up to buying our own house.

Anne sees her prime responsibility as being to her child and, indeed, to any future children which she intends to have. She knows that it is her responsibility for looking after her child which prevents her from returning to work. She sees her role not only at the level of day-to-day reproduction but also at the level of generational reproduction. She talks about the 'business of having a family' as something to be 'got over'. She has a definite notion of skills which she has to transmit to her children and this would prevent her from considering even part-time work until they are at school. The same woman talks about the split in her experience of housework and child-care and its effects on her sexuality:

DH I mean do you think that doing housework and that sort of side of your life is different from when you're looking after the baby?

AB Yes that's different.

DH And do you think that there's another you, this you that wants to go to work?

AB Yes, I mean I'm not sitting here feeding him and thinking, 'I'd love to go to work,' you know, it's just a phase that I go through for about five minutes and I forget it. But when I pick him up I'm a different person from when I'm doing me housework. I get quite moody I suppose when I'm doing me housework. If me husband comes in, you know trying to mess about with me, I . . . (laughs) you know, 'get lost!' sort of thing. But if he comes round when I've got the baby I don't mind. I can't really say much more than that really.

Women often *recognize* their oppression but *refuse* to challenge or confront the situation, even to the extent of refusing to accept the feelings which indicate their oppression. Anne is conscious that she is performing roles and duties which are at variance with how she thinks of herself but when the thoughts come into her mind she shuts them out. She does recognize that housework affects her moods but she puts the blame on herself – she is 'moody'. She recognizes that housework affects her sexuality – she does not want sexual or affectionate advances from her husband when she is doing housework but these are acceptable when she is with the baby. She has a sense of herself as being a different person but she does not let her mind dwell on the contradictions within which she experiences her life. Sheila Rowbotham (1973) identifies this aspect of women's consciousness:

> Women have devised particular resistances within the framework of their lives as they are. There is the switching off, the half-there swimmy feeling, the barriers round yourself, and there is illness.

Conclusion

This article has attempted to look at the effect on some working class women of their 'invisible' but essential contribution to the process of capital accumulation. It has necessarily been a very fragmentary account of women talking about their experience of living the contradictions of their situation. It has sometimes been very difficult to comment on the extracts because of a consciousness that any commentary may appear banal and superfluous. What I have felt is that in many cases the words spoken by the women are more forceful when left to stand on their own. For this reason this article is concluded with a long extract, spoken by one woman, left without detailed comment because I think the woman speaks her own oppression. In doing so, she reveals her own experience of femininity through the move from the control of her father to that of her husband and the change in her life since having her children. Her account synthesizes the points which I have tried to make in this article about the lived experience of these women.

DH   Erm, these questions are about, well just about you really. Is being married and being a mother as you expected it would be or if not, how is it different?

BW   I don't really know, 'cause I never really thought about it before I had the children, about being a mother, and being married. I 'spose it's the same as I thought 'cause I thought, 'Well you have more freedom when you're married 'cause you can do more or less what you like, you've only got your husband to tell you what to do and, sort of, and you can more or less stand up to him and say, 'Er, no! if I don't want to do it I won't.' ((Yes)), you know, whereas, if your Dad tells you what to do then you sort of do it, you don't say 'No, I won't,' you sort of do it. (laughs) ((Yes)) Y'know, its sort of different, but with the children I never really thought about having children sort of, till he came.

DH   Erm, so is your life how you expected it would be with the children and . . .?

BW I s'pose it is really 'cause I never really thought about it much, about the children, I just thought I'd just carry on going to work and that really.

DH Before you had the children how had you thought things would be?

BW Well I just thought it would be just like it was when I was single but I'd be married so I could please myself what I done y'know. ((Yes)) We'd just sort of go on holiday together and that and things like that. Do just more or less what I wanted to do instead of having to get home at a certain time every night. ((Mm)) I never really thought about having children and having to look after them and stop going to work. It never occurred to me. (laughs)

DH If I asked you what you were, what do you, what do you think of yourself?

BW I don't know, just an ordinary housewife, just doing like what other people do ((Yes)) y'know, just ordinary.

DH And do you think, do you think of yourself as having one job or a lot of jobs?

BW I don't think much about it. I s'pose I do lots of different things, but I don't really think about it, I just sort of do it. ((Yes)) I don't think. In fact, me husband says I don't think much. (laughs) I says, 'I haven't much to think about!'

DH Do you, used you, I mean did you ever plan things and think about what you were going to do?

BW I used to before I was married. I used to plan everything for months. Like, we planned the wedding months in advance ((Mm)) and any holidays, they used to be planned well ahead and like, we used to plan ahead for Christmas. Or if we was going out I used to plan like, what I was going to wear and if I was going to go to the hairdressers and have me hair done and all that. But I don't now, I don't think about anything till it just comes and then at the last minute it just hits me, 'Oh dear, I've got nothing ready,' you know ((Yes)) and it's just one mad rush. I don't know, I think it's just since I've had the children, I don't seem to think about anything really much.

DH Why do you think you've changed in that way?

BW I don't really know. Me husband says I've changed an awful lot since I've had Shane, y'know, but I don't sort of think about things like outside the house. All I can think about is like, babies and children and sort of how to keep nappies clean (laughs) and sort of boring things like that. . . .

Acknowledgements

I would like to thank Stuart Hall for his comments on the draft of this article and Paul Willis for his discussion of this article and discussions of research methods, but mostly for the example of his own work. Thanks also to Mrs Lemon of the Mother and Baby Clinic and particularly the women without whose co-operation the research would not be possible. Finally to Charlotte Brunsdon for her friendship and intellectual support during the past year which has been invaluable to the development of my work.

Notes and references

1 The women are originally contacted at a council 'welfare clinic', where the health visitor kindly allows me to approach the women while they wait to see the doctor. I explain my research to them by saying that I am interested in how women experience being wives and mothers and ask if they would be prepared to help me by allowing me to visit them at home and ask them questions about their lives now and before they were married.

2 Because of the limitations of space, I have not concentrated on many aspects of these women's lives which I do recognize as being important. Other areas which are covered by the interviews include: family and educational background, leisure activities before marriage, attitudes to housework and detailed discussions of housework routines, social networks, present leisure activities, the role of the media in their lives, their feelings about their present lives and their future. The most obvious omission is any reference to forms of resistance which women may negotiate in terms of, for example, sexual resistance or fantasy, particularly through their relationship with the media (see footnote 4). However, I do not think that these omissions would alter the main arguments of this article (see forthcoming MA thesis).

3 See also Gavron (1966): 'In conclusion, it can be said that although the middle-class mother may encounter psychological difficulties concerning her role as an individual with her first baby, she very soon makes a deliberate effort to assert her own rights as an individual. The working-class mother who sees motherhood as inevitable is in fact less prepared for the ties of children and is less able to cope with the isolation that follows.'

4 Mass communications in the form of radio and television have emerged as an important aspect of the day-to-day experience of the women in the study. Television and radio are never mentioned as 'spare time' or leisure activities but are located as integral parts of everyday life. To take radio as an example, Radio 1 and local radio are listened to during the day while the women are engaged in domestic labour. From a reading of their comments about the role of radio in their lives it would appear that they see the radio disc jockey as another 'person' in their privatized world. Phone-in programmes are also important in counteracting isolation. One woman said, 'I like listening to the people that phone in, I like the conversations (. . .) I suppose it's 'cause I'm on me own.' These programmes not only provide a contact with the 'outside' world; they also reinforce the privatized isolation by reaffirming the

consensual position – there are thousands of other women in the same situation, a sort of 'collective isolation' (for a more detailed analysis of this aspect of the women's lives see forthcoming MA thesis).

5 The number of manual workers engaged in shiftwork increased by more than half during the decade 1957–67 and since then has been increasing (Cliff 1970). Kinnersley (1973) gives examples of the effect on workers of shiftwork and makes some comments on disruption of family and social life of the worker, but neglects the effects of shiftwork on the *wives*. See also Young and Willmott (1973, Chapter 7: 'Shiftwork').

6 This lack of leisure activities is also in sharp contrast to their lives before they were married, when they often went out every night of the week and only stayed in to wash their hair and 'do their ironing'.

Key to transcripts

. . .	pause
( )	non-verbal communication, e.g. (laughs)
*	taken from field notes, not transcript
. .	speaker interrupted
(( ))	phatic communication, e.g. ((Mm))
(. . .)	passage edited out

5 Working class girls and the culture of femininity

Angela McRobbie

He's got a crush on my best friend but she don't care because she loves someone else
I'm standing on the outside looking inside where I want to be
Love's unkind . . . 'cos he's not mine.
Just the other day I was praying he would give me a chance,
Hoping he would choose me for his partner for the High School dance,
I was standing outside the class but it wasn't me but my best friend he asked
Love's unkind . . . 'cos he's not mine.

> Donna Summer, Giorgio Moroder,
> Pete Bellote, *Love's Unkind*
> © Heath-Levy Music Publishing Co.

This paper is based on a piece of work carried out in a Birmingham youth club over a period of six months (April 1975–September 1975) (1). The study itself was prompted by a recognition that throughout a range of disciplines dealing broadly with youth (including ethnographic studies of education, delinquency, subcultures and youth culture) there was a whole missing dimension, namely girls. Adolescent girls tended to appear fleetingly, and often through the eyes of 'the lads' in chapters dealing with *their* views on sex or 'birds' (Fyvel 1961, Willmott 1966, Parker 1975, Patrick 1973, Willis 1977). Otherwise, girls were allotted brief consideration in family or community studies (Hoggart 1957, Willmott and Young 1964), a significant enough indicator of where they were *assumed* to be rooted.

As a preliminary attempt to redress this balance, my work focused on a sample of girls (fifty-six in all) aged between fourteen and sixteen who were regular members of the Mill Lane youth club, lived on the adjoining council estate and attended the same school. In most cases both the girls' parents worked. Their fathers tended to be employed directly or indirectly in the car industry, and their mothers were engaged in shift or part-time work (waitressing, bar-work, cleaning, office and clerical work). My aim in this exploratory project was quite simple: I wanted to look at the culture of these working class girls, at their 'peculiar and distinctive way of life . . .' and at 'the meanings, values and ideas embodied in institutions, in social relations, in systems of beliefs in mores and customs, in the uses of objects and material life' (Hall and Jefferson 1976) which were associated with them. The intention was then to map out the ways in which they experienced and made sense of the social institutions which they inhabited, and to consider in some detail their inter-personal relationships. But underpinning this concern with their culture was an awareness that regardless of its nature or form, it was in no sense a free-floating configuration. Instead it would be linked to and partly determined by, though not mechanically so, the material position occupied by the girls in society; their social class, their future role in production, their present and future role in domestic production and their economic dependence on their parents. And because cultures, though referring to the essentially expressive capacities of the group in question, are not created from scratch by the group but instead embody 'the trajectory of group life through history; always under conditions and with raw materials which cannot wholly be of its own making' (Hall and Jefferson 1976), then it was important to situate the girls from the start within the pre-existent culture of femininity which they, as females in a patriarchal society, are born into and which is continually transmitted to them over the years by their mothers, sisters, aunts, grandmothers, neighbours and so on.

Clearly this cultural formation would comprise a rich and complex network and to ensure that this complexity was grasped in the field work, a whole range of sociological techniques were employed. These included participant observation, taped and untaped interviews, questionnaires, informal discussions and diary-keeping. The absence of relevant literature on the subject meant that there were fewer presuppositions and assumptions upon which the study could be launched than is typically the case with 'participant observation' studies. Sociologists, for example, looking at male youth cultures can normally expect to find some clearly visible features such as an orientation towards football, motorbikes, vandalism, violence or simply 'doing nothing' (Corrigan 1976) (2). But with girls there existed no such 'easy lead'. Given this situation it was necessary to be as reflexive as possible methodologically; this meant continually questioning the means by which the data was collected and checking at every possible instance to make sure that what the girls actually said and meant was being clearly understood.

It is not my intention in this paper to offer a systematic profile of the research in all its stages; to do so adequately would clearly be untenable in such a short piece. Instead I want to concentrate on the contradictions and apparently unresolvable conflicts which the girls' culture had to deal with and somehow accommodate. But a word should be said about the broader strands which did emerge from the work as a whole. In fact the picture which was revealed displayed a remarkable, if complex, homogeneity. The repertoire of responses was typified by an ultimate if not wholesale endorsement of the traditional female role and of femininity, simply because to the girls these seemed to be perfectly 'natural' (see Article 2). As one girl put it,

> If I had me own I wouldn't put them in a nursery. I mean its all you've got. They're your own aren't they? It's up to you to look after them. I wouldn't trust anybody with my baby. You don't know what they're doing when you're not there.
>
> 'Sue', 15 years

She went on,

> Me Mum stayed at home until we was all at school then, she got a job cleaning

out the laboratories. She always says its not right to leave them when they're that young, they don't know who their mother is, it confuses them.

What this suggests is that the woman's 'natural' biological capacities are extended to include also her *social* location in the household as domestic labourer. So, to summarize, although aspects of the female role were constantly being questioned, such criticism precluded the possibility of a more radical restructuring of the female role because ultimately it was women who had the children. This biological 'fact' and its social implications (also experienced as natural) – housework and child-care – meant that the oppressive features of the female career seemed equally intransigent and unavoidable, unalterable facts of life. Two factors 'saved' the girls from what they otherwise envisaged as an unexciting future: first, their solidarity with each other, their best-friend relationships which they saw as withstanding time and married life; and second, their immersion in the ideology of romance. Each of these figure significantly in the following discussion where the focus is on specific instances (class, sex and, less importantly, age) in the girls' experiences. The bulk of this piece will attempt to chart and make sense of the articulations of the first two of these with and against each other, and will look at the girls' developing class and sexual identities.

However, age as a kind of 'common sense' structuring category does merit some attention. First, not yet members of the labour force, the girls, like their brothers, are still economically dependent on their parents for their maintenance and welfare. But their parents' wages tend not to cover the cost of their children's leisure and consequently all the Mill Lane girls had to earn their pocket money. Their limited resources for spending also meant that they had to rely on the state to provide them with facilities outside school where they could meet, dance, drink Coke and get to know boys. The more glamorous world of consumption based round 'town' discos and fashion are all attendant on their entering production and becoming wage labourers.

Age also plays a role in structuring the girls' sexuality. That is, what is expected of them sexually is socially understood in terms of whether they are at the 'going steady' stage (fifteen onwards) or at the 'one night stand' stage (thirteen/fourteen). There are of course always exceptions, but this study suggested that between the ages of fourteen and fifteen, girls occupy a kind of twilight zone sexually. They interpret their sexuality in sub-sexual terms, in the vocabulary of a boy 'trying it on', 'trying to get it' or, more commonly, having 'wandering palms'. Sex education, with its emphasis on 'human biology', clinical sexuality and, as one girl put it, 'bathing babies', clearly has little to offer here. The girls cannot easily 'cash' any of its prescriptions because it completely ignores the social and brutally sexist environment within which this emergent sexuality is experienced. If you haven't got a steady then contraception is simply not an issue. Any girl who consciously 'took precautions' with a casual 'date' would be laying herself wide open to savage criticism since such calculated, premeditated action totally contravenes the dominant code of romance. As one writer discussing pregnant teenagers put it,

'They reckon that if you are in love and you get carried away, it is alright, – but if you are on the pill then you have planned it' (Melville 1974).

This linking of general social experience with particular ages or 'phases' finds its fullest expression however in the official ideologies of youth where, to put it crudely, age consciousness pre-empts and thereby seeks to negate any more fundamental divisive elements which could separate out young people along more problematic lines like class. Nowhere is this ideology more apparent than in *Jackie* (as in girls' and women's magazines as a whole).

Here adolescence itself is an ideological construct whose connotations are immediately identifiable and made comprehensible through those topics included in the *Jackie* repertoire: 'problems', 'romance', 'jealousy' and so on. Indeed the whole range of consumer goods directed at female youth is intricately sub-divided into 'phases' and 'stages'. Not surprisingly then the girls who are the subjects of this ideological commodity-based offensive do operate within these categories.

Well I buy *Jackie* and *Fab* now, but my sister, she's 17, buys *Honey* and *19* so I usually read them too. Once you go to work you start getting magazines with more on fashion than love stories.

'June', 15

Similarly pop was experienced differently according to, sometimes, minute differences in age:

I used to like the Rollers more than anyone else. But I think I've changed. I mean it don't get you anywhere. You spend all your money on them and you're lucky if you even get to see them. You can't get them so what's the point? I still like Rod Stewart but I don't go mad over him. You grow out of that.

'Chris', 16

Finally, the girls did see themselves in terms of following a linear career culminating in marriage.

It's not so much that I mind. But I think it'd make me Mum happy if she saw me with a boyfriend, steady like, by the time I was 16-17. I think she worries I'll be left on the shelf, see me sister, she's dead pretty, she's had a steady since she was 14½ . . . . There's a girl down our way and everyone feels sorry for her, she's 26 and she's never had a boyfriend yet.

'Maxine', 15½

Age is then an important factor on the feminine map; not only does it hold together groups of friends, it also defines for them their expectations, hopes and aspirations.

Class, sex, school and family

This consciousness of age as a socially cohesive force does not however obliterate other differences which the girls observe as existing between them and others. In fact it seems to operate within a wider framework of already-shared class and gender values. That is, *within* this group of *working class girls,* they relate to each other on the grounds of common expectations of, and experience of, the female role. Consequently it is more useful and productive to explore just what this 'working class-ness' means and how it binds them together and informs their culture, than to concentrate simply on their feminine, adolescent consciousness.

Two questions are central to this discussion; what are the determinations acting upon the girls, 'interpellating' (Althusser 1971) them as class subjects, and how do the effects of this positioning find expression at the level of a developing class cultural identity? To answer these we have to look first at their material position. As I mentioned earlier, the girls are dependent for their livelihood on their parents and thus on where they fit into the capital/labour relation. Instead of being given pocket money, the girls were expected to earn it, and with the current shortage of Saturday jobs, the most common 'employment' consisted of housework where the girls were 'hired' on a sub-contractual basis by their mothers. So, although a few girls did spend their Saturdays behind a counter in Woolworth's or 'passing up' in the local hairdressing salon, the majority were given on average £1.50 a week for performing a series of household tasks throughout the week. This involved cooking the evening meal for the family Mondays to Fridays, tidying the house while their mothers were at work, helping with the shopping, and even washing younger brothers and sisters and putting them to bed. From my calculations it was quite normal for them to spend between twelve and fourteen hours per week engaged in some form of domestic labour (several baby-sat for neighbours and relatives as well as for their own mothers). Not surprisingly the girls were not joined in this work by their brothers.

Me brother doesn't do a thing in the house. He makes a mess and I clear up after him. He doesn't even make his own bed, waits for me mum to do it when she gets in from her work.

'Jill', 15

This dependence on domestic and more or less home-based employment for leisure money meant that the girls were rooted in their immediate environment, the estate. They simply did not have access to other parts of the city and to the general experience which flows from doing things together and going places with each other. In contrast, their brothers earned their money for football matches (which of course involve a great deal of travelling about the country) by delivering newspapers, working unofficially in off-licenses and betting shops, 'stacking up' in supermarkets and so on. But, at least partly because of these material limitations, the girls rarely left the estate. They bought their clothes from the local shopping centre or more often from catalogues ('clubs'). Apart from visiting an older married sister, which they often did in groups, their days and evenings were spent moving between school, youth club and home with monotonous regularity. Not only, then, is their experience in sharp contrast with that of their brothers, but it also differs significantly from that of their middle class peers, the small group of girls who also attended Mill Lane School, but who lived in a small strip of private housing on the periphery of the estate.

From the accounts of the girls in my sample, it was clear that the middle class girls, none of whom attended the club, were in a very different position. It was impossible to say whether they earned their pocket money by doing housework, but it did seem unlikely that they spent as much time in domestic labour as the others. Several girls talked about the amount of home work which 'they' did and others described how they went in the evenings to a city Arts Centre where they could play table tennis, do pottery, drama and dance, as well as 'chat up' boys. The point I am trying to make here is that the width of the experience of these girls is bound to be much wider than that of the youth club girls, even if they *do* share a common interest in femininity, simply because their material horizons are much broader. Boys may well dominate their consciousnesses at the present moment, but there are also possibilities for a career other than just marriage. Frith, describing a group of middle class schoolgirls in the following terms:

> Allison and her friends . . . had a busy and self-contained social life, meeting weekly at the folk club (most of them picked at guitars themselves), at parties in each other's houses, at concerts.
>
> Frith (forthcoming) (3)

The Mill Lane girls knew very little of life outside their direct environment and regarded everything that was not familiar with suspicion, even hostility. Thus women who were known to them in situations other than the domestic were seen as figures of social control - teachers, social workers, youth leaders, careers advisers and so on. Likewise students were seen as shadowy characters, like hippies, dirty and untidy.

> I could never go out with someone like that, me Dad would go mad if some fella comes to the door to take me out in scruffy jeans and with long dirty hair.
>
> 'Sue', 15

Not surprisingly this did make it difficult to enter their culture as a participant observer; a woman who did not introduce herself to them in terms of her domestic status was, at least to begin with, an unknown quantity. And there was more to this than class differences or simply the usual difficulties experienced by researchers as they 'enter the field'. There was the added and hidden dimension stemming from their being female and inhabiting a culture of femininity. That is, there is something about their culture which shuns outside interference of any sort, and this, I would argue, is gender-specific. Unlike the boys at the club who played football and table tennis with the male youth leaders, the girls guarded their free time and privacy jealously and consistently refused to join in 'official' club activities (4). And so, what starts off as a material limitation or restriction stemming from their class position and their sex takes on specifically cultural dimensions which in turn reflect both these features.

Nowhere is this complex interweaving of class and sex more clearly articulated than in the *school*. Indeed this is the site of so many contradictions that there is no way in which I can do justice to its complexity here. Rather I merely want to draw attention to the different levels at which contradictions appear and which have a direct bearing on the experience and culture of the girls.

First, and briefly, at the level of the official schooling ideology there exists a whole body of educational thought which has focused on the school's role in preparing the girl for her career in the home. This is best summarized in Newsom (1948), and its suggestions have been implemented in the form of special domestic subjects for girls in the curriculum: grooming, housewifery, health and hygiene, food and nutrition, fashion, needlework and even interior design. Underpinning this official ideology is the 'hidden curriculum' which also operates to the disadvantage of girls. As Sue Sharpe (1976) points out, they are expected to be tidier in their work than boys, producing work which looks good more or less regardless of its content. This Sharpe sees as a means of restricting the expressive capacities of young girls, boys being allowed a freer range of expression with the emphasis for them on the quality of the content rather than the prettiness of the form. Turning to look at the internal dynamics of schooling, contradictions emerge. These are (1) where class variables operate in the school alongside, and on top of, the sexual divisions sketched out above; (2) where the school is placed against the family, the informal agency of education for girls; and (3) where the school can be seen as a progressive force and in particular where feminist teachers can attempt to introduce girls to the ideas of the Women's Movement.

First, then, class. One of the central features of the school is to prepare pupils for the position they will occupy in the labour force. This process is obviously not simply a matter of feeding pupils automatically into some slot in the labour market, and several writers have acknowledged the problems and complexities involved in this move from school to work (5). But for our purposes here, it is enough to point to the fact that in this process working class girls are separated out from their middle class counterparts. So although both may be the targets of sexist practices in the school, there are also differences in the way these oppressive factors operate and in the way they are responded to. To put it crudely, middle class girls are directed to different kinds of jobs than working class girls although *both* may also be, indeed are, pushed in the direction of the home. Wolpe (1976) describes schooling for working class girls as an attempt to produce 'an adaptable, pliable and docile labour source with only marginal skills'. In contrast, middle class girls, destined for even a short-lived career in the professions or 'female semi-professions', will necessarily have a different and slightly less 'domestic' experience of schooling. But in outlining such a clear-cut division I am necessarily simplifying. Schools cannot and do not operate at *all* points and at *all* times on a kind of class and sex apartheid basis. Indeed because teaching has traditionally been a career open to women, often single 'career women', then it could be argued that here the girl is more likely to be encouraged to think in terms of having a separate, independent identity than elsewhere. And so the possibility which the school offers for the introduction of feminist critiques in the classroom should not be underestimated, a potential which is now being explored by groups of feminist teachers (6).

This picture is further complicated when we turn to look at the girls themselves. First, as Sue Sharpe describes, there is the sudden 'under-achievement' expressed by girls right across the board as they approach adolescence. Despite the problems involved in using this term (what is 'achievement' anyway?), it does have some purchase in signalling the force of the pressures, mounted on girls at this moment, to conform to the feminine ideal and to think more and more about boys, their own attractiveness, popularity, and so on. For the Mill Lane girls this 'under-achievement' consists of a whole set of class, sex and 'anti-school' articulations. To begin with they saw themselves as 'naturally' occupying an antagonistic relation with the middle class girls, commonly known as the 'swots' or 'snobs'. They were at once competitive with them and contemptuous of their application, diligence and conscientiousness.

> They all think they're brainy but they're not. I mean Karen and me, we do no work but if we wanted to we could be top of the class. We're just interested in other things. They just want to be top, they're not . . . they don't like boys or nothing.
>
> 'Maggie', 14½

The girls also looked down on 'their' lack of style:

> They wear horrible clothes, I mean they don't know what fashion is. They're not like us at all. They don't wear platform shoes and skirts - mid-calf length. They always wear the uniform proper-like.
>
> 'Sally', 15

And they thought little more of 'their' taste in boys:

> I don't understand it, when they go out with a boy it's, like, one from the same class, you know, boys the same age or even younger than them. I couldn't do that! Imagine going out with a fella that was 14.
>
> 'Linda', 14

Two other girls talked about 'their' performance in the school:

> They suck up to the teachers, never do a thing wrong. . . . If they get caught reading a magazine under the desk, they're sort of ashamed.
>
> 'Meg', 15

> They never swear, use language like we do.
>
> 'Debbie', 14

When it came to their own schooling the girls felt simultaneously that they were failures - according to 'Maggie',

> They don't care, nobody in this school cares, the head said to me last week she just wants us to leave, they treat you like you was dirt. . . .

– and yet paradoxically successes. This latter hinged on their ability to work the system and to transform the school into the sphere, *par excellence,* for developing their social life, fancying boys, learning the latest dance, having a smoke together in the lavatories and playing up the teachers.

Their developing sexual identities also lend greater weight to this oppositional stance. To put it briefly: one way in which the girls combat the class-based and oppressive features of the school is to assert their 'femaleness', to introduce into the classroom their sexuality and their physical maturity in such a way as to force the teachers to take notice. A class instinct then finds expression at the level of jettisonning the official ideology for girls in the school (neatness, diligence, appliance, femininity, passivity, etc.) and replacing it with a *more* feminine, even sexual one. Thus the girls took great pleasure in wearing make-up to school, spent vast amounts of time discussing boyfriends in loud voices in class and used these interests to disrupt the class. In answer to the question, how do you spend your time during the maths lesson, two girls replied:

Carve names on me desk, anything that comes into me head – boys' names. Woody. Eric. Les. Then when I've done that I start writing on me plimsolls.

'Sue'

Comb me hair under the lid of the desk, put on make-up, look in me mirror.

'Karen'

And a constant source of fascination to them was the girl who got married two months before she could leave school.

Like, she's really happy, you can see it on her face, last week I walked up to her and said, 'How's Billy?' Then I asked her what it's like to go to school and then go home to your husband. It must be really funny having to go home and get the dinner ready for him coming in.

'June'

Marriage, family life, fashion and beauty all contribute massively to this feminine anti-school culture and, in doing so, nicely illustrate the contradictions inherent in so-called oppositional activities. Are the girls in the end not simply doing exactly what is required of them – and if this *is* the case, then could it not be convincingly argued that it is their own culture which itself is the most effective agent of social control for girls, pushing them into compliance with that role which a whole range of institutions in capitalist society also, but less effectively, directs them towards? At the same time, the girls are expressing a class relation, in albeit traditionally feminine terms. As one girl, 'Wendy', put it,

We don't need the teachers to tell us. But we like to have a good time. There's plenty of time to study when you're older. Me dad would like me to study more. He wants me to get a good job. He's a shop steward and he's always telling me about his union and that. Getting me to read the papers. But I'm not interested now. I like to go out every night with Christine. We like to have a good time at school. Play up the teachers, talk about boys.

In the *family* however, many of these tensions and contradictions disappear. For a start the girls experience no conflict around their sense of 'being working class' here. And while family life is by no means unproblematic, it is not grounded on a fundamental disagreement over values, expectations and assumptions about the female role. (It's also interesting to note the importance placed on parental attitudes by the girls. Even if they seem to disagree with them, they do repeatedly refer to what 'me Mum' or 'me Dad' would think.) Moreover in this domestic environment they have no need to adopt defensive strategies, the hallmark of their 'outside face'. Here they learn a whole body of 'really useful knowledge', they become familiar with all the facts of pregnancy, childbirth, child-care and domestic life through informal channels, and in the protective emotional atmosphere of the home. In general their relations with their parents (especially mothers) were good, and great emphasis was placed on maintaining these warm and satisfying relationships. Nonetheless this did not blind the girls to the fact that marriage did not measure up to its claims. One girl, 'Jill', talked about scenes of marital violence in her street: 'They've only been married for six months and he knocks her about. If that's what it's about I don't want to know.' Another described her father's possessiveness and her mother's ensuing misery:

> He had her in tears this morning. He won't let her over the doorstep. He always thinks she's going to go off with another man. And me Mum's not like that at all. All she wanted to do was go to the ladies' sauna, up at 'Manyana', with her sister and me cousin. And me Dad! He went about with a face like fizz all day, so that she ended up not wanting to go. It's not fair. Just 'cos she looks young and pretty. He works with about fifty women and me Mum never says 'who's Lizzie then?' She never bothers but he goes mad thinking she goes out looking for someone else.
>
> 'Maxine'

And two girls talked about their elder sister's marriage with surprise:

> We all thought that Carol would be just the one to get married. You know she'd keep a nice house, but I wouldn't have believed it. She's always hitting Dean and her house is a mess, she never does any cleaning.
>
> 'Gail', 15

It also became apparent in the course of the research that the girls didn't really expect the romance of marriage to last indefinitely.

> He goes his way and I go mine. That's how most of my married cousins are. They go out together now and then. I mean take the kids to their Nan's on Sundays. When I go round to babysit he's always going one place and she's going somewhere else.
>
> 'Vicki', 15

And, speaking of 'the future', 'Suzanne' said: 'As long as he don't mind me having friends round while he's out I don't mind if he goes out every night.'

Yet despite this 'realism' the girls were still fascinated with marriage, partly because of the status it would confer on them and partly because it was the only possible means through which their sexuality could be expressed legitimately.

'Me Mum says she doesn't mind me being on the Pill if I was engaged or just about to be married, but she'd hit the roof if she thought I'd go on it just, you know, for anyone, for someone that wasn't a steady or me fiancé. I wouldn't anyway, you just get known for being like that.

'Anne', 16

To sum up, I have argued that class and sex impose on the girls in such a way as to force them into contradictory positions: in the school they express their class identity by and large in female and feminine terms, and in the family they recognize that somehow the code of romance doesn't deliver the goods. Yet despite this they cannot envisage a future without marriage or children.

I worry a lot about not getting married. I mean what if no one wants me and I had to stay with me Mum and Dad?

'Marge', 15

The culture of femininity

What then are the distinguishing features of the girls' own private culture and how do these relate to our discussion of class and sex identities? First, it is characterized by a tremendous sense of solidarity between the girls and in particular between 'best friends'. Despite all the pressures on them to take a boyfriend, several girls described how loyalty to a friend came first.

If I had to choose between a fella and me friend, I'd choose her any day. I mean fellas are all the same. They just want the one thing and if they don't get it they pack you in. It's always the same. They always 'try it on' and if you say no, they give you the push.

'Sally'

At the same time the motives surrounding tight-knit female twosomes are not so altruistic. Both partners know that, although they are not looking out for 'steadies' at the present moment, it is this unit (two girls together) that is most suitable for finding a 'fella'. The female twosome, then, anticipates future boyfriends, but for the moment its members are thoroughly involved in each other. In fact there is a huge emotional investment put into these relationships by the girls; it is as though they transfer all their emotional energies later to be focused on a boy, on to the 'best friend'. In a similar way pop stars and idols are used as substitute boyfriends, in anticipation of the 'real thing'. Clearly, both the 'best friend' unit and the immersion of these partners in pop culture and fantasy relationships exist at least partly as a response to the brutally sexist attitudes held by adolescent, and in this case working class, boys. In short, these attitudes push working class girls further into compliance with the traditional female role and force marriage upon them as the only legitimate channel for the expression of their sexuality.

These sexist responses operate quite simply and within the terms of the classic 'double standard' (7). On the one hand boys naturally seek sexual experience but any girl who willingly participates sexually with them is branded and later denounced as a 'whore' or a 'tart'. This means that every time one of the Mill Lane girls goes out on a date she is confronted with a situation not easily resolved. If she gives into the boy's demands she stands not only to become pregnant, but also to lose her reputation – still, it seems, a valuable asset on the marriage market for working class girls. As 'Sue' put it, 'If you get known for being like that you lose all your friends. Girls don't want to know you and the boys just want the one thing. It's not worth it.' This sexual exploitation they are subjected to is hidden and concealed because it operates through individual degradation and humiliation. Their whole self-esteem is at risk, making it difficult for them to talk to one another about it openly and frankly. Only in the intimate relationship with the best friend can such problems be divulged. Hence the culture of exclusion, secrecy and resentment. And so, on top of the material limitations placed upon the girls which are experienced in and through the ideological apparatuses they inhabit (family, education, media, etc.), there is an invisible level of oppression which stems directly from their explicit experience of sexual relationships; these too, I would argue, have specifically material and class dimensions.

These limitations are best explained if we return for a minute to the general expectations of the Mill Lane girls. Most of them realized that for them marriage would be an economic necessity. They saw clearly that the wages they would get would be quite insufficient to keep them, for example, in a flat. Instead they would have to strike up a good deal with 'Mum', and hope that she would take as little from them for their 'keep' as possible. The rest of their wages would go on those consumer goods considered necessary to attract a 'steady' (make-up, clothes, drinks, discos, magazines, etc.).

Moving into a flat with a girl friend was quite out of the question; they would simply move, when the time came, from one man's house (their father's) to another's (their husband's). Recognizing their own economic dependence, and aware of the problems which girls and women experience sexually outside of marriage, the working class girl, by the time she is ready to leave school, automatically thinks of marriage. She is denied that crucial space, the privilege of her middle class peers, the few years spent at college or university where thoughts of marriage are at least temporarily suspended and where sexual experience outside marriage is quite permissible. As Mungham (1976) observes,

. . . there is not much place for a single working class woman in society. This is not simply a question of economics . . . though it will mean a life lived on the low wages of women in working class jobs . . . but of being forced to live as a marginal person in working class society.

And, as he goes on to illustrate graphically,

The girls themselves know full well what this meant, 'I've got this auntie – Auntie Elsie, she's ever so nice but she never got married. So she misses out on a lot of things really. I mean she goes round with me mum and all the family and them, but, well, she just sort of has to watch. Know what I mean? I don't want to be like her.'

The culture of adolescent working class girls can be seen as a response to the material limitations imposed on them as a result of their class position, but also as an index of, and response to their sexual oppression as women. They are both saved by and locked within the culture of femininity.

Notes and references

1   See McRobbie (1977).

2   See Corrigan, P. (1976) 'Doing nothing' in S. Hall and T. Jefferson (eds.), *Resistance Through Rituals*.

3   See S. Frith's forthcoming book, *The Sociology of Rock*.

4   This resentment was clearly illustrated when a new leader at the club attempted to join in dancing with the girls at the weekly disco. The girls, astounded and dismayed at this interference in the one activity which they completely immersed themselves in, quickly moved en masse to a different part of the floor, leaving the leader to dance alone.

5   See D. Finn's unpublished paper, 'Training and skills', presented at the first meeting of the Conference of Socialist Economists' Education Group, University of Birmingham, December 1977. See also Willis (1977) and Hussain (1976).

6   Recently there has been a series of one-day conferences organized by feminist teachers interested in tackling sexism in schools and in working with school students.

7   Parker (1974, pp. 135-8) describes how 'The boys would thus enforce, by physical force if necessary standards they themselves were not willing to keep or observe.' He goes on: 'The second category of girl the boys identify is the "dirty ticket", "the randy", "the good screw", "tear yer back out", "little raver", designated for sexual exploitation.'

6 Psychoanalysis and the cultural acquisition of sexuality and subjectivity

Steve Burniston, Frank Mort and Christine Weedon

Introduction

Psychoanalysis has been severely criticized by feminists for the nature and implications of its account of the development of female sexuality, in which women's subordinate position is located in the structures (Oedipus complex, penis envy, etc.) through which sexual identity is acquired. These psychoanalytic structures are posited by psychoanalytic theory as fundamental to civilized culture and as a result, women's subordination becomes an inevitable consequence of the development of human sociality. Nonetheless Freud has been recognized by many feminists as the first theorist to bring the question of sexuality to the fore and to show that sexual identity is socially constituted rather than biologically innate. In this article we intend to look briefly at developments in psychoanalysis since Freud in relation to the acquisition of sexuality, language and subjectivity, and to examine its usefulness in the development of a materialist theory of sex/gender relations - a theory which might explain ideologies of sexual identity in such a way as to point to useful political strategies against women's subordination and sexism generally.

Like much of the rest of the book, this article is located in a space between Marxism in its present state of theoretical (under)development and what, from a feminist political position, we envisage as marxist-feminism. The move which many marxist-feminists have made into the area of psychoanalysis has often been precipitated by the existing state of marxist theory and politics, in which there is no definite space for questions of sexual oppression. This absence can be seen historically as a consequence of an over-evaluation of economic factors which directly determine, in an expressive way, the political and ideological superstructures. The revolution in marxist theory precipitated by the work of the French marxist philosopher, Althusser, in which the importance of politics and ideology as relatively autonomous levels of the social formation has been reasserted, together with a fuller notion of ideology as material practices, has opened up the possibility of examining sexual ideologies in their own right. Nonetheless, in the absence of a full theorization of the relations of sex, gender and biological reproduction (the impetus for which has come largely from the Women's Movement), the feminist element is always in danger of being lost. By this we mean the recognition that gender too (in articulation with class) structures and is structured by ideologies, and that gender relations in their present form imply the subordination of woman to man. It is in the light of this need for a full theorization of sex/gender relations that we are looking at psychoanalysis. We begin with a critical exposition of Freud and Lacan and move on to consider feminist assessments of psycho-analysis. Following from this, in the concluding sections, we examine some of the political and theoretical questions raised by psychoanalysis in relation to feminism and Marxism.

Freud: anatomical or cultural privilege?

The current re-emergence of Freud's work, and its particular Lacanian developments, from within the Women's Movement, has meant that psychoanalysis is now defined in an explicitly political context. The insistence by Juliet Mitchell and others that psychoanalysis is a feminist theory by default, and that it contains a unique set of concepts for an investigation of the construction of human sexuality and the development of sexual asymmetry has encouraged a *symptomatic reading* (1) of Freud's works of sexual theory — a reading which interprets and delivers ambiguities and absences. In such an analysis, the valorization of the male genital (against which in the Oedipal phase the infant is defined in its specific sexual identity), the castration complex, and the concept of female penis envy, are given a socio-cultural interpretation. They are read as the symbolic representations at the level of the unconscious of the overall patriarchal form of social organization: that is, of the terms in which women are, and have been, subordinated to male control. Freud's theory is, in that sense, seen as specific to the historical development of patriarchal structures.

Yet the difficulties which a feminist reading of Freud's text on sexuality must confront still centre on the problems of biology and anatomy, insofar as they inform Freud's specific theorization of the acquisition of sexual identity, and as they constitute an implicit part in his overall psychoanalytic theory. Freud's discovery of the original bisexuality of the drives in the pre-Oedipal phase provides a valuable political argument against ideological concepts of innate masculinity and feminity. However, as feminists, we experience major difficulties in any investigation of the process by which, according to Freud, bisexuality becomes unisexual in its object-choice, in the movement towards the acquisition of a masculine or feminine identity. Central to the structure of the Oedipus complex is the dominant role awarded to the penis in the father's intervention in the mother–child relationship. The significance of the penis is such that, as Laplanche and Pontalis (1973, p. 313) point out:

... its absence or presence transforms an anatomical distinction into a major yardstick for the categorisation of human beings ....

The little girl's discovery of her 'organic inferiority' (Freud 1977, p. 379) — the fact that her own 'small penis' will not grow and that she has in effect been castrated — and the consequent move into a passive 'feminine' role, is dependent on the significance of the male genital in an anatomical rather than a cultural context. For Freud, the primacy of the penis is located in its role in biological reproduction:

... the penis owes its extraordinary high narcissistic cathexis to its *organic* significance for the propagation of the species .... [our emphasis]

Freud (1977b, p. 341)

Though the distinction is marked between anatomical sex differences and the mode of their psychic representation, the structuring of the Oedipal triangle is nonetheless based on anatomical rather than social privilege.

In the context of Freud's original theorization, the work of some of the early female psychoanalysts who engage critically with Freud at precisely that level of anatomy and physiology seems more than justified. The studies made by Karen Horney (1974) and Helene Deutsch (1976) in the twenties attempt to refute biologically what they interpreted Freud's theory to be: that is, a theory of the anatomical inferiority of the female. They mark the terms of a literal level of engagement with Freud's work. Horney, in particular, follows the logic of a biological critique of Freud, to insist in turn on the physiological basis of a newly founded 'femininity'.

Ultimately, there is no sense in which a symbolic interpretation of Freud's theory of sexuality such as Mitchell conducts in *Psychoanalysis and Feminism* (1975) can appear as anything other than a partial reading. Certainly Freud's work in this area does *not* mark any progressive movement from the anatomical and physiological hypotheses to a specifically socio-cultural theory of the acquisition of sexuality. Biology is a continually significant factor in Freud's work on sexuality, as it is in his general psychoanalytic theory. Furthermore, we should be aware that Freud never makes a completely clear distinction between anatomical sexual characteristics, the psychic acquisition of a masculine or feminine identity, and the type of object-choice.

This ambiguity between the biological derivation of sexual difference and the terms of its psychic representation marks, more generally, distinct points of divergence in Freud's general psychoanalytic theory, and in the schools of development post-Freud. Broadly speaking, we can refer to the instinctual dynamic in Freud's work as the model for the functioning of the unconscious in which the psyche is located firmly within the biological functioning of the organism. With specific reference to sexuality, associated concepts here include: the location of the development of mental sexual characteristics in a corresponding physiological base, the investigation of the biochemical determinants of human sexuality (see particularly Freud 1977a), and the notion of sexual libido as the quantitative movement of psychic energy towards a specific object-choice. According to the instinctual model, sexual drives are directed to a particular form of object cathexis (attachment) in the Oedipal phase by the determinants of physical anatomy (i.e. the possession or lack of the penis).

Specifically symbolic readings of Freud (such as that of Althusser 1971b), maintain that the instinctual model is merely the ideological and 'home-made' schema used by Freud at the inception of the new science of psychoanalysis. In fact this model consistently informs Freud's study of sexuality in works as distant as the 'Three Essays on the Theory of Sexuality' (1905) and the essay, 'Female Sexuality' (1931). It marks the extent to which Freud never wholly removes his science from its origins within orthodox medical practice. Freud's concern with anatomical privilege, in isolation from the total *social* situation, should be seen partly in the light of his inheritance from traditional physiology.

There is in fact a distinct dualism in Freud's psychoanalytic theory which is exemplified by his ambiguous conceptualization and location of the unconscious. Further, the position occupied by the Oedipus complex forms a significant point of intersection in that psychic-biologistic duality. It is clear that a conception of anatomical determinancy is central to Freud's view of the acquisition of sexuality in the Oedipal phase. Yet the Oedipus complex is also the major point of reference for the investigation and analysis of symptoms in the case studies. It is seen by Freud as the formative element in the deep structure of the neurosis. Neurotic symptoms are, for Freud, the expression of a psychic conflict, the origins of which lie in the Oedipal phase of infantile sexuality. It is in the attempt to comprehend the determinants of neuroses (through presented symptoms, through jokes and slips of the tongue and, most significantly, through the interpretation of dreams) that Freud develops the psychoanalytic method, and constructs a model for the unconscious which contrasts with the physiologically based quantitative energy model.

The psychoanalytic method consists of bringing out the unconscious meaning of the words, the actions and the products of the imagination of a particular subject (dreams, fantasies, delusions, etc.) according to a theorization of the unconscious in which linguistic and verbal structures are a crucial determinant. It is this 'linguistic' model which forms the basis for non-biologist developments of Freudian theory, such as the work of the French psychoanalyst, Jacques Lacan, who insists that 'the unconscious is structured as a language' (Lacan 1972, p. 188). More significantly it is the model which has formed, via Lacan, the major point of entry for psychoanalysis in recent feminist debates on sexuality.

What we would argue here, with regard to the distinction between the dual conceptions of the unconscious as they appear in Freud's work, is that there can be no easy integration of the two systems. We cannot simply assert that Freud's *representational* model for the psyche is always predicated on an *instinctual* base, for as Althusser suggests (1971b, p. 207) the specificities of the particular model (i.e. instinctual or representational) result in radically different conceptions of the unconscious, which are not reconcilable. It is precisely because the two theories are continually present in Freud's work (often in the same text), and in terms that are not resolved, that we would maintain they exist as a *duality* in psychoanalytic theory.

Furthermore it seems crucial here to indicate the difficulties of Freud's theory in relation to the physiological/psychic and instinctual/representational distinctions, precisely because these dualities are the starting point for mutually exclusive post-Freudian developments in psychoanalytic theory. The current feminist demand for the theoretical inclusion of the psychoanalytic categories of sexuality has been posed largely through Lacanian concepts. This stresses the linguistic side of Freud's original programme, and the potential in Lacan's work for the development of a theory of sexuality which is rooted socially rather than biologically. But the work of Herbert Marcuse, for example (as characteristic of the Frankfurt School's approach to psychoanalysis), takes Freud's instinctual dynamic as an implicit model for the theorization of sexuality, in what is ultimately a political strategy for the liberation of instinctual drives. For Marcuse, the Ego of consciousness co-operates with the social forces of ideological manipulation and sexual repression, while the Id preserves the potential for liberation in the sexual instincts. Both Wilhelm Reich and Marcuse attempt to demonstrate, practically, the potential for 'political' action contained in such a theorization. Reich, in his Marxist period, conceives of the structures of the unconscious as historically specific to particular forms of social and economic organization. His original programme, conceived of as the attempt to 'understand the way in which social institutions, ideologies, life-forms, etc., mould the instinctual apparatus' (Reich 1972, p. 21) remains a valuable point of departure in any attempt to locate the structures of the unconscious within material social practices (2). Marcuse sees instinctual liberation, and specifically the liberation of repressed sexuality, as part of an explicitly political programme. Contemporary forms of sexual repression, Marcuse maintains, channel the sexual drives into compulsory heterosexual and monogamous forms of object-choice. What is demanded in *Eros and Civilisation* (1964) is a non-repressive expression of the original 'polymorphous perversity' of the drives in a variety of sexual orientations (homosexual, narcissistic, etc.).

The problems implicit in the instinctual model for a theorization of sexuality centre on the way in which Marcuse poses the *innate* structure of human drives *in opposition* to the historically specific structures of social organization. Sexual drives, for Marcuse, may be rearranged, or to a greater or lesser extent socially repressed, but their structure remains safely fixed within physiology. In that sense, the free flow of libidinal energy is conceived of as the biological extension of the 'truth' or 'essence' of 'human nature'. A non-repressive form of social organization would, for Marcuse, both rationally and instinctually express the essence of each individual subject. This location of the unconscious within the physiological processes of the organism places psychoanalytic theory once again firmly back in the problematic, in which the individual is defined *in opposition* to the movement of social forces. And the problem of sexuality and sexual liberation thereby appears as the problem of individual liberation, rather than as necessarily involving the transformation of social structures.

In contrast, it is the Lacanian system (however questionable in its present form), with its emphasis on the linguistic construction of the psyche, which provides the potential for a material location of the unconscious. For Freud it is centrally the works on dreams that provide the impetus for a conceptualization of the unconscious in which the role and function of language is crucial (e.g. *The Interpretation of Dreams* (1965) and the dream studies in the *Introductory Lectures in Psychoanalysis* (1975)). In specific relation to these works, two elements should be distinguished in an attempt to identify the centrality of linguistic and verbal concepts. Firstly, there is Freud's constant reference to the *dream work* as a script in which the *latent dream content* 'seems like a transcript' of the manifest dream thoughts. Freud's comparisons and analogies here are continually linguistic: dream thoughts have 'a mode of expression, whose characters and syntactic laws it is our business to discover by comparing the original and the translation' (Freud 1965, p. 312). Secondly, verbal elements are quite literally central to Freud's theorization of the movement of unconscious impulses, through the processes of condensation and displacement (see Article 7, footnote 4) to the form of their representation at the level of consciousness. The unconscious idea is displaced along a chain of associative paths, to be represented ultimately in consciousness as symptoms, fantasies or dreams. In that process, word presentations (the verbal residues of memories and perceptions) are the crucial determinants in the movement of the repressed idea from the unconscious proper to the system of consciousness. The pre-conscious is defined by Freud as the point at which the unconscious idea is brought into connection with these word presentations. Repressed unconscious impulses are represented in consciousness by becoming attached (cathected) to word presentations in the pre-conscious system (Freud 1961, p. 20). A major part of the work of psychoanalysis (the bringing to consciousness of the repressed wish) involves supplying the pre-conscious system with the intermediate verbal links to which impulses from the unconscious proper may become cathected.

Lacan: sexuality, language and subjectivity

Lacan sees his work as a return to this 'essential' Freud, the impact of whose work had been lost in the post-Freudian biologist development in psychoanalysis. The essential theoretical advance made by Freud is identified by Lacan as his theory of the unconscious and the challenge it offers to the notion of a unified, self-present subject, an 'I' who exists unproblematically in and for itself. This conceptualization of the subject, exemplified in Descartes's premise: 'I think, therefore I am,' makes the subject the source of meaning and language, rather than, as Lacan would have it, socially constructed in and through language (see below). In Lacan's reading of Freud, centrally his work on dreams and jokes, etc., the unconscious is not the site of biological drives but rather their manifestation in the mind, through the primary processes of which condensation and displacement are most important. Freud uses linguistic analysis to uncover latent meaning, which has been transformed by condensation and displacement and appears as the manifest content of a particular dream. In his approach to the unconscious, Lacan is not, however, searching for *latent* meaning, since he insists that meaning can never be original and fixed. He is rather seeking to understand the way in which *apparent* meaning has been organized through the action of condensation and displacement, Freudian concepts which are reformulated in Lacan's theory as the linguistic concepts of metaphor and metonomy (3). This reformulation marks the difference between Lacan's theory of representation and that found in Freud's work (see below).

The biological basis of the drives, the importance of which for Freud varies at different stages of his work, is not seen by Lacan as coming within the terms of the object of psychoanalytic study. The shift in emphasis in Lacanian theory is towards the problem of the social structuring of the unconscious through language. Lacan sets out to read Freud's work on dreams and parapraxis in the light of Saussurean linguistics and to develop further the notion of the unconscious structured as a 'language', the specific cultural form this structuring takes and its importance for a theorization of subjectivity. 'Language' in this context refers to the formal linguistic structures, of which the speaker is usually unconscious, which underpin and enable individual speech acts. The essential principle of language, according to Saussure, is that it consists of signifying chains, the individual elements of which are called 'signs' and consist of the unity of signifier and signified. Within the two systems of signifiers and signifieds, individual signifiers or individual signifieds are distinguished by their difference from all the other elements in the system. There are no pre-existing positive terms in which meaning is located prior to its enunciation in the signifying chain. On the contrary, the sign receives its meaning from its place in the signifying chain. The Saussurean concept of the sign is however criticized by Lacan (together with Derrida 1973 and Kristeva 1974) for being open to the suggestion that meaning is fixed prior to its articulation in the signifying chain. The notion of a pure signified - a concept existing outside of its articulation in language - relies on a fixed source of meaning, a unified, transcendent consciousness, which can guarantee meaning and which it was Freud's achievement to question. Lacan suggests that in effect there are only signifiers which stand in a relation of difference to one another and that they are endowed with meaning retrospectively when the signifying chain is cut (4).

The unconscious in Lacanian theory is structured in the form of signifying chains, organized around what Lacan calls nodal points. These are certain privileged signifiers whose position is given by the law which is the precondition of the structuring both of the unconscious and of the symbolic order of language, meaning and human culture. Both the unconscious and the symbolic orders are founded through the organization of desire specified by this law. The law in question is what for both Lacan and the French anthropologist Lévi-Strauss founds culture and sociality and is the source of meaning, which supports the symbolic order. It is in effect that law by which desire is controlled, i.e. what Lacan calls the law of the phallus (the phallus being the symbol of the control of desire). It takes the universal cultural form of the Oedipus complex and the incest taboo, which results from it and which, in Lévi-Strauss's anthropology, is consolidated in the universal law of the exchange of women between kinship groups. It is referred to by Lacan as the law of the 'Other', i.e. the law which sets up the limits within which the 'I' as subject can function. Lacan uses this formulation of the 'Other' to stress that meaning in the symbolic order of language does not originate in the subject who speaks. This assumption is a result of a misrecognition by the speaking subject of itself as occupying the place of the 'Other', i.e. of being the source of meaning. In effect the terms within which the subject can function in the symbolic order are pre-given by the law that founds this order and determines the way in which the subject is constructed, as a sexed individual, in and through language.

Thus the place that the individual can occupy as a subject in language and culture is fixed by the law which structures the symbolic order. This law organizes desire, and by extension sexuality, through the Oedipal triangle. Lacan locates the source of this law as the symbolic position of the 'Father', which is the source of meaning and the precondition for language and culture. (The Judaic notion of 'God the Father', who is absent, who is the law-giver and whose name is so sacred that you cannot even speak it, is an example of what is meant by the symbolic 'Father'.) This position of control is not to be confused with that of the real father in the Oedipal triangle since this position, and the triangle itself, are but effects of the organization of the cultural realm according to the symbolic laws. Nonetheless, at the resolution of his Oedipal complex, the male child identifies with the position of the symbolic 'Father', imagining himself as potentially able to occupy this position. In doing so he collapses the position of symbolic 'Father' into that of the real father of the patriarchal family and misrecognizes himself as being able to control desire at some future date.

In the development of the human infant the unconscious is constituted, along with subjectivity, at the moment when the child, having resolved the Oedipus complex and accepted a heterosexual love-object through repression of aspects of its bisexuality, is able to enter the symbolic universe and can position itself within language. This is the culmination of a process of development from the pre-Oedipal phase, through the mirror phase, the Oedipus and castration complexes. At the moment of resolution of the Oedipus complex, the presences and absences which the child has experienced in relation to the zones of the body (e.g. having or not having the mother's breast), which led it to distinguish between itself and the world, are retrospectively given meaning. At this point the representation in language of presence and absence enables the child to exercise some degree of control over its situation, by representing what it experiences to itself (5). Thus the Oedipus complex is the point in the development of the child, when a third figure, that of the father, intervenes in the relationship between the child and the mother, and for the boy, taboos any incestuous relationship with his mother. This is effected by the threat of castration. In the case of the girl, it is a question of her recognizing that she can never sexually possess her mother, the object of desire. This possession requires having the 'phallus', which she can only hope to receive in the form of a penis or baby, if she changes her pre-Oedipal sexual attachment to her mother for a heterosexual love-object – in the first instance her father. At the point of resolution of the Oedipus complex, the child enters into subjectivity – the position of 'I' in language – which it can now distinguish from the second and third persons (you, she and he). This entry into language is sex-specific and sets the child on the path to femininity or masculinity, according to the laws of the symbolic order.

Both Lacan and Lévi-Strauss stress that the laws and positions which constitute their theories of human culture are *symbolic*. Thus the organization of human sociality, according to the Oedipal triangle, which serves to order desire in the unconscious and thus found sexuality and meaning, is (they stress) a *neutral* structure. This means that although Lacan cites the 'Father' as the source of the law, this does not necessarily imply the subordination of women. Similarly,

Lévi-Strauss insists that his fundamental law of the exchange of women by men is also neutral. However, in the development of the human infant, its entry into a specific form of sexed subjectivity, in accordance with the laws of culture, is predicated on a specific resolution of the Oedipus complex, which functions through the recognition of *anatomical* difference. This difference, having or not having the penis, comes to mean, in cultural terms, having or not having the phallus. Although this position is based on misrecognition, in the sense that no one can actually possess the phallus, i.e. become the source of the laws which structure human sociality, it is nonetheless men, as possessors of actual penises, who are able to identify with this position of control.

Thus the phallus can in effect never be a neutral signifier of difference, since the anatomically grounded elision between the phallus and the penis implies a patriarchal organization of desire and thus of sexuality. Because Lacan's theory ultimately rests on the biological difference between the sexes, manifest at birth, it is impossible to detach the phallus from this particular physical difference and give it any non-oppressive, cultural significance for women. As it stands, Lacanian theory necessarily implies a power relation between men and women, in which women are subordinated; yet for Lacan it is not a historically specific privileging, but an eternal law of human culture. The supposedly *pure symbolic* function of the phallus cannot be explained solely in terms of the internal logic of Lacanian theory whilst it relies on an anatomical difference. It is this which constitutes the *phallocentrism* (privileging of the phallus/penis), of Lacan's theory. Once we reject the notion of a necessary, ever pre-given patriarchal structure for the organization of desire (and it is here that a feminist critique of Lacan, as of Freud, must centre), the dominance of the phallus, in its equation with the penis, can only be explained historically and materially, by an analysis of the structural relations between the sexes, which are manifest in material practices. It is only this materialist analysis which can ground the phallus as a symbol of the social organization of sexuality at the level of the unconscious.

Feminist assessments of psychoanalysis

The relation of feminism to psychoanalysis is discussed most fully, and in the light of Marxist, Lacanian and anthropological concepts, by Juliet Mitchell in *Psychoanalysis and Feminism*. The feminist assessments of psychoanalysis which predate this are examined by Mitchell herself (1975, pp. 303-56). Before we present our account of Mitchell's work we would like briefly to review the general problem of the relation between psychoanalysis and feminism as it is treated in these works. Certain basic objections to Freud's work are common to all, but outright dismissal of psychoanalysis is more rare – only Germaine Greer (1970) and Eva Figes (1972) take this position. Other feminist writers retain a sense of the possible usefulness of Freud's work, often on broadly similar grounds. Each text presents its own general thesis about the extent and nature of women's oppression and the necessary strategies in the struggle against it. Thus in each case, the detail and emphasis of the discussion of psychoanalysis is determined by wider feminist arguments. (Perhaps the most ambitious of these is Shulamith Firestone's (1972), which envisages a dialectic between the Male Technological and Female Aesthetic principles, ending in a synthesis.)

In the chapters on psychoanalysis, attention is mainly focused on Freud's account of the construction of femininity and its implications. The feminists say less about general problems such as that of the relative importance, within the theory, of physiological and psychic determinations. The general charge against Freud's work is that it reinforces, ideologically, the oppression of women by describing the characteristics of feminity in terms of the immutable structures of the psyche. The point is made that the dominant and positive significance attributed to the penis or to its symbolic representation by Freud (and by Lacan) constitutes the extension into psychoanalytic theory of cultural and historical notions of male superiority. To this objection is added the argument that psychoanalytic theory should be seen as a product of a social and historical situation, in a way which comprises it, as a supposedly objective and scientific theory. The suggestion is strongly resisted by Mitchell (1975, pp. 322-3), who counters it with claims as to the scientificity of the theory, which owe much to Althusser's notion (1971b, p. 184) of science as breaking from ideology. In this way Mitchell removes it, as a science, from the restraints of the particular historical conjuncture.

A related objection made by Kate Millet (1970), among others, is to the ahistorical nature of the Freudian theory of psychic development. Here the problem of the effectivity of biology versus that of psychic representations is raised. Millet accuses Freud of biologism, and advances the alternative notion of socialization, effected solely through the historically specific forms of social relations, although, unlike Mitchell, she omits a consideration of Freudian representations, or language, as part of this process:

> What forces in her experience, her society and socialization have led (a woman) to see herself as an inferior being? The answer would seem to lie in the conditions of patriarchal society and the inferior position of women within this society. But Freud did not choose to pursue such a line of reasoning, preferring instead an etiology of childhood experience based upon the biological fact of anatomical differences.
>
> Millet (1970, p. 180)

Mitchell rightly objects to the reduction of Freudianism to biologism, although her own reading of Freud also presents problems, as we shall see.

A further issue, in the feminist discussions of Freud, is the question of the consequences of psychoanalytic practice. Some feminists make the distinction between Freudian theory, and psychoanalysis as practised by later analysts in various countries, especially the USA. Figes sees the later developments mostly as ameliorations of true Freudian repressiveness; for her the problem is that 'not only are there still many orthodox Freudians practising and writing, but Freudian ideas have also become very popular currency' (1972, p. 160). Under these conditions, she says, women are 'brainwashed' into an acceptance of their own supposed inferiority intellectually, personally, and sexually. Her argument contrasts with the Lacanian view of American analysis, as a corruption of Freud's original practice which, it is maintained, was concerned not with conformity to social or sexual norms, but with self-knowledge (cf. Lacan 1977, p. 7; Mitchell 1975, p. 337).

The questions raised by Freudian theory of sexuality are seen as crucial by the feminist writers because, throughout their works, they locate sexuality as an important site of women's oppression, inasmuch as it is conceived as passive, receptive, dependent on the active, stimulant male presence, even masochistic. This conception of female sexuality seems to be the point at which all notions of women's inferiority meet and condense. The Freudian theory of the vaginal orgasm, as the mature form of feminine response, is regarded as a major factor in the reinforcement and reproduction of these repressive notions of female sexuality. This was clear for the first time following the findings of Masters and Johnson that 'all female orgasms originate in the clitoris' (Greer 1970, p. 96). Until this recognition, as Greer points out, 'the woman who knew that all her orgasms originated in the clitoris was shamed by the imputation of immaturity and penis-envy' (1970, p. 93).

On the other hand, if Firestone calls Freudianism 'the misguided feminism', part of the reason is her appreciation of the revolutionary implications of the Freudian stress on sexuality. The fact that Freud treated sexuality in overt separation from questions of morality, and in an analytical fashion - however unsatisfactory his conclusions - was important in laying the basis for subsequent feminist developments of the kind that Firestone outlines. Freudian theory offers at least the prospect of an account of the construction of sexuality which shows it to be a social and historical rather than a natural phenomenon.

The tendency to see Freud's work as flawed but potentially useful for a theory of feminine socialization is inseparable from overall political tendencies. An account of socialization and of sexuality as it is developed in the individual is thought to be necessary, not only because feminists recognize that sexuality and sexual practices are an important terrain of political struggle. These accounts are seen as also contributing to an understanding of political action as the conscious effort to change personal relationships. It is necessary to be aware of both the positive and the limiting aspects of this conception of political action. This point is developed later.

Feminists continue to evaluate and appropriate psychoanalytic concepts in a non-Lacanian and non-Althusserian context. Ann Foreman's *Femininity and Alienation* (1977) is a recent important example. Here both the appreciation of Freud's work on sexuality, and the ultimate rejection of his ahistoricism, reappear - this time combined with an anthropologically based attack on the universality of the Oedipus complex (Foreman 1977, pp. 18-23). While Foreman's critique of Mitchell is perceptive, her own thesis suffers from a tendency to reduce Marxism to a theory of human alienation - the economic category 'labour power' becomes 'a term expressing the alienation of productive activity', and the class struggle is 'the historical working through of the process of alienation' (1977, p. 130). There is a danger, with this kind of terminology, of retaining an unspecific and utopian conception of political action as the necessary expression of inevitable historical progress (7).

Juliet Mitchell: the material location of the unconscious

In terms of recent history, it was the Women's Movement of the sixties and early seventies, with its emphasis on the *ideological* forms of sexual subordination, and the development of strategies for ideological struggle, which utilized psychoanalysis politically, in the move towards a theorization of sexuality and sex-oppression. As Juliet Mitchell insists polemically in *Psychoanalysis and Feminism* (1975, p. 362):

> The longevity of the oppression of women must be based on something more than conspiracy, something more complicated than biological handicap and more durable than economic exploitation (although in differing degrees all these may feature).

In many ways, the theoretical developments achieved within the Women's Movement, in the move towards a theory of the construction of sex/gender identity in its historically specific ideological forms, parallel in a broad sense recent advances made in Marxist theories of ideology. Both represent an increasing disillusion with the various forms of reductionism and economism, in their inability, in this specific context, to provide anything other than a partial analysis of women's subordination, together with their restrictive potential for political practice. *Exclusive* concentration, for example, on the 'domestic labour debate' (7) leads to a merely partial analysis of woman's oppression which, within a wider perspective, fails to preserve the historical specificity of female subordination as it predates capitalism. As Gayle Rubin insists (1975, p. 163):

> To explain women's usefulness to capitalism is one thing. To argue that this usefulness explains the genesis of the oppression of women is quite another. It is precisely at this point that the analysis of capitalism ceases to explain very much about women and the oppression of women.

It was in the context of this theoretical absence that *Psychoanalysis and Feminism* opened the way programmatically within a section of the Women's Movement for an inclusion of the categories of Freudian psychoanalysis in the investigation of the functioning of sexual ideology. In general terms, psychoanalysis is posited by Mitchell as the repertoire of concepts necessary for a more extended analysis of the functioning of the ideologies of sex and gender. In what appears to be an Althusserian reading of the social formation, Mitchell usefully insists that the relationship between specific forms of sexual *ideology* and the structures of *political* and *economic* organization is not one of direct correspondence, but rather that each specific level exists in a state of *relative autonomy* from the others. Thus particular ideologies are not seen as mere direct reflections of the economic base of society, but possess their own internal laws and dynamics, and their own material location within specific social practices. Furthermore, Mitchell maintains that it is the developments in psychoanalysis made by Freud and Lacan (together with existing Marxist concepts of ideology), which provide the point of departure for the understanding of the social organization of sexuality.

Arguing that the wholesale rejection of Freud, made by some radical feminists, is in fact fatal for the overall development of a theory of woman's subordination, Mitchell insists that Freud's discoveries provide a unique conceptual schema for an investigation of the construction of human sexuality. Although she acknowledges that biologism does exist in Freud's work, Mitchell argues that the continual denunciation of Freud's patrocentric bias halts any movement towards an evaluation of the *potential* of psychoanalysis (8). Freud's theory, Mitchell states (1975, p. xvi) is inherently social:

> ... psychoanalysis is about the material reality of ideas both within and of man's history; thus in 'penis envy', we are talking not about an anatomical organ, but about *the ideas of it that people hold and live by within the general culture.* It is this ... factor that also prescribes the reference of psychoanalysis. [our emphasis]

She argues for a decisive break from concern with anatomy and biologism, and points to Lacanian developments in psychoanalysis, as a theory of the cultural acquisition of sexual identity (though as a feminist, disturbingly uncritically in the light of Lacan's explicit phallocentrism). For Mitchell, as for Lacan, it is the 'symbolic' Father (only imperfectly incarnate in the presence of the 'real' father), who embodies the law that constitutes human society and culture. The specific history of the individual in fact takes place within this larger structure, which embraces *all* historical forms of social and cultural law. The Oedipus complex is the terrain on which, at the level of the unconscious, the infant acquires her/his place as a sexed subject within the human order, which is simultaneously the acquisition of a place and nomenclature within language and within culture.

In her attempt to ground Lacanian concepts more explicitly within material and social practices, Mitchell turns to Lévi-Strauss for an account of the way in which the patriarchal Oedipal invariant is internalized at the level of the unconscious. Her claim is that the material organization of kinship structures, and specifically the exchange of women, are in 'structural homology' with the structuring of the unconscious according to the law of the symbolic 'Father'. The exchange of women in the social order finds its internal equivalent in the constitution of the unconscious within the structures of patriarchal law. The problem with Mitchell's analysis is not that it is in any sense wholly misdirected, but that it is not sufficiently developed, and in a quite specific sense, given what appears to be her initial Althusserian reading of the social formation. The structures of kinship and familial organization are recognized by Mitchell as the principle material practices which determine the construction and development of the unconscious in its patriarchal form. Yet those kinship structures are themselves posited by Mitchell as forming a *wholly autonomous* system of social organization, and as unrelated to developments at other levels within the social formation. Quite specifically, they are not seen as the crucial site for the location of the terms under which *economically, politically,* and *ideologically,* women are subordinate to male control. Rather, the forms of kinship/familial organization are the site of *patriarchal structures* which are seen to form a separate system.

The crucial point in Mitchell's theorization here concerns her use of concepts derived from Lévi-Strauss. Lévi-Strauss himself argues (significantly in terms which form the basis for Lacan's own developments), for a theory of the symbolic exchange of women, which conceptualizes that system as synonymous with the constitution of culture and human society itself. Kinship structures are *not* seen by Lévi-Strauss as overdetermined by the overall form of social and economic organization, but rather: 'the rules of kinship and marriage are not made necessary by the social state. They are the social state itself' (Lévi-Strauss 1969, p. 490). This emphasis on the importance of the *structure* of the act of exchange fails to locate the fact that *within* that structure women exist in a relationship of subordination to men, which is a *power relationship* (9). Furthermore, it is in fact precisely this type of 'structuralist' analysis that Mitchell herself performs: 'The act of exchange holds a society together: the rules of kinship (like those of language to which they are near-allied) *are* the society' (1975, p. 370).

From her reading of Lévi-Strauss, Mitchell maintains that kinship structures are not themselves articulated in their historical specificity on the larger structures of social and economic organization. Kinship, for women, at any rate, appears in Mitchell's theory as the *equivalent* of the concept mode of production, *not* as its dependent structure. Certainly in *Psychoanalysis and Feminism,* kinship/familial structures are never conceptualized, either in the historical or the contemporary analysis, as functioning at a variety of levels within the social formation. Specifically here, Mitchell seems to show little awareness of the crucial *economic* function of the family under capitalism in reproducing labour power (both biologically and in the production of use values). It is precisely the lack of this larger articulation that enables Mitchell to argue that the structuring of sex and gender relationships, in contemporary forms of familial organization, are obsolescent and archaic, and in no way related to the demands of the capitalist mode of production. Furthermore, it is this separation of the structures of kinship from the specific forms of economic and political organization, which leads Mitchell to search for the 'origins' of patriarchal structures, both as they determine the forms of the unconscious, and the forms of the social exchange of women. That search leads, by default, not into a materialist analysis, but into the anthropological–mythical realm of Freud's *Totem and Taboo* (1961), where we find an account of the 'world historical defeat of the female', the defeat of the primitive matriarchies, and the subsequent rise of 'patriarchy', and hence of civilization itself.

It is from these theoretical developments that Mitchell derives her particular political position; women are located within the social structures of 'patriarchy' rather than within class structures. Hence the trajectory for feminist political struggle is predicated on a terrain independent from that of class struggle:

> ... men enter into the class-dominated structures of history while women (as women, whatever their actual work in production) remain defined by the kinship patterns of organization.
>
> Mitchell (1975, p. 406)

In her attempt to preserve the specificity of the oppression which women experience as theirs and theirs alone, Mitchell moves from a position of scrupulous relative autonomy, towards total autonomy, the implications of which appear to be separatist. The terms of Mitchell's political programme are directly derived from her theorization of women's subordination as located within the autonomous patriarchal structures of 'human society'.

Marxism and Lacanian theory: feminist developments

Juliet Mitchell's work is important for British feminists and marxists as an introduction to Lacanian and Althusserian concepts. Since the appearance of her book, feminist discussions of psychoanalysis, inasmuch as they have accepted the general argument of *Psychoanalysis and Feminism,* have been prompted to return to the original texts of Althusser and Lacan for a clarification of the specific marxist and psychoanalytic concepts used in Mitchell's work, in relation to a theorization of women's subordination (10). In addition, attention has been focused on the work of Julia Kristeva, who has taken up Lacan's theory of the constitution of sexed subjectivity in a specifically feminist way and attempted to unite it, at least in principle, with an Althusserian theory of the social formation.

Kristeva claims to complement Althusser's theory of ideology, in the sense that she sets out to theorize the nature of the 'always-already' given subject, which constitutes Althusser's theory of 'ideology in general' (Althusser 1971a). She locates the subject as constituted through what she calls (1974) the mode of sign production. (This is the process of 'significance', which consists of both the symbolic, and semiotic, i.e. unconscious, feminine, aspects of signifying practice.) It is ultimately determined by the laws of Lacan's patriarchal, symbolic order. Although Kristeva is still working with a notion of an 'individual' subject, constructed in the mode of sign production, she does recognize that the constitution of subjectivity is part of a *social* process, which involves other levels of the social formation. Yet she does not adequately theorize the relationship between what she terms the mode of 'socio-economic' production and the mode of sign production.

Yet, inasmuch as Kristeva attempts to deal with the constitution of subjects, in a certain relation to the order of language, or symbolic representation in general, her work has had vast implications for the analysis of texts, in particular artistic texts. The specificity of artistic texts, in which the semiotic (unconscious, repressed, feminine), determinations are more pronounced, lies in their particular property of undermining the experience of fixed subjectivity at unconscious levels of identity and desire. This has led Kristeva (1974), Barthes (1970), and in Britain, contributors to *Screen,* among others, to develop Lacanian readings of film, poetry and prose narrative.

The work of Julia Kristeva is significant as an attempt to clarify and develop the Lacanian theory of subjectivity in a feminist direction, in the context of the construction of a specifically marxist-feminist concept of aesthetic and political practice. Her work on subjectivity goes much further than Lacan's, in trying to readdress the problem of the drives (which she translates into her concept of *pulsions*), and their psychic representations. At the same time, she retains the sense of the effectivity of symbolic – i.e. culturally determined – significations. The implications of this for feminism lie in the fact that, for Kristeva, the *pulsions* and their significations, which constitute the repressed realm of the semiotic, are to be valued at the expense of the fixing, repressing agency, the symbolic. Kristeva retains the Lacanian account of femininity, seeing it as constituted through a different form of acceptance of castration, involving a less complete subjection to the patriarchal laws of rational discourse. She describes (1974, esp. pp. 209–350) a revolt against these laws in the works of the French *avant-garde* writers, Lautréamont and Mallarmé. Their works, she argues, are dominated by the sensual and rhythmical semiotic process, which relativizes logic and meaning. Kristeva maintains that the same challenge to meaning is presented on a historical scale by the feminist revolt against the patriachal laws of family, state and language itself.

Kristeva, in her theorization of sexed subjectivity, attempts in principle to hold to an Althusserian reading of the social formation. In this sense, her work contrasts with that of another Lacanian feminist, Luce Irigaray (1977, pp. 62–77). Kristeva accepts the notion of an *unsexed* libido, effective at the pre-Oedipal stage in children of either sex. According to her theory, women are not so much fundamentally different from men, as constituted by the relative dominance of a semiotic mode, which is present, but less effective, in the male psyche. By contrast, Irigaray asserts that: 'it is in order to establish their difference that women are claiming their rights' (1977, p. 68). She sees women as having a specifically *feminine* libido and language, the recognition of which demands a separatist political stance, in opposition to a phallocentric culture.

The problem of the centrality of the phallus in Lacanian theory (posed afresh by Anthony Wilden 1972), and of its universal and essential nature, remains central to feminist appropriations of Lacan. We would argue that a solution to this theoretical problem would necessarily involve a fundamental recasting of the whole conceptual system, far more radical than that undertaken by Kristeva. Yet a more basic problem, even than this, from the position of marxist-feminism, is that of the relation between the two theories, which both Mitchell and Kristeva attempt to hold to: Marxism and a psychoanalytic theory of the constitution of sexed subjectivity, however recast. We would argue that the problems in this area have not, in any way, been resolved by the assertion of the necessity to marxist theory of a *general* conceptualization of the constitution of the subject (see Irigary 1977), and we will return to this point in our concluding section.

Political and theoretical perspectives: psychoanalysis, feminism and Marxism

What then is the political and theoretical importance of psychoanalysis? Disregarding its ahistorical phallocentrism, for the moment, the initial recognition, that forms of sex gender are cultural, rather than biologically innate, makes a potentially greater control of our own sexuality a viable proposition. We are made aware of the ideological nature of sexual stereotypes, and led to question their social functions, i.e. ultimately to place forms of sexual relations and emotional behaviour in relationship to social and economic relations.

A rejection at an individual level of dominant sexual ideologies can offer a framework in which to understand one's emotional life, too, as culturally formed in response to certain social ideologies, which may be repressive or contradictory. Sexual identity is linked in Lacanian theory with forms of subjectivity, which are understood as socially constructed in language in relation to sexual difference, rather than ever pre-given. This notion, also, can have important political effects on how we see ourselves in relation to ideologies, which function by fixing the individual as subject, within the structure of their own meanings. It is these meanings which, though constructed to intervene between the individual and her/his 'material conditions of existence', appear 'true', natural and eternal, and which we feel 'privileged' to share (Althusser 1971a).

Once we move beyond the level of useful personal–political insights, to examine how adequate psychoanalytic concepts are for a theorization of the acquisition of sexual identity, we are confronted by all the problems of the ahistorical phallocentrism of psychoanalysis. Nonetheless it is important to realize that psychoanalysis does preserve the particular dynamic of sexuality and gender relations, structured in dominance and subordination, with their own history and development, in way which other theories of the social construction of sexuality do not. The various specific sociological approaches to the acquisition of sexuality (11) all, in a general sense, insist that sexual identity is learned and reproduced by the interaction of the individual with various social and cultural practices, in the overall process of socialization. The problem here is that attempts to particularize this form of analysis, i.e. to articulate a relationship between specific forms of gender characterization and the structure of social relations, often tend towards either reductionism of a form of sociological functionalism, in which the family appears to regulate sexuality and sexual identity in the 'interests' of capitalist production.

The patriarchal eternalism of Freudian theory is not sufficient reason for marxist-feminists to disregard it. When applied in a historically specific way to the patriarchal nuclear family - clinical evidence of which founded the theory in the first place - it can offer a useful analysis of women's position, and a symbolic reading of the power of the penis can generate a way of focusing actual structures of male power and control. We must nonetheless be aware that such a shift involves a real transformation of the original psychoanalytic concepts.

However, it is not a question of *either* socialization *or* psychoanalytic theory. We need both elements in an analysis of the construction of sexuality, the ideological conditions of which structure women's subordination and the sanctioning of selected sexual practices. Furthermore, we need an analysis which is *not* reductionist and yet attempts to articulate the *relationship between* historically specific ideologies of sexual identity and sexual practices, and other levels within the social formation.

Psychoanalysis and Marxism

Throughout this article we have been mainly concerned with examining the limitations of psychoanalysis and locating its appropriation or rejection by feminists. Psychoanalysis has been valued because of its attention to sexuality as a social construction, to the problem of language and ideology as factors in the oppression of women, and to the vital role of the family and kinship structures in the reproduction of that oppression. But what are the possibilities of marxist analysis in these areas? And what is the relation between Marxism (as a theoretical method and a materialist philosophy), and psychoanalytic concepts? Are they mutually contradictory, antagonistic, or can they be seen as complementary?

The situation is affected in an important way by Althusser's use of concepts which closely resemble those of psychoanalysis, especially of the Lacanian type (cf. Althusser 1971a). His work in this respect must be seen in the context of his attempt to specify the nature of the ideological instance, and its relation to the economic and political levels. In accordance with his attempt to think of ideologies as material social practices, Althusser presents an analysis of these practices. What concerns *us* is his awareness of the family as one of the material social practices which constitute the ideological level (1971a, p. 252). What is also implied, albeit in an unsatisfactory way (12), is the importance of these ideological practices, via their role in social reproduction, as a terrain of political struggle. But the implications of the Althusserian argument for the struggle against the oppression of women are buried *rather deep*.

There is another dimension to Althusser's analysis of ideology; this is his theory of 'ideology in general' (1971a, pp. 262-78). Althusser's attempt to analyse the internality of specific structures of the ideological level - as distinct from its place or role in the social formation as a whole - involves him in efforts to theorize the unchanging and ahistorical aspects of ideology. Here the echoes of Lacanian theory are louder. Ideology in its most general aspect is theorized in relation to the individual, to language and the nature of subjectivity. The general role of ideology, most importantly performed through language, is to 'interpellate' the human individual, that is, to enable the individual to imagine her/himself as a unified, central point from which experience and being radiate, i.e. as a subject (1971a, pp. 272 ff.). Althusser stresses the extent to which expectations and roles, embodied in linguistic and other practices, pre-exist the development of the individual, pre-forming the limits and possibilities of that individual's conception of her/himself.

In Lacanian terms, Althusser's article relies on an impermissible dislocation between problems of subjectivity and language, which seem to remain in part ahistorical and universal, and the structures of kinship and familial relations (including, presumably, relations of sexuality), which are located in the historical and political sphere. But does Althusser's attempt indicate the possibility of a merger between Marxism and psychoanalytic theories of the constitution of the subject, from which feminist analysis would benefit?

Later work, developing Althusserian problems, has involved an increasing awareness of their implications for feminism (13). However we would argue against any notion of a merger between the two theories in this specific context. Marxism is characterized by its attention, for fundamental reasons, to the historically specific. Historically general concepts, such as productive labour, are necessary for Marxism, but are formulated only in so far as they are needed in the analysis of the specificity of, for example, a particular mode of production. From a marxist point of view, the fact that the human individual uses language and is constituted as a member of a system of ideological, political and economic practices, when considered as general, is a necessary and sufficient starting point. The detail of the entry of the individual into a social position, understood as an eternal and universal process, does not have to be explicated for any politically useful analysis.

It is precisely because psychoanalysis is implicated, at its inception, in those *eternal* and *universal* questions that the attempt to develop concepts of subjectivity in a marxist direction is so fraught with difficulties. If we are able to retain the term psychoanalysis in what follows, this is conditional on our awareness of its inherent idealist dynamic. The Lacanian use of the term, for example, refers to a discourse which centres around the conditions of human life in general (notions of desire and alienation): a metaphysical discourse of little political relevance. Such considerations must be seen to depend on historically and politically specific situations.

The basic project of psychoanalysis - to understand the *process of constitution of sexed subjectivity* - is fundamentally flawed as a philosophical starting point. Where the attempt is made both to retain this basic project, and to develop a wider conception of political action, it is hindered by the individualist structure of the original theory. This structure is seen in its purest form in the patient-analyst situation, where all action is ideally conceived of as the transformation of intersubjective relations. Marxism should articulate some concept of intersubjective relations, but with a conception of political, economic and ideological relations, which together constitute the field of political action. Our contention would be that Marxism can be developed in such a way as to extend and refine its analysis of women's oppression, and that these developments would not depend on a theorization at a *general* (i.e. ahistorical) level of the constitution of sexed subjectivity.

Conclusion

Finally, we would wish to indicate programmatically the ways in which the concepts of psychoanalysis could be transformed and integrated into material and concrete analyses of the construction of sexuality and the forms of sexual oppression. We would see this work of historical and conjunctural analysis as crucial in determining the forms of political action to be taken, in the attempt to transform existing structures of sexuality. Furthermore it is a project which would preserve as its *absolute precondition* the historically specific location of the forms of subjectivity within material practices. Throughout the exposition of Freud and Lacan, we have insisted on this task as the continually necessary correction to tendencies in both theories, which, either through biologism or universalism, return us to a static conception of patriarchal structures. More positively, now, we would indicate the need to move towards a theorization of the terms in which psychoanalytic structures of the unconscious could be materially located – as a stage in the overall investigation of the construction of sex and gender.

Althusser himself, in 'Freud and Lacan' (1971b), tentatively provides a framework for that type of theorization. The line of development, outlined in that essay, attempts to articulate the relationship between the structures of the unconscious, the concrete form of kinship structures, and the form of sexual ideology conceived of as contributing to the maintenance and reproduction of particular social relations. Ultimately, Althusser's theorization of that relationship remains at the level of a structural homology. However, his framework returns us usefully to the project, outlined by Mitchell in *Psychoanalysis and Feminism,* of materially locating psychoanalytic structures, but in terms which insist on a fully marxist theorization of the social formation. Althusserian developments in marxist theory provide precisely that structural analysis which avoids a simplistic collapse of certain *ideological* functions of the family with its *economic* role. Yet the concept of relative autonomy does not, of itself, enable a sufficient theorization of the relation of sexual ideology and sex-oppression with the political and economic levels. What is needed beyond that, is the necessary task of tracing, concretely, the relationship between historically specific forms of sex/gender identity (including their unconscious representation), the material practices which structure the acquisition of that identity (the media, the educational system, the labour process and primarily the mode of kinship/familial organization), and the organization of economic and social relations which constitute the mode of production. The crucial determinant is the multi-functional aspect of the family, as the point of intersection of the economic and ideological levels. It performs significant tasks within the circuit of economic production and reproduction and, also, it is the primary material practice within which sexual identities are constructed.

Work performed by marxist anthropologists has already noted the various economic, political and ideological functions of kinship structures (i.e. the socially transformed variants of genealogical and blood relations) in pre-class societies (14). What is now needed is to extend the terms of that analysis, to include an investigation of the way in which the nuclear family still preserves a multi-functional purpose under capitalist relations. For it is in this type of interrelated analysis of the family that one can begin to locate materially and structurally the psychoanalytic determinants which contribute to the acquisition of a sexual identity.

Current analysis performed by marxist-feminists still tends to separate out as a duality the economic and ideological functions of the family. We are now in a better position to comprehend the terms under which the specific form of domestic labour performed by women, together with women's role as biological reproducers, contribute to the circuit of capitalist production. Further, the psychoanalytic theory of the construction of sexuality, and the various socialization theses, insist that it is primarily in the family that sexual identity is acquired and 'learned'. Yet beyond posing that duality of functions, little attempt has as yet been made to analyse concretely, within a Marxist framework, the way in which a dominant sexual ideology is effective in maintaining and reproducing the structure of social relations, within which women find their subordinate place in the circuit of capitalist production and biological reproduction (15). Tentatively here we would outline *one* specific structure in which to 'think through' that articulation between the economic function of the family and the social and unconscious acquisition of sexual identity.

Working on the terrain provided by Althusser in the essay on 'Ideology and ideological state apparatuses' (1971a), we should ask not only the question, 'How is the reproduction of the relations of *production* secured?', but also, 'How is the reproduction of the relations of (biological) *reproduction* secured?' Part of the answer, to draw further on Althusser, is that these specific relations, which are relations involving the subordination of women to men, are secured and controlled by the legal, political and ideological superstructures (located in specific material practices) and also by direct intervention of the state (16). But, we would argue further, that these relations are massively maintained and reproduced by the functioning of the dominant form of sexual ideology. The ideological interpellation of the individual, into a masculine or feminine identity, operates *socially* (with all the attendant baggage of maleness, and the reciprocal ideologies of motherhood and femininity) and through the structures located by psychoanalysis as articulating a 'living out', *at the level of the unconscious,* of a specific form of masculinity or femininity. Furthermore, these sexual structures (operating socially and unconsciously) contribute to the maintenance of the specific form of social relations, necessary for the (biological) reproduction of labour power.

Such a conceptualization provides one tentative schema for a theorization of the terms under which an ideology of sexuality, in its conscious and unconscious structures, is articulated with a given structure of the social relations of production and reproduction. Beyond this, what is required is the massive empirical task of a precise historical and conjunctural analysis of the functions and structures of the family – that is, the class-specific forms of its economic, political and ideological effectivity, under determinate historical conditions. Most urgently of all, we require that type of *conjunctural* analysis for political purposes, in the movement to transform existing sexual ideologies and practices. It is to that programme that this study is tentatively addressed.

Notes and references

1 A symptomatic reading is a reading which actively constructs the theoretical absences, inherent in the way in which the object of study is originally conceptualized. See Althusser 1969. Althusser's method relies on the model provided by a Freudian analyst's reading of the patient's utterances.

2 We refer here specifically to the period of Reich's work which broadly covers the years of his involvement in the Sex-Pol clinics in Berlin, in the 1920s and early 1930s, up to his expulsion from the Communist Party in 1933. Thereafter, Reich's increasing dissatisfaction with both Marxism and orthodox Freudianism led him into very different fields, which are characterized by the attempt to liberate the repressed sexual instincts through his self-styled 'Vegetotherapy'.

3 Metaphor and metonomy are the two processes whereby language functions and through which meaning is constituted. The terms were first used in this way by Jakobson, and correspond to the concepts of condensation and displacement in Freud.

4 Lacan does ultimately have to discuss the relation of a signifier – the phallus – to the real. Why should this vital signifier of desire bear any relation to the anatomical feature, the penis? Lacan provides only a few unsatisfactory comments:

> It can be said that this signifier is chosen because it is the most tangible element in the real of sexual copulation . . . by virtue of its turgidity, it is the image of the vital flow as it is transmitted in generation. (1977, p. 287)

5 Cf. Freud's description in *Beyond the Pleasure Principle* of the 'fort/da' game. The child's action of drawing a cotton reel to itself and throwing it away again, whilst articulating the words 'da' (here) and 'fort' (gone), enabled it to symbolize a control over the presence and absence of objects, in particular the mother.

6 For an Althusserian critique of such theoretical tendencies, in a related context, see Molina (1976, p. 236 ff.).

7 See the section, *Women working in the home,* Article 3.

8 In fact we would argue that Mitchell's position in relation to Freud's biologism is rather too one-sided in its polemical insistence that psychoanalysis is *nowhere* concerned with physiological and instinctual processes. It appears that in her attempt to demonstrate the usefulness of psychoanalytic categories, for an analysis of sexual ideology, Mitchell underplays what, we have insisted,

forms a continual part of Freudian theory: namely, that definition of the instincts, which locates them within physiology.

9   Mitchell's *structuralist* use of the concept of exchange has a long history, which can be traced via Lévi-Strauss and the group of the *Année Sociologique,* to part of Durkheim's original programme in *The Elementary Forms of Religious Life* (1961) and, with Marcel Mauss, in *Primitive Classification* (1963). For a valuable survey of the history of developments in Structuralism, see Hall (1977).

10 See for example the chapter of Lacan in Coward and Ellis (1977) or the paper on psychoanalysis given at the Patriarchy Conference 1976 (Ros Coward, Sue Lipshitz and Elizabeth Cowie, in 'Psychoanalysis and Patriarchal Structures in *Papers on Patriarchy,* Women's Publishing Collective, Lewes 1976).

11 Examples here would include Plummer's theory of the 'learning' of sexual roles in *Sexual Stigma* (1975), and that of Gagnon and Simon (1973) on the construction of sexual identity through 'sexual scripts'.

12 See Hirst's objections to the essay: Hirst (1977).

13 At the time of writing, a proposed new journal, *m/f,* promises to contribute to this work.

14 See Article 8 on anthropological approaches to the theorization of the relations of reproduction.

15 Some progress towards a materialist history of the family has been made by Eli Zaretsky (1976).

16 Examples of state control of specific forms of sexuality would include, for example, the political-juridical intervention on the question of male homosexuality, and the economic/ideological legislation, which constitutes the Beveridge Report of 1942 (where ideologies of motherhood and domesticity are crucially linked to the economic position of women, both in the home and as wage labourers).

© *Woman magazine. Reproduced by permission*

7 A woman's world: 'Woman' – an ideology of femininity

Janice Winship

We are, perhaps, only too familiar with what we recognize on the crowded news-stand as a typical *Woman* cover (1). Always a white woman's face: young but somehow ageless; skin smooth and plastic as a doll; pretty - though not beautiful as in *Vogue*; smiling widely - having fun perhaps; red, shiny lips framing the perfection of white-toothpaste-ad teeth; clear eyes gazing at *you*, addressing you intimately (2).

As potential buyers, we women casually peruse that cover for its verbal indication of the contents, but we 'read' the visual image only as the sign of the magazine *Woman*. As feminists we may dismiss the cover and the magazine it invites us to as yet another 'exploitation' of women: a patronizing abuse and trivialization of women's 'real' position in society. Yet if we consider it as an ideological construction, it is already a *work* of ideology (3) which, both consciously and unconsciously, has constituted this *condensed* representation (4). If we deconstruct this representation, we can begin to reveal some of the important contradictions of women's patriarchal subordination (5) under capitalism with which the magazine as a whole must necessarily engage.

First it is a woman on the cover looking primarily at us, its *female* consumers and readers. Not only is it the most personally revealing part of the body that is represented - the face - but it is the most personal aspect of the face - the *eyes*, which steadily catch our eyes (6). Eyes, and lips as well, supremely shouting 'woman', pointing us the way inside to a world of woman: woman to woman.

But that representation of woman is no ordinary woman - yet she is a woman all the same; she has a glossiness and perfection about her that we, however many layers of beauty cream we daub on (and off), never achieve. We are failures in comparison with this woman, who in her perfection is a *man's* woman. And this in two senses: although it *is* women who look at and buy this magazine, the cover represents woman with the seductive expression directed, not to women, but to men; second, however, it is an idealized woman as defined by men, but which we, in vain, emulate. As John Berger (1972, p. 47) writes:

The surveyor of woman in herself is male: the surveyed female. Thus, she turns herself into an object - and most particularly an object of vision: a sight.

And Eva Figes (1970, p. 13):

Woman, presented with an image in a mirror has danced to that image in a hypnotic trance. And because she thought the image was herself it became just that.

Finally, the woman is not simply an 'ideal' woman but also *not* a woman: it is not her as a live, fluctuating and enigmatic *person* that is represented, but her as a *thing*. She is constructed from commodities: make-up by . . . , clothes by . . . , hair by . . . ; reified, her person denied her as she becomes the *named* photographer's (usually male) constructed feminine commodity. She is also *the* commodity - the magazine itself which is to be consumed.

This image encapsulates, then, patriarchy in its articulation under capitalism, as it positions women as feminine subjects. What appears to be *central* - the relation of women to women - is simultaneously defined in relation to absent men/masculinity - they are feminine; and in relation to an absent reality of capitalist production - they are consumers to be themselves consumed as commodities which appear 'natural'. As Marx describes this fetishism of commodities:

> The mysterious character of the commodity form consists therefore simply in the fact that the commodity reflects the social characteristics of men's own labour as objective characteristics of the products of labour themselves, as the *socio-natural* properties of these things. [my italics]
>
> Marx (1976, p. 164)

This characterization begins to suggest why it is important that as feminists we consider women's magazines seriously. We are directed to the problem of feminine subjectivity in the *particular* attempt magazines make to construct our *presence* out of an absence - primarily through the construction of 'motherhood'. They both express and cope with the fragility of that absent presence. They recognize the problem of femininity, yet finally refuse it as a problem (7).

If in the Women's Movement we are challenging the construction of our 'absent' femininity, our feminism does not and cannot break wholly from it. Our femininity is not something any of us can escape. All of us as women 'achieve' our subjectivity in relation to a definition of women which in part is propounded by women's magazines. We may be struggling against such a definition, but none of us, though we might like to, can eliminate the modes of subjectivity in their patriarchal form by disparagingly ignoring them; as if we too do not live within them, having to find our place within the parameters they set. As feminists we frequently negotiate the tension between our secret reading of magazines for their 'useful' diets and zany fashion, and our attempts to break with the modes of femininity they represent.

While women's magazines can deny subordination by *acclaiming* femininity and the centrality of women in society (is it not true that women, indispensably, bear and bring up children?), feminism embraces certain aspects of that femininity - including 'child-care' and 'personal life' - as central sites of political struggle. The specificity of feminism is partly constituted through the struggles by which it draws on these aspects of women's oppression, but transforms them into aspects of *feminist strength*. As part of understanding that movement from femininity to feminism and the relation between them, we need to explore the processes by which femininity 'manoeuvres' within and against masculine hegemony (8) in its capitalist forms, i.e. that femininity is not merely a passive acceptance by women of patriarchal domination but represents an *active subordination*. Unless we understand those processes, as Louis Althusser affirms, 'down to the effects of the fetishism of ideology . . . in which men [sic] consciously or unconsciously live their lives, their projects, their actions, their attitudes, and their functions as social' (1970, p. 66), we have no hope either of challenging them or building from them.

Furthermore, to dismiss women's magazines as make-believe and trivial is not only to discount and disregard those women who in their millions (9) read them, who we might think are easily deceived by them, but also to mistake the necessarily intimate relation between magazines and their readers as a causal one. It is not magazines in themselves that determine what women are. Their 'peculiarity' - note there are no men's magazines of a comparable kind (10) - is constituted from the marginality of women's position 'outside' the magazine, which in turn contributes to that subordinated position (11).

The ideology of femininity

In Article 3 of this book we have attempted to explore women's subordination in terms of their 'economic place' in patriarchal relations under capitalism. We were not centrally concerned in that article with the focus of our attention here, in relation to women's magazines: the representation of those relations in the specifically *ideological* domain which women inhabit and construct. While not wanting to argue a direct correspondence between the social relations of re/production (12) and ideology, I do intend to hold to the notion that ideology places the individual in relation to those relations (13). As Althusser describes ideology (1971a, p. 165), it

> represents in its necessarily imaginary distortion not the existing relations of production (and the other relations that derive from them), but above all the (imaginary) relationship of individuals to the relations of production and the relations that derive from them. What is represented in ideology is therefore not the system of the real relations which govern the existence of individuals, but the imaginary relation of those individuals to the real relations in which they live.

Ideology is a 'level' relatively autonomous from the economic and political instances so that, for example, we can conceptualize women's magazines as primarily ideological production. But the work of ideology, which is organized through, and places the subject in, an imaginary relation, operates at different levels. Furthermore, it provides a coherence by eliminating and negating social contradictions through operations which are themselves contradictory. Here, in relation to women's magazines, we are concerned both with the contradictory representations of femininity in the magazine, and also with how the means of representation are contradictory. In a wider study than this, we would need to look at the contradictions between the representations of femininity in *Woman,* which is the focus of concern here, and those in *Cosmopolitan* say, and between those in magazines and TV soap operas, for example, and so on.

First, however, I want to sketch out the broad parameters within which, contemporarily, the ideology of femininity operates. Although it is the representations of femininity in *Woman* that I am engaging with, these general features extend outside that terrain. The ideology of femininity as it is constructed through patriarchal capitalist determinations must always be seen both in relation to its overdetermination by 'masculinity' and as it is simultaneously included but set apart from the capitalist construction of the 'free' individual. Ideologically, women, as women, whatever their actual place in production, are negatively placed within the social relations of re/production. Mitchell (1974, p. 404) notes that 'men enter into the class dominated structures of history while women's . . . is the sphere of reproduction . . .'.

The 'subdomains' of ideology which contradictorily contribute to it, and which can only be separated out for the purposes of analysis, consist first and dominantly of 'motherhood'. This slides into 'personal life', 'everyday life' and 'domesticity', all of which place women as mothers at their centre, while also *differently* addressing men. Second, 'femininity' concerns 'sexuality' - in the sense both of 'attractiveness' and 'availability' - which are 'hidden' from 'motherhood'. Third, 'femininity' is *inscribed* within 'masculinity' which determines it, so that it takes over in a mediated/transformed way aspects of 'masculinity': 'femininity' is represented in some of its manifestations as masculine (see 'Indoor Sports' photo p. 132). Finally, the ideology of the 'free' individual cuts across this composite ideology of femininity, to contribute an ideology of 'feminine independence/individuality'.

The construction of the 'feminine' position for women is contradictory in a mode different from that in relation to 'masculinity' and men. As a subordinated group defining ourselves through our absences, we know first what it is we are absent from (14). As it has been described within psychoanalysis, 'the place she is in is one of referring to an image of herself that is always not-male' (Coward, Lipshitz and Cowie 1976, p. 12). Women learn to define themselves in relation to men first as they are fathers within the social relations of reproduction within the family, and second as that position is consolidated at the moment they become 'breadwinners' within the social relations of production: women become 'mothers' and 'dependants'. Marx argues (1973, p. 244) that it is out of the act of 'exchange' of commodities that 'the individual each one of them is reflected in himself as its exclusive and dominant (determinant) subject. With that, then, the complete freedom of the individual is posited.' But it is the moment at which men, as breadwinners, 'freely' exchange their labour power for a wage, that their individuality specifically 'arises'. That relation from which women are largely excluded (because their position is always mediated through men *even when* they too are wage labourers - see Article 3) represents the potential 'split' that has developed under capitalism: production/consumption; work/leisure; work/personal life; work/everyday life (Marcuse 1969, 1964; Zaretsky 1976; Lefebvre 1971; Red Collective 1971). It is a split which operates for *men* but which is dependent on women's patriarchal subordination - their confinement to family, home, personal and everyday life (Brunsdon and Morley 1978; Davidoff, L'Esperance and Newby 1976; cf. Article 2).

Women inhabit this area contradictorily. On the one hand, they make sense of their 'lack', their absence from the social language of politics and production, by taking on the 'marks of womanhood' (Mitchell 1975): narcissism, masochism and above all motherhood – when becoming a mother compensates for this lack. They justify their lack as well as recognize it as such: women as well as men 'glorify' motherhood but women also apologize for it – 'I'm only a housewife'. On the other hand, these 'marks of womanhood' are always overdetermined by masculinity. Mitchell's psychoanalytic analysis of this phenomenon, also apparent in the social acquisition of femininity, makes this clear: 'femininity is in part a repressed condition that can only be secondarily acquired in a distorted form . . .' (1975, p. 404). Masculinity always 'runs through' femininity. Thus in the work/personal life split women are defined/confined by men to be entirely *within* personal life. However, women themselves recognize that collapsed within personal life is the *work* they must perform to establish *men's* personal life. In relation to their own lives women both do and do not operate according to that divide structured through men. What Pierre Bourdieu writes of the Berber house is, despite its cultural separation, illustrative of 'home' here too:

> The orientation of the house is fundamentally defined from the outside, from the point of view of men and if one may say so, by men and for men, as the place from which men come out. The house is an empire within an empire, but one which always remains subordinate because, even though it presents all the properties and all the relations which define the archetypal world it remains a reversed world, an inverted reflection. 'Man is the lamp of the outside and woman the lamp of the inside.'
>
> (1973, p. 110)

In the magazine context it is a divide which is constantly managed: the home is simultaneously *just* an arena of leisure for women, and one of leisure and *work*, where 'work' is justified as such (even when we might not think of it as work – the work of beauty) by resort to the masculine concepts of work – efficiency, planning, etc. (cf. Conran 1976, Davidoff 1976).

But the mode in which 'masculinity' structures 'femininity' is complicated by the position of men as *a site of coincidence* between patriarchal and capitalist relations. Since it is the male labourer who is 'freely' able to sell his labour power, that ideological relation of capital is conferred on 'masculinity', i.e. the particular ideological form which 'individuality' takes under capitalism – that of the 'free' individual as the source of individuality – is historically *gender-specific*. The individual who is 'interpellated as a (free) subject' in order, as Althusser (1971a, p. 169) says, 'that he shall (freely) accept his subjection', is *indeed 'he'*.

Nevertheless, women also live, contradictorily, within that ideological construction *through their femininity*. For example, narcissism for women as the 'mark of womanhood' in which you 'love yourself as you-would-like-to-be/your-man-would-like-you-to-be' – the sexually attractive and available woman – can in one sense be an evasion of 'true' femininity as 'mother' who is sexually unavailable: you 'work' at narcissism to achieve an ideological independence from men through a specific feminine construction of 'individuality' – what Freud calls 'self-sufficiency' (Freud 1961, S.E. vol. 14, p. 94). Under contemporary capitalism that work is carried out through the consumption of commodities, which itself contributes to 'individuality'. It is of course a 'self-sufficiency' which aims ultimately to be *dependent* on men (see discussion of 'Indoor Sports' photo below). In *Woman* these contradictory processes of ideology centred on the ideology of motherhood are, as we shall see, intricately worked on and organized to legitimate women's subordination. It is that legitimation which provides the magazine's *raison d'être*. The organization however depends on the magazine as a media production.

'Woman' as media re/production of ideology

We can point to the ideological specificity of women's magazines through their content. For *Woman* in 1977 that would be something like: letters page, fiction, ads, beauty/fashion, and home features, things to make/bake, feature on a celebrity, the story of a 'brave and valiant' family/individual, horoscope and problem page. It is a content already suggested to us in the text on the cover. But if we were to *define* it as that complete whole, we would be positing an object 'out there' separate from the producers on the one side and the readers on the other. Of course it *is* that: the object we casually pick up in the doctor's waiting room or avidly pounce on as it drops through the letter box each week, without considering how it is produced. As a cultural object, however, we have to consider three modes of relatively autonomous production which separate and relate it to women who read it.

Firstly, women's magazines are a particular commodity produced within a cycle of capitalist production and consumption in which ultimately women must be the consumers. In part, then, the specificity of a women's magazine is shaped by a series of technical determinations: photography and reproduction, the size of letter boxes, etc., and economic determinations – that it is a capitalist profit-making enterprise which 'needs' advertising and regular consumption. That consumption depends on the success of a second process making it 'readable' and 'enjoyable' enough for it to be bought.

The second process is that of media production. Initiated by the editorial team who write and design the magazine, it employs visual and verbal forms, selects, transforms, neglects material according to certain media criteria, which set it up as a women's magazine and not a newspaper or wholly practical do-it-yourself journal. In particular, women's magazines are primarily concerned to *entertain,* although on the terrain of *women's work* (15). In addition, they provide entertainment which offers (although not in all the features) a more idyllic world. As Richard Dyer suggests, writing particularly of Hollywood entertainment (1976, p. 3):
'Entertainment offers the image of "something better" to set against the realities of

day to day existence.' But simultaneously '... the ideals of entertainment imply wants that capital itself promises to meet'. The general criterion of 'entertainment' determines the balance of features; the limits to serious topics which can be discussed; the kind of casual, chatty language that is employed; the use of colour, titles, design, etc.

But while it frames the overall shape and conservatism of the magazines – as one editor said, 'You don't give readers what they *want,* but what they *enjoy'* (White 1977, p. 70) – nevertheless the magazines are finally determined by, and constructed through, the ideology of femininity. The third level of production is that by which the ideology of femininity, in its contradictory aspects, is worked through the constraints of media production. That production of ideology finally delivers us the specific 'complexly structured unity' (Althusser 1970; Mitchell 1971, p. 101) which is the magazine's list of contents. The construction of 'femininity' as a represented content – women's lives – is narrated to and represented from particular 'feminine' standpoints which women reading the magazine are constituted by and live within. The magazine, however contradictorily, therefore has a meaning for women in relation to the ideological representations which they live as their everyday life.

What I shall focus on here is the magazine as discourse(s) in which ideology, positioning the reader as the feminine subject who is included within it, is constructed through the different modes of representation that make up the magazine in its constituent parts. As Geoffrey Nowell-Smith writes, again about film:

> The spectating subject requires the relation to an other in order to situate itself, and somewhere the film must provide it with that other. (The objection that the spectating subject is comfortably in an armchair and knows perfectly well that it is so situated is here beside the point.)
>
> (1976, p. 28)

It is from the centrality of woman – woman addressing you the individual woman as mother: past, present, or *yet-to-be* – that the dominant discourse of the magazine is organized. It is, however, a *selective* construction of 'motherhood': an idealization in which the customary *dependence* of women as mothers on men is minimized or absent and the essential function in society that women perform as mothers is defined as *natural.* It is a discourse *confined* to certain parts of the magazine, *separated* from others. For example, it is not usually 'spoken' by the visual of the cover – unless it is a 'celebrity plus baby', or by fashion features – except at its limit: woman attracting man. These *displacements* and boundary *constructions* are a means by which the magazine tends to avoid or negate both the appearance of the more burdensome aspects of motherhood which it contradictorily deals with, and potentially disruptive discourses of 'you the free individual'; 'you the sexually attractive woman'.

In managing these contradictions, the magazine operates within a representation schema of fantasy/reality or practicality (which overlaps with, but is distinct from,

139

a leisure/work division), where into fantasy are displaced both the ideals and resolutions which the reality of subordination does not deliver. But, at the same time, our understanding as readers of this schema is *recognition* of that subordination. It is that recognition which Henri Lefebvre in his astute appreciation of 'experience and make-believe' in women's magazines fails to appreciate. Thus, in the following quote, it is he who wonders in 'utter bewilderment', not women who read the magazines:

> ... experience and make-believe merge in a manner conducive to the readers' utter bewilderment. Indeed a single issue may include practical instructions on the way to cut out and sew up a dress or precise information such as where and at what price to buy another, alongside a form of rhetoric that invests clothes and other objects with an aura of unreality: all possible and impossible dresses, every kind of dish from the simplest to those whose realisation requires the skill of a professional.... The reader, according to his personal taste, invests this subject matter with a concrete or an abstract interpretation, sees it as pragmatic or imaginary, imagines what he sees and sees what he imagines....
> It is a fact that women do read these practical texts on make-believe and these make-believe sections (including publicity) on practical fashions.
>
> Lefebvre (1971, p. 85)

It is this noticeable division that has led Cynthia White to describe *Woman* in recent years as 'uncertain, even schizophrenic' (16). The magazine's schizophrenia, however, is *already rooted in women's lives* (17).

The fantasy/reality schema immediately confronts us on the cover in the condensed image of a woman: perfect and *not* like you, but a woman and *like* you; in the headlines luring us to the contents: the sexual fantasy of 'Clint Eastwood – what goes on behind those icy blue eyes?' and the down-to-earthness of 'Telling your child about sex – before it's too late'. Inside it intervenes in the representation of sexual relations of women with men: fiction romance, in contrast to the abrasiveness of 'love' affairs on the problem page; family life as lived by celebrities in one feature, juxtaposed with more mundane family life of 'ordinary' people in another, and so on.

A prime means by which fantasy and reality, and, therefore, contradictions, are held together is through the *differential* use of verbal and visual material. Visuals are consistently of young, attractive women; verbal content is not necessarily about or addressed to such women. Fashion features pose models in bizarre/exotic surroundings, in everyday or fairly outrageous garments but overleaf provide instructions to sew/knit. The same form is applicable to food and recipes: ordinary food or 'ornamental cookery' (Barthes 1972, p. 78) in an out-of-the-ordinary environment with 'simple' recipes provided. Ads, particularly, use these means while simultaneously contradicting editorial features: an ad for 'cushion floor' *illustrated* with two extraordinary and expensive bathrooms, sandwiched between the letters pages with their *written* theme of everyday life (18).

In constructing the magazine in its constituent parts, we work through the contradictions of the ideology of femininity and the magazine's means of representing them, beginning from their organization into the dominant discourse which places *you* as 'mother'. This description of the magazine's 'contents' divides the magazine into six sections which cut across the list of contents as it is spelt out by the magazine, but attempts to embrace it.

A woman's 'stronghold': consigned to everyday life (Lefebvre 1971, p. 92)

While 'motherhood' is central it is also the fulcrum for an ideology of everyday life which it works through but with which it is not quite synonymous. As we turn the pages of the cover and then an ad we are embraced 'In a Woman's World, by the editor' (19). The editor sets up the intimacy of 'we're all women together whatever our station in life', through our similar position and memories as mothers/cooks/ housekeepers concerned with the details of everyday life, whether it be packing for a holiday or worrying about our cash outflow in the home. The extraordinariness and fantasy of some of the articles that are pointed to is balanced against this practicality: you are brought into the excitement through your everyday life which, in one of its *actions coincides* with other women's more exciting experiences – that action through its place within the fantasy illusorily 'elevates' you. Thus a fashion team is flying off to Israel; you relate to them through the 'problems of packing your suitcase' (*Woman*, 9 July 1977) – whether it be for Israel or Brighton.

On the same page is the renowned space for readers' letters, 'Woman to Woman': this is the page where you have your 'say', where the common terrain of everyday life is explored. These letters are from women to women, concerned with those aspects of life women can only say to women and which will only be of interest and entertainment to women: laughing at their own feminine foibles, importantly mocking men's behaviour, as well as recounting the humorous, detailed escapades of their children. It reads as antidote to any radio or TV news bulletin – everyday life as it does not appear in the news: it is organized around the family and personal life, it is cheerful, it deals with 'trivia', 'good deeds', 'generous and ordinary people' as opposed to the 'famous', 'disasters', 'important events of state and industry', and 'crime'. It is not presented as 'progress', the development of the world, history in the making, i.e. as *news,* but as a cyclical repetition through differences – women's life is always the same, its values apparently almost untouched by capitalist production (although there is nostalgia for the past). Everyday life has its own moments of drama and extraordinariness which disrupt, enliven and enrich what seems a monotonous closed trajectory. They are in some sense what keeps us going: they make everyday life, which we all live, worth living each day. As we are given it here, it is through these differences that you as a woman live your individuality: everyday life which is paradoxically never the same, but always the same each day, concerns both events which *happen* to you but also events which you determine and have *control* over.

PEACE PLEASE
I was one of eleven children and we used to save up for special occasions such as Christmas and birthdays to buy mother a present. We'd usually ask her what she'd like and never could understand her answer: 'Just five minutes peace'. We couldn't buy that so what did she mean?

Now I have a family of my own and know exactly what she meant. But we couldn't have afforded it - peace is priceless.

Hilary Kennedy, Houston (30 July 1977)

As entertainment, the letters' page seeks self-reflexively to affirm the selected point of view of 'women in the home' that it sets up. While it is idealized and cut off from the world outside it is precisely because women are peripheral in the 'real' world of masculine concerns that the place they do have in everyday life is so central here. There is recognition of the *different* access women have to everyday life, but that is something to be valued, not spurned as 'oppressive': it is men's lack, not women's.

In its different aspects, everyday life underlies all the magazine: the practicalities of knitting and buying clothes for children, the 'common sense' approach to illness ('In Dr Meredith's surgery'), the 'domesticity' of cooking and 'home building' and, above all, 'personal life'.

Personal life is . . . motherhood . . . is nationhood

The emotional experiences of 'personal life' as they are represented on the letters' page are not about relations with friends - women or men, but about boyfriends and husbands, parents, and centrally about 'the family' in which you, as a person, are 'mother'. On the letters' page everyday life as family life is cheerfully endorsed. However, it is recognized elsewhere that its reproduction is secured neither without encountering problems nor without challenges to this status quo. These problems are the ups and downs that any family, even if not like yours or mine, might experience and which threaten to disrupt the self-satisfaction of family life. Yet through adversity, the family is re-established in the closeness of its relationships: the family is reconfirmed as a *national* institution.

'Real life' families appear in features such as 'The right to love (see photo p. 132) a ten-year struggle to adopt a foster child'; 'Living without him - two widows whose husbands were killed by terrorist bombs'; 'The baby with ten lives'; and 'Two for the road: the couple who gave up city life, for a caravan in Wales'. As 'documentaries' these features are usually illustrated by black and white photos (often the only illustrations in the magazine to show 'ordinary' rather than famous people or young models) which suggest 'having-been-there' (Barthes 1971) (20). Emphasis is on the emotional strength of women who, not without initially exhibiting weakness, learn through the 'trials' that appear to have been sent to 'test' them. So you, another 'weak' woman can/will also conjure up hidden reserves of emotional power when misfortune befalls your family. The misfortunes dealt with are your worst fears as mother and wife realized, but nightmares which turn out successfully: your attempt to adopt a child thwarted by her real, biological mother; your child dying from cot death; you are widowed; your marriage is falling apart. But at the end of the tunnel a bright light shines yet and you gain in experience and the quality of your life - almost through a religious salvation.

These features recognize the problems of marriage but simultaneously see those problems as reinforcing the marriage bond, not challenging it as an institution which confines such problems to a private torture. As Sheila in 'The baby with ten lives' says,

> I'd never expected marriage or motherhood to be a bed of roses . . . I'd seen how hard my mother had to work with us five children and I'd helped her after my Dad had his accident when I was 13. But I hadn't expected the troubles Ray and I had had.

But:

> As for Ray and me, we've been brought much closer through all our trouble over Donna.
>
> (23 July 1977)

Women's actions in these features often border on the masochistic but for altruistic purposes - usually for the sake of the children. It is on their behalf that mothers put on a 'brave face' and continue in the daily grind of everyday life despite their emotional loss. In this case, it is the loss of a husband: '. . . they need Jane's determined cheerfulness and reassurance badly. Weekends are still the hardest to get through' (16 July 1977). Yet it is also children who make that life worth living again.

Sometimes the difficulties concern the family as the *economic* unit of capitalism, through which personal relations are precariously constructed. 'Two for the road' features a couple who find themselves caught up in the ethic of material possessions:

> Geoffrey Edwards was obsessively dedicated to his job and the material possession it provided. With growing dismay, his wife Josie watched as his burning desire to make money undermined their marriage. Then came the decision which changed everything.
>
> (23 July 1977)

While this problem is a common one that the reader can identify with, their 'decision' to solve it is extreme, in the sense that it is out of the range of possibilities for most women. They give up their jobs, sell all their belongings and attempt a self-sufficient, travelling life through which they regain the 'romance' in their relationship. In this return to 'pre-capitalism', which makes an individual rejection of capitalist values, the family nevertheless is strengthened. As Josie says: 'In fact we're so close now that we're thinking of having a baby to make our happiness complete.' Family life represented as lived right across the country, irons out class and cultural differences. The several 'family' features that I have already mentioned span the spectrum of class, but, while we can identify characteristics which define these families in class-specific terms, those potentially conflicting differences are minimized through what they are seen to have in common - 'the family', not as historically and class-specific but the 'natural' unit of all time. In this context, it is royalty and celebrities to whose family lives we gain a keyhole view. For *Woman,* the Jubilee highlight (19 November 1977) was the Queen's visit to the home of an 'ordinary' family in Glasgow. She is adored with a 'religious' fervour, but what contributes to her 'power' for women is her simultaneous distance from most women and her proximity as wife and mother. She, at the head of the nation, like you at the 'bottom', is a family woman who supposedly speaks the same language of being a wife and mother. It is this aspect which in part creates 'the nation' of families.

Polly Toynbee, writing of *Woman's Realm,* has condemned such an approach in which even Margaret Thatcher is discussed in terms of her 'preoccupation with trivia'. Toynbee (1977, p. 11) calls it:

... a kind of nonsensical conspiracy to bring all women, however high-flying, right down to the lowest common denominator. ... It implies that there is no escape from *real* womanhood.

What is absent here is the recognition that women who regularly read women's magazine are likely to be *more* trapped within the social relations of reproduction in the family than Margaret Thatcher. The 'trap' of motherhood is also consistently posed as one of the 'fruits' of life: *even if* women wish for more than just family life, they would not want to forsake it in the black and white choice of either/or (see Article 4). Features on, say, Lulu becoming a mother are reassuring because she is *combining* the values of a mother with those of a top salary earner in the competitive, ruthless world of pop. It is finally children who make the world go round. Nevertheless, as Toynbee maintains, these features do glorify motherhood as if no woman can be fulfilled or mature until she is herself a mother: it is the only 'fruit' in life for women: it is what makes a house a home. As Lulu comments: 'Now they'll have to accept that I'm grown up. Having a baby is proof of that isn't it? I'm not a little girl any more, I'm a woman' (15 October 1977).

Work at femininity . . . beauty and fashion . . . cookery and home . . . and catch your man

Simone de Beauvoir writes that for a woman:

to care for her beauty, to dress up is a kind of work that enables her to take possession of her person as she takes possession of her home through housework; her ego then seems chosen and recreated by herself.

de Beauvoir (1972, p. 543)

But, as Shulamith Firestone insists, though not specifically in relation to 'beauty':

It takes one's major energy for the best portion of one's creative years 'to make a good catch'. (To be in love can be a full time job for a woman, like that of a profession for a man.) Women who choose to keep out of this race are choosing a life without love, something that as we have seen, most men don't have the courage to do.

Firestone (1972, p. 155)

Working at beauty is both the means by which you achieve a 'creative' individuality and the mode through which, in making yourself loved as an object, you find a man. It is also a work, like housework, which can only be carried on through the consumption of commodities; like housework too it is repetitious and invisible work (McRobbie 1977). Unlike housework, however, you work at constructing *yourself* into the commodity men will 'consume'. Fashion, like ads, then, directs us in a complex way to capitalism in its patriarchal form. Boldly extravagant in colour and design, fashion does not generally address you as 'mother' but as 'a gay young thing out for a good time'.

In the 'Indoor Sports' example (see photo) our attention is directed to the women dressed in their capitalist commodities, explicitly the glittery wool, implicitly the other accoutrements: make-up, pink jeans, jewellery, which complete the 'glamour' of femininity. Second, we are given those commodities as the models become them in their relation to men. The charged, almost garish colour accentuates the heightened but undeclared *sexual* atmosphere between these 'glamorous' women and 'classy' men. This takes a particularly complex form of masculine hegemony which contradictorily both accepts and subverts. The whole scene is premised on women's absence from the game of billiards, which provides the setting, and from most of the other predominantly male games which the sweaters depict. That absence is recognized even though it is constructed as a presence – the models are *not* playing the appropriate games, they are posing for men. The process sabotages masculinity, makes fun of it, employs guerilla tactics, but only to acknowledge masculine dominance – to achieve femininity by getting a man.

Our sports wear never saw a playing field – and is never likely to. These are glamorous versions of what the men usually wear and are absolutely right in a party setting. Score your points for femininity, don't play according to the rules and keep him from watching Match of the Day.

(12 November 1977)

While men engage here in the world of sport, women engage in a mediated form – the sport of catching men, which through its common denominator of 'sport' constructs the *appearance* of equality between women and men.

Third, this fashion item operates through the schema of fantasy/reality into which you are implicated. It is a spectacle: a staged scene which is not one of everyday life, but whose meaning utilizes knowledge of that everyday life in its masculine form, and whose objects – the 'absurd' sweaters – are incorporated into everyday life by *you knitting* them (patterns overleaf). By association you too become sexually provocative and catch your man.

The achievement of individuality, through the narcissistic construction of *you*, the *particular* loved object, relies not on work at the point of production as it does for men, but on work at the point of consumption. As consumers women 'work' with the acumen that is generally attributed to business, not to receive a wage but to receive compliments; 'cutting the cost of coats', 'cut capital outlay' – on clothes; budgeting for the cheapest buys. We are given suggestions for 'rational' action: 'think of your cheeks in terms of three sections'; for adopting techniques which smack of the underside of big business: 'with a bit of clever cheating . . .' (in relation to hair colour). Contradictorily the aim is both a 'false' look, because the use of cosmetics is not denied, but always within a 'natural' genre, assisting the natural – which is women's true attribute – not destroying it. It is not a beauty 'au naturel' but a beauty of deceit: as if (to men) it were natural, but in fact a total construction (21).

Cookery and do-it-yourself home features which use similar means of representation, although this time they address themselves to you as housewife/mother, carry the same ambiguity as the fashion features: work for women is represented as pleasure/leisure. At one level they are eminently practical but are set within a framework of fantasy so that you, the reader, transfer the meaning of 'adventure', 'nostalgia', 'extravagance', to what is by itself an everyday creation – a work of production, not consumption for women. Thus 'Berry ripe' (16 November 1977) is a double-page colour spread mostly taken up by close-up shots of woven baskets full of luscious fruit you can almost taste. Above are small illustrations of the completed dishes you can bake from the fruit. Even without the accompanying text, we are transported both to the past and to the depths of the country, where such rural life as signified by the rural baskets and the abundance of fruits still goes on. The work of picking the fruit and that of baking are hidden – the recipes are overleaf (22).

In control – 'Actionwoman' – with rights and power . . . and duties

The magazine's representation of women's 'individuality' is constructed through women's negotiation of their lives in relation to fashion and the home. It is an individuality represented as *independence* while circumscribed by masculine domination. The arena where 'independence' is strongly affirmed, apart from some do-it-yourself tasks more commonly performed by men which you are encouraged to tackle, is in the 'Actionwoman' column. It has taken over (significantly in the period since the Women's Movement has gained some respectability as well as visibility – it first appeared in 1974) from what used to be called in the 1950s 'How it's Done', a feature primarily concerned with appropriate etiquette, whether at home entertaining or making funeral arrangements (White 1970). It may now seem to have considerably shifted its terrain, focusing predominantly on consumer issues in terms of how women can *act* to establish their rights, but also casting its net wider to include more general legal rights, and problems of paid work. On the one hand, it is concerned with women as individuals with equal rights to men, in a way that 'How it's Done' could not conceive. On the other, the consumer emphasis tends to undermine that, as it defines women primarily in their position as housewives. Nevertheless, the image of 'Actionwoman' - actually Lynn Faulds Wood's team, but by implication you - is of 'getting tough', 'delivering ultimatums', generally of being in control and dictating terms.

The feature devoted to 'On going back to work' (15 October 1977) suitably illustrates the contradictory pulls in play. First it was a 'special' feature, i.e. did not rest easily within the weekly format and focus of consumers in the home. Yet, as indication of the topic's importance, it was much longer. *Woman's* recognition of the need for women's independence is clearly stated:

With children back at school and time possibly hanging heavily, many mums are beginning to feel the need to go back to work, either to earn more money or even just to provide a *little* independence . . . [my italics]

but it is a very qualified independence that is envisaged. The article never considers paid work as a right for women with children and, therefore, considers it within the framework of, 'Any hope of part time work or even work at home?' Jobs considered all fall within the category 'women's work' and there is nothing about unions or Equal Pay and Sex Discrimination legislation. Yet the article is encouraging to women - suggesting they have acquired more skills from running a home than they might think, posing the problems involved in returning to paid work: the economic situation, hours available in work, children and husband. In the end, however, the problem is presented as an *individual* one for you in your family: 'You could be the biggest obstacle of all by letting yourself by daunted by all these drawbacks.'

The horoscope, always appearing towards the end, also begins from this position of the individual. It poses for you that you as an individual must recognize the potential opportunities or disasters which your star influences have structured for you. *If* you take the appropriate *action,* which you are directed towards, then you are likely to keep on a steady keel and have some sense of *progress* into the future. In part, you are in control of your own life; if you take the wrong initiative, the resulting upset in your daily life is partly your fault. Life then is represented as a delicate combination of fate and the stars but finally of *your* own judgements and actions. It deals with the areas you would expect: relationships to boyfriend/ family/friends; finances; work/career; leisure/social life and health, organizing them as a composite of ups and downs, action and passivity, which never wholly soars to the heights of pleasure or plummets into total despondency. As an obvious 'fun' feature in the magazine, it carefully follows the work/leisure boundaries of our lives.

Love is . . . romance . . . is marriage and children

'"Come away for the night," said Cary Grant', 'What goes on behind those icy blue eyes?' On these cues, as we gaze at large close-up photos we are no longer a spectator just about to peel potatoes in the kitchen, but are whisked away on a magic carpet and drawn into the personal lives of these male filmstars, Cary Grant, Clint Eastwood, Muhammad Ali, Telly Savalas. These fantasies are distanced from us, spatially (they are frequently in the States and most often in Hollywood) and by class (see *Personal life*... section above), but like dream fantasies, they are emotionally and sexually charged. On our behalf the interviewer, usually a woman, intimately discusses their relationships with women, and imaginarily we identify and change places with those women.

These relationships are sexual. *Woman,* unlike *Cosmopolitan,* cannot easily handle women's sexual relationships except on its problem page, or in an almost biological context of having babies – 'Tell your children about sex before it's too late' (12 November 1977). Motherhood and sexuality are ideologically separated: for mothers sexuality is hidden, if anywhere, in the privacy of husbands' beds. However, they are more easily managed from the obverse position of *men's* relations with women, when it is men who are sexually active, women passive, or from the position of a female *celebrity,* although the 'management' still involves little more than sexual innuendoes and acknowledgement of sexuality.

But the sexual relations of these men that are hinted at are always finally overdetermined by family life. Either it is their wives who see them, despite their sexual recklessness, as primarily 'good fathers' to their children, or they themselves place the 'still point' (Davidoff *et al.* 1976, p. 175) of home – their wives, or consider their children as first in their lives. Thus we learn of Telly Savalas: 'Who would have guessed a doting father lurked behind that tough image' (8 October 1977) and Veronica Porche, Ali's 'new woman' comments: 'They think the way he acts is the way he is. Wild and talkin' when he's really quiet and shy.... He's the most wonderful father' (23 July 1977). For women reading these articles, this final containment of sexuality within the family form allows the fantasized extramarital sexual relation to be 'experienced' but to remain at the level of fantasy, reconciled with their affirmed position as wives and mothers. Compare here 'The right to love' photo – love is loving a child within a family.

The short stories (I am not here intending to deal with the serials – usually historical/thriller/romances) have much in common with the fantasies above (23), although they range more widely, extending over the problem of femininity in *all* its contradictions. They employ a means of representation analogous to the dream work of dreams which Freud describes, giving the illusion of describing a 'reality' but only alluding to that reality: condensation, displacement, representability and secondary revision (24). They are fantasy – initially indicated by the visuals, hazy, impressionistic, another world, too 'simple' for 'real' life; they are egoistic: the construction of the stories is from the point of view of an individual, usually a woman; they are about sexuality – masculinity/femininity – but only allude to sex; they are bereft of much detail which would locate the scenes in more accurate class terms, say, but are rich in other; they are *symbols* onto which the emotions of relationships are displaced, and are punctuated by 'magical' moments which allow a resolution (wish fulfilment) to be achieved.

They tend to concentrate on three moments in a woman's life: the problem of getting a man and its relation to wage work and 'independence' for women; the difficulties within marriage, particularly when children are small; and the dilemmas of middle age when children are leaving home. With the shift to a younger readership of *Woman* it is the first two which are now more frequent. Here we consider an example of each, very schematically, taking them as particular stories constructed in a general way.

'The right man' (9 July 1977)
The story sets up the situation where Julie is *in competition* with Matt, in relation to a *job*: they've both got social studies degrees. At the same time, she is in competition with a 'lovely brunette' for *him*.

The problem is compounded when:
1 Matt wins in the job market through his *masculinity* – he's good at games. The 'swinging' tennis racket however makes its first appearance as a symbol of male virility – when he waves good-bye with it to the 'lovely brunette'. It now takes on the characteristics of domination. Julie has to resort to the typically feminine occupation of temporary secretarial work.
2 The 'lovely brunette' who is successful with Matt is also wealthy – she's driving a sports car. Failing on both fronts: femininity and the larger (masculine) world of work, Julie then checks out her assets: a) attractive enough in the mirror – NB also fair in opposition to the 'lovely brunette'; b) she's got brains – OK.

We then shift back in time (cf. dreams) to the history of her relationship with Matt which *she* terminated over the problem of *sexual relations,* although this is never explicitly stated:

Julie had become rather sensitive to the way things were going. Considering that Matt had never spoken of love and marriage, they were going much too fast.

The problem of 'sex before marriage' is fused (condensation/displacement) into that of 'independence': all the difficulties of a woman achieving 'independence' or being trapped by 'dependence' are focused into 'not having sex'/'having sex', i.e. premarital relations cut short a woman's 'independence'. 'She wanted to be her own woman before and after she became a wife.'

Back to the present. Matt is visiting her parents, a device which indicates that, welcomed by parents, he will soon be accepted by her. He again makes advances towards her and sexual innuendoes are made: 'she was turning to jelly', but then she *gets the better of him,* by putting an ice cube down his back. That 'coldness' decisively cuts off the 'warmth' of any relationship. However, she's upset. Matt, i.e. her relationship with a man, is seen as a *disturbance* in her life. Her attempts at 'independence' in terms of a job and *not* bothering about men have been thwarted.

She then finds a job and simultaneously meets a man who is impressed by her *mind*. In contrast when Matt comes to say cheerio to her family (he's off to his new job), he laughs at Julie's dishevelled appearance as she leaps out of bed, i.e. at her *non-femininity*. Good at her job she achieves 'self-respect', 'a place in the world', i.e. the masculine world. In addition there is no worry over Bill, who makes, we assume, no sexual advances: 'she was safe and comfortable with him'. Nevertheless, she feels this isn't her 'real' self, i.e. not fulfilling her femininity – she misses Matt.

Now comes the moment of fate intervention, necessary to 'resolve' the problem which is unlikely to be neatly resolved in 'real' life. She catches her mother sadly turning out *her* old love letters and her mother explains how because of her pride and stubbornness, she and her boyfriend had misunderstood each other, never declared their love before he went off without her ever seeing him again. Julie recognizes the comparison and her attempt at 'independence' is collapsed into 'getting your own back, how nasty it sounded'. So she rings Matt . . . .

The story finishes at a moment of 'balance' and 'equality' between Matt and Julie: the problems of work/marriage-family for a woman are finally evaded although they have been raised.

'The Meringue' (30 July 1977)

On to this meringue are displaced the problems of marriage: 'marriage is a confidence trick – a trick that gives you confidence'.

The scene is set with Becky slaving away on a Friday evening waiting for her husband, who is already two hours late after a week away at his work: 'travelling, selling, meeting people, seeing'. He bounds in joyfully, completely *insensitive* to how she feels, trapped at home. He makes excuses for being late: '". . . traffic, you know . . .". Only she didn't know. Becky was never there, only here.' She knows he's lying: he's been drinking with friends. She's cool and unfriendly, tells him the meal is already overdone, their child Maidie overtired. . . . The kitchen having been swamped by his homecoming is now 'small and empty' again as he exits. Ambiguously she has her 'space' back again.

Over dinner, she forces herself to chat: 'She heard herself underlining the *trivial*, just to show how trivial her life was compared to his'. He, realizing she's upset, asks what's the matter.

No use saying 'nothing'. They both knew. And they both knew he knew. And probably, she thought bitterly, he knew, she knew he knew (25).

Rather than say anything because she does not want him to think she's nagging him, she sighs, goes out and brings in

the elaborate meringue pudding she'd made with such excitement and anticipation in the morning. The whole meal a hymn to love, a tribute to the homecoming. An empty gesture now.

The cake stands between them; like their marriage a fragile but complicated structure. He refuses any and sulkily leaves the room. Then Maidie, who had been kept up 'to make the reunion complete', i.e. children *make* a marriage, symbolically destroys their marriage by banging the meringue to pieces, i.e. children are also the *source of the problem* of marriage for women.

However, a few minutes later when she watches Maidie asleep Beckie smiles:

'The baby was worth all the disappointments of marriage.' Returning downstairs, she grudgingly washes up while *he* sleeps in front of the TV.

She wanted to cry, to scream, to bang doors, break plates, make him understand the terrible frustration that built up inside during every week he was away and exploded each time he let her down.

She doesn't because she remembers how her own *mother* had, and had frightened the *children:* Becky doesn't want to upset Maidie.

She returns to the living room where he's asleep – *as Maidie was.* The similarity of the sleeping state takes on the added meaning of a *child* asleep:

A man? He was more like a bewildered boy. Like Maidie. . . . Both of them, she thought; all of us perhaps as she remembered her pride in her meringue, need our own confidence tricks. Things to boost our egos, keep us reassured, secure. And if she had to control herself for Maidie, surely she must do the same for this equally sensitive man too.

So her anger leaves her, she kisses him and they go to bed; the meringue is still edible for tomorrow.

Thus at one level women's oppression in the family is *experienced* and understood, its implications of subordination are finally denied, resolved only within the personal relations of individuals. The work/family split in which women and men are placed on opposite sides is recognized, but work is seen to be 'just as bad' as being trapped in the family: her husband is judged an 'individual' *like* her and their child, both of whom she masochistically 'mothers'. But it is mainly the child who makes any other conceptualization of the problem impossible, i.e. having children is synonymous with *mother* at home (see Article 4). What other mode is there. . . ?

Dear Anna Raeburn, femininity catches me, traps me . . . oppresses me – but I keep crying for more . . . .

'Problems? Anxieties? Difficulties?' spill out into real life as we close the magazine's last page – the last feature, uncontainable and irresolvable; in contradiction with the final ad: 'Insist on *Hoover* for good looks and reliability. *Hoover* makes things better for you.' Here is everyday life as it weighs down on women – its 'misery' (Lefebvre 1971, p. 35): personal life in its privacy of torture; motherhood as masochism; sex experienced as men's power over women; women isolated from each other. These are aspects of femininity as oppression but in their representation as 'individual', particular problems the magazine copes with a potentially explosive last couple of pages. This is not Anna Raeburn's 'fault': she does her best to de-individualize the problems, point to organizations, groups to join, suggest friendships as important/more important than the claustrophobia of the nuclear family. She encourages women to have confidence in themselves, to take initiatives. But in the context of a magazine which, while constantly negotiating the tensions of these problems, does not admit to them except here, the deduction that recognizes them *as common* oppression can never be made by women: the problems will continue to be reproduced and experienced by women as 'individual' problems. The contradictions of femininity which women recognize, experience and seek advice about cannot be challenged from *within femininity* – which is finally, through contradictions, what the magazine as a whole endorses.

NOT LIKE MEN (19 November 1977)

We've been married for 27 years and I've brought up three children. I never went out to work because I thought it was my duty to look after the family. But now that they're married and off our hands, is it too much to expect my husband to take me out sometimes? He still thinks I should be content to stay at home doing the household chores. The only entertainment a woman needs, in his opinion, is a gossip at the local shops. Our sex life is far from satisfactory. He has his girlie books and pictures but when I ask what satisfaction I have, he says women don't need stimulants like men. He also seems to think I should need as much sex now as I did in my 20s which is making me very tense.

Notes and references

1 This article focuses contemporarily, not historically on the magazine *Woman*, using illustrative material from July, October and November 1977. It relies however on a much wider reading of *Woman* and other women's magazines, and hopefully its relevance extends to include them.

2 In the last three years, the cover has often broken with traditional format. Recently for example we have seen the Queen; Lulu and baby; Muhammad Ali, girlfriend and baby, in that prime position. In addition cover women are posed much more seductively – cf. *Cosmopolitan*.

3 See Barthes (1967, p. 92): 'Ideology is the form of the signifieds of connotation.' For work on ideology see Althusser (1969): 'On the materialist dialectic'; 'Transformation of a determinate given raw material into a determinate product. . . .'

4 See *Screen* (1975) vol. 16, no. 2, p. 26. 'Condensation', as a concept taken from Freud's analysis of dreams, is best understood in the context of that 'dream work'.

   The manifest content of the dream is the product of the dream work which transforms . . . the materials of the dream. Analysis works backwards from the analysand's account of his manifest dream to the materials of the dream. The main mechanisms of the dream work are condensation (accumulation of a number of dream thoughts, etc. into a single manifest representation), displacement (shift of cathexis [energy/attention] from one representation to an associated one, or replacement of the former by the latter), considerations of representability (translation of abstract thoughts into concrete images) and secondary revision (assembly of the result of the three other mechanisms into a relatively coherent and comprehensible whole).

5   By 'patriarchal subordination' we understand men's domination of women through control of their sexuality, procreative potential and their labour - organized economically, ideologically, and politically.

6   See Millum (1975, p. 57) who considers the 'personal' aspects of 'face' and 'eyes'.

7   See Butcher, Coward *et al.* (1974), particularly the introduction which poses some of the problems we are confronting here on the cover, and the sections on 'Women's magazines', and 'Ads' which cover the ground we are working through here.

8   While the term 'hegemony' originates in Gramsci (see Article 2), 'male hegemony' has been used by Rowbotham (1973). Here we use the term *'masculine* hegemony' to suggest the contradictory acquisition of *gender* for women and men in which 'femininity' resists the 'dominant masculine' order as well as being subordinated by it - right down to the level of the 'unconscious' where hegemony must 'start' and 'terminate'. See Article 3, footnote 25 to *Women working in the home* (p. 74).

9   See White (1975, p. 50). The mass weeklies, *My Weekly, Woman's Weekly, Woman* and *Woman's Own,* together with the monthlies, *Annabel* and *Woman and Home* have a combined sale of 7.2 million copies per issue.

10 Men's magazines are of the 'fantasy', 'girlie' variety, or of the 'specialist' practical kind, e.g. *Hi-fi,* or *Do-it-yourself.*

11 White (1970, 1977), Faulder (1977), Toynbee (1977) all tend to conceive of magazines as 'causing' women's subordinated position.

12 By social relations of re/production, we mean social relations of reproduction of the individual - mainly in the family, which includes the production of use values, *and* social relations of capitalist production. See Article 3, *Equal Pay* section.

13 See Hirst (1976) who argues against a direct correspondence but is left with no concept of 'determining in the last instances by the economic'.

14 As a subordinated group, women bear this in common with other subordinated groups. For example, blacks 'know' the 'colonial culture' in which they are colonized. See Fanon (1967).

15 Although we would claim that for women buying a magazine has always been a 'treat', however much it may assist in the 'work' of femininity, IPC has only recently, in the face of falling sales, reassessed the long-held priority of 'service' to be replaced by 'entertainment'. However, it would seem to be

implemented not as a change in topics, but in the mode in which it is presented (see White 1977).

16 White is specifically talking about the contrast between the 'cosy' editorial features and the 'shock treatment' meted out on its final page by 'the most stringent of all agony column writers, Anna Raeburn' (White 1977, p. 52). However, that clash is only a modified form of the fantasy/reality representation.

17 See Laing (1961), where all his schizophrenic cases are women but he makes no mention of that fact.

18 The consideration of advertisements is a considerable omission in this article when they take up about a half of the magazine. However, they are particularly complex in their ideological construction of femininity. They both support and contradict other constructions in the magazine. I have considered it better to omit an analysis of them here than to too briefly 'explain' them. For the present, see Millum (1975), Butcher *et al.* (1974), and Williamson (1978).

19 Curiously because of the 'personal' address that is made here, 'the editor' is never 'personalized' and named. However, this is by no means the case in all women's magazines.

20 As Stuart Hall suggests in relation to news photos, photos play a crucial role in this form of personification for people where 'personalisation . . . is the isolation of the person from his relevant social and institutional context, or the constitution of a personal subject as exclusively the motor of history' (1972, p. 78).

21 For more on this ideological work constructing 'the natural' see Article 2 and Williamson (1978), who specifically considers its operation within ads.

22 Cf. 'the natural' above, this time not in relation to 'femininity' but to a similar ideological work – see ads, and Williamson (1978).

23 As Mirabel Cecil writes, '. . . reality is not what magazine stories have ever been for. They provide women with a world which is larger than life, more romantic, more exciting or more ordered than their own world. They want to lose themselves in it for the moment and then come back satisfied, to their own familiar lives' (1974, p. 236).

24 See footnote 4 above.

25 Cf. Laing (1970).

8 Relations of reproduction: approaches through anthropology

Lucy Bland, Rachel Harrison, Frank Mort and Christine Weedon

In this article, we set out to examine the usefulness of recent marxist and marxist-feminist anthropology for the development of concepts with which to theorize women's subordination in both pre-capitalist and capitalist societies. Given the political urgency of theorizing women's position under capitalist social relations, we could be asked: why anthropology at all? The answer lies, as we see it, in the logical tendency of Marxist theory, as developed in *Capital,* to place interpersonal relations — specifically those of dominance and subordination between the sexes — outside the sphere of socially determined relations. In *Capital,* social relations are theorized solely as economic relations of which individuals are the bearers. The sphere of sexual relations and biological reproduction is excluded from this definition of social relations and in consequence, it has *often* been assigned a 'natural' status (1). In this way, the sexual division of labour and the social relations of biological reproduction have been held to be naturally pre-given, rather than socially constructed through economic, political and ideological practices (2).

The lack of a full theorization of the juridico-political and ideological forms taken by the relations of biological reproduction is evident in marxist approaches to anthropology itself. For example, the concept of the exchange of women, which might be expected to lead to a recognition that both reproduction and female sexuality are structured in terms of a power relation of domination and subordination between the sexes, is taken over unproblematically, i.e. as natural, by Hindess and Hirst (1975, 1977) and Godelier (1975), among others, to support economic and demographic analyses. From a feminist perspective, the concept of the exchange of women poses the need for an analysis of the relations of biological reproduction and highlights the need for an analysis of the articulation of the relations between production and biological reproduction.

The starting point for such an articulation has often been seen to lie with Engels's formulation, in the *Origin of the Family, Private Property and the State,* in its apparent avoidance of reductionism:

> the determining factor in history . . . is the production and reproduction of immediate life. This . . . is of a twofold character: on the one side, the production of the means of existence . . . on the other . . . the production of human beings.
> Engels (1972, p. 71)

However, the nature of the relationship *between* these two parallel structures, production and reproduction, was never clearly theorized in the subsequent text.

Furthermore, although Engels was using the concept of 'reproduction' to refer here to biological reproduction, certain marxists and feminists alike have tried to theorize women's subordination in terms of a *general* notion of reproduction, thereby conflating procreation with a wider conception of reproduction. However, unlike Engels, we would not hold to the notion that women's subordination arose with father right, private property and class society. Recent feminist anthropology (3) has shown that women's subordination exists in pre-class social formations, even in matrilineal societies. In fact, women's subordination appears to exist in all societies known to anthropology and history.

We would argue that, given the 'obvious' separation of economic production and biological reproduction of sexed subjects under the capitalist mode of production, and the form taken by marxist analysis of the capitalist mode of production, which concentrates solely on the sphere of economic production, there is no way in which we can get at the multifunctional role of the family under capitalism, without a prior knowledge of the history of the structures of kinship in pre-capitalist and pre-class societies, where economic and biological reproduction are interwoven in the very structures of kinship.

In our attempt to denaturalize the sphere of biological reproduction and to see the patriarchal form it takes as historically determined at the economic, political and ideological levels, we use the term 'relations of (biological) reproduction'. By this we mean the reproduction of human beings and the control of sexuality. We hope here to go some way towards developing this concept and posing the problem of its inter-relation with the economic mode of production. The focus of the article is kinship as the site of biological reproduction, its attendant conditions and effects, and its location in relation to economic production. We begin by looking briefly at a marxist approach to anthropology, derived from the concepts of *Capital,* and at its limitations. From here we move on to examples of marxist-feminist anthropology, and examine how far they have been successful in theorizing women's subordinate position as socially and politically constituted through economic, ideological and legal practices. We conclude by considering exactly what we mean by the relations of biological reproduction and their complex location in the social formation, and the implications of this for looking at the position of women under the capitalist mode of production today.

Social relations of production: absent concepts, absent sex

Hindess and Hirst, in their specific discussion of the mode of production under primitive communism in *Pre-Capitalist Modes of Production* (4), provide what at first sight appears a valuable point of entry for the analysis of the subordination of women in primitive societies. Their general insistence on a type of conceptual clarity in the use of marxist concepts, their reading of the social formation as a complex structured unity, and above all, their emphasis on the social *relations* of production as they are articulated with the structures of kinship, all seem to provide a framework for the theorization of the specific position of women in these societies.

In their critique of extant forms of marxist anthropology, notably the work of Meillassoux (1972) and Terray (1972), Hindess and Hirst draw attention to the terms under which the absence of certain crucial concepts can lead to an unsystematic theorization of the structure of primitive communist societies. Their primary insistence is that the analysis of any mode of production must rest on the double articulation of the forces and relations of production. That is as:

> ... structured by the double articulation of the mode of appropriation of surplus labour, which defines the structure of relations of production, and the mode of real appropriation, or productive forces, which defines the form of organisation of the labour process.
>
> Hindess and Hirst (1975, p. 21)

Within that articulation, the mode of appropriation of the surplus (with its structure of social relations) is seen by them as the dominant element, in that it defines the limits of development of the productive forces. Hindess and Hirst argue that the concept of the mode of production offered by Meillassoux and Terray is informed by a 'technicist' reading; that is, that the social relations of production are conceived as 'dominated by the productive forces'. Hence in such a reading, the shift in primitive communist societies from land as the *subject* of labour (i.e. direct extraction of the surplus) to land used as the *instrument of labour* (where human labour is invested in the land) is itself seen to determine the changes in the relations of production. What such a formulation fails to acknowledge, Hindess and Hirst stress, is that the movement from one form of real appropriation to that of another requires as its precondition a corresponding change in the relations of production.

It is that emphasis on the social relations of production in Hindess and Hirst's theorization which should provide the point of entry for analysis of the specific place occupied by women within those societies. Certainly, their examination of primitive communism contains a detailed discussion of kinship structures, and their operation as a moment within the circuit of economic production, but it is in terms which almost totally omit any discussion of the question of sexual division and subordination. Their analysis maintains that, because the mode of appropriation of surplus labour under primitive communism is collective, then there can be no form of *social* division between a class of labourers and a class of non-labourers; hence no political level, and no state. The emergence of a political level and the apparatuses of the state is dependent on the appropriation of surplus by a non-labouring class. They maintain that

> the coercive apparatus of the State is necessary to its role in the maintenance of exploitative relations of production.
>
> Hindess and Hirst (1975, p. 34)

Yet it is their initial failure, in the construction of the problematic, to reveal that sex and gender relations are *power* relations (involving domination and subordination) which enables Hindess and Hirst here to consider the maintenance and reproduction of social relations as relatively unimportant. The crucial absence in their analysis of the mode of production in primitive societies is that of the role played by women both within the labour process and as biological reproducers. And further, the recognition that women's position in both processes is one which involves a form of subordination to male control. We are arguing specifically here for a recognition that pre-class societies do include forms of social relations which are power relations, and that the invisibility of women in Hindess and Hirst's analysis renders the theorization of those social relations as unproblematic.

The specific difficulties in Hindess and Hirst's analysis centre on the terms under which kinship relations are located within the primitive communist mode of production. In general terms, they argue for a conceptual analysis of kinship structures within a marxist theory of the social formation, as against the 'fetishistic treatment of kinship in idealist anthropology' (where a notion of kinship may be substituted for that of the mode of production itself). Given their insistence on the primacy of the *relations* as opposed to the *forces* of production, then the structure of the economic level is determined by the form taken by the redistribution of the product according to a set of 'ideological social relations' (1975, p. 44). In that sense, kinship relations (originally and autonomously the ideological relations of genealogy) are conceptualized as being annexed to the circuit of the production and redistribution of the surplus. The distinction is made between 'simple redistribution', where a surplus is distributed through 'a network of relations established on a temporary or semi-permanent basis', and 'complex redistribution', where the distribution of the surplus follows the structural patterns of kinship. For Hindess and Hirst, both forms of redistribution define the limits of development of the productive forces, since, as they insist in their critique of Meillassoux and Terray, the shift to a more developed form of the *productive forces* is itself dependent on a more developed form of social relations.

However, within their theorization of the role and functioning of kinship structures in the mode of production, certain inconsistencies should be noted. Hindess and Hirst maintain that in the shift from the form of simple to that of complex redistribution the development of kinship structures are the crucial determinant. Under simple redistribution, kinship relations may or may not exist, but are not seen as essential to the reproduction of the economy. (Though we are never informed as to what social structures do perform the essential function of redistribution here.) But the movement to the form of complex redistribution requires as a precondition the intervention of the structures of kinship at the economic level. By this process, existing genealogical and blood relations are transformed to perform the function of the distribution of the surplus. Furthermore, for these structures of kinship to be reproduced, Hindess and Hirst insist on the construction of a determinate set of ideological practices; specifically those of the ritual and the ceremonial necessary for the regulation and control of marriage exchanges. However, the crucial problem here concerns the terms under which the semi-permanent band collectives are transformed into the wider and more complex network of kinship structures, which are themselves a prerequisite for the move into the form of complex redistribution. Hindess and Hirst maintain that this transformation may be achieved under the form of simple redistribution at the point at which the quantitative development of the *productive forces* has reached a certain level. The reading here, contrary to all the earlier assertions, appears as quite specifically based on the primacy of the *productive forces* in determining the development of the *relations of production* of kinship structures. Indeed, their assertion of the eternal primacy of the relations over the forces of production, at the level of general concepts, would seem to ignore the specific *historical* instances in which the productive forces are in fact instrumental – at points of transition within modes of production. The transition from simple to complex redistribution outlined here appears to be a case in point (5).

More generally though, it is the narrow definition that Hindess and Hirst award to kinship, as effecting merely the redistribution of the surplus, that militates against any analysis of women's subordination. In fact, they consider as almost wholly unproblematic those elements in the circuit of economic production in which women are located under conditions of male domination. These include the sexual division of labour within the labour process itself, the control of women as biological reproducers, and the ideological practices necessary for the maintenance of determinate forms of kinship structures, which involve the restrictive control and subordination of women.

The sexual division of labour within the labour process is noted by Hindess and Hirst in their analysis as the characteristic form of co-operation under conditions of simple redistribution, but it is a form which is *not* defined as consisting of *unequal* social relations. As Maureen Mackintosh points out (1977), women's subordination is invisible in the terms of their analysis. What Hindess and Hirst maintain (1975, p. 63) is that:

In the band collective men and women have different technical specialisms. They are employed in the production of different foodstuffs and each depends on the other to sustain a complete and more or less regular food supply.

Similarly, the role of women as biological reproducers, and the male control of female reproductive power, lie beyond the terms of the analysis. In fact, the part played by women in biological reproduction is a crucial determinant in the development of kinship structures themselves, but Hindess and Hirst (1975, p. 74) fail to problematize the relations of biological reproduction:

All that is required for the reproduction of the economic level is some *system of social relations* in which children are reared by adults. [our italics]

Finally, if kinship systems are theorized by Hindess and Hirst as the ideological form of social relations whereby the surplus is redistributed under the form of complex redistribution, then what are the precise structures which constitute these social relations, and by which mechanisms are those structures maintained and reproduced? Anthropology has long since demonstrated what in fact Hindess and Hirst omit from their analysis: namely, that kinship structures are forms of social relations within which women are exchanged by men. Thus, though they rightly insist that the social relations of kinship must be maintained and reproduced by a determinate set of ideological practices, the absence of the position of women from their analysis prevents any examination of the ideological practices which are effective in securing the control of women. Here we would include the whole cluster of taboos and restrictions placed on women in primitive societies, together with the sanctioning of specific forms of sex/gender identity, which we would maintain are ideological conditions necessary for women's subordination.

In fact it is at the level of the initial constitution of their object of analysis that we would wish to engage with Hindess and Hirst here. Politics, and the existence of a political level, is defined by them as absent from primitive communist societies *precisely because* relations of sex and gender are rendered almost wholly unproblematic. In a sense, the internal consistency of Hindess and Hirst's conceptual framework can remain intact by virtue of the absence of what is perhaps the most significant determinant in those societies, that is, the level of gender politics. What we would question here is not merely an *omission* from their analysis, but their overall conceptualization of the political level itself. Furthermore, it is precisely this omission which remains a problem for feminists working with marxist concepts in examining the capitalist mode of production.

It is that absence which specifically informs Hindess and Hirst's limited definition of kinship solely as the ideological structure through which the form of economic distribution is achieved. Such an analysis thus almost wholly neglects the specificity of kinship structures as the material ideological practices within which relations of sex and gender are lived out as power relations, and in terms which have crucial effects at the economic and political levels. Yet what we do need to hold to in Hindess and Hirst's analysis is the conceptual clarity of the structure of their theorization, however partial that analysis ultimately remains. The attempt to trace the nature of the *articulation* between the economic and ideological levels remains a crucial point to retain in the analysis of the position of women in pre-class societies, *and* under capitalism. It is the point to which we shall necessarily return in our subsequent analyses.

Marxist anthropologists such as Terray, Godelier (1975) and Meillassoux do include certain of the anthropological considerations which are absent from Hindess and Hirst's analysis of the primitive mode of production. Thus, for example, Godelier, in investigating Australian hunting and gathering tribes, takes into consideration demographic and ecological constraints on the structure and formation of kinship. Yet these determinants on the economic functions of kinship are not articulated with a theorization of the precise nature of the relations of production, because Godelier consistently sees the determinacy of the mode of production in terms of *forces* of production (as is true of Terray). However, Godelier's anthropological use of concepts such as demography and ecology does lead him to outline specific forms of constraints placed on women - for example, ecological determinations on the frequency of childbearing and by extension *ideological* restrictions on female sexuality. But, he fails to recognize how these restrictions are *socially* constituted as forms of subordination.

In the next two sections, we look at the work of two marxist-feminists who deal, in different ways, with the absences that we have indicated with respect to Hindess and Hirst. Firstly, we examine Bridget O'Laughlin's (1974) analysis of women's subordination in terms of women's role within the reproduction of the labour force, and the relation of this to the reproduction of the forces and relations of production. Secondly, we examine Rubin's analysis of women's subordination in terms of the acquisition of sex/gender identity, and argue that her account fails to relate to other levels of the social formation.

Before turning to these accounts in detail, we would like to mention the usefulness of the paper given by Kate Young and Olivia Harris at the Patriarchy Conference in London in 1976. It appeared at a strategic moment for some of us who felt that feminist theory seemed to have reached an impasse, both in psychoanalysis and in marxist political economy. In their paper, 'The subordination of women in cross-cultural perspective' (Young and Harris 1976), they use the concepts of the exchange of women, rules of marriage, and the sexual division of labour, as theoretical tools for understanding asymmetrical relations between the sexes. In this way they extend the repertoire of marxist concepts to include those for dealing with sexual asymmetry.

Women in reproduction

O'Laughlin, in 'Mediation of contradiction: why Mbum women do not eat chicken (1974), attempts to apply specifically marxist concepts in an analysis of women's subordination in a particular society, the Mbum Kpau in Tchad, in Africa (1974, p. 301). The Mbum 'are primarily shifting cultivators (6), but also practice hunting and gathering, livestock raising, and craft production' (1974, p. 303).

Arguing that 'a Marxist framework (questions, categories, and causality) facilitates analysis of the structures of any society - Capitalist or pre-Capitalist ...', O'Laughlin nevertheless has to bring into play concepts developed in the discipline of anthropology, in order to unravel the problem of *sexual asymmetry* in food prohibition. The object of her analysis is to show how a particular ideological practice, the sexual skewing of food consumption, in which males eat privileged surplus foods (chickens and goats), serves to mediate a particular contradiction with respect to women. Thus she writes (1974, p. 315):

The paper is not an attempt to interpret a symbolic system but to demonstrate how one particular set of ideological representations may serve to mediate contradictions.

The analysis begins by examining the way that the *technical relations of production,* the work process itself, is organized. Little sexual differentiation is found in agricultural practices (direct forms of production), either with respect to labour input or subsistence derived. There is greater sexual differentiation however in secondary forms of production, crafts, and food preparation and in trade (1974, pp. 304-6):

> The economic subordination of women to men was shown not to be technologically determined, for within production as a whole there are few sexually assigned roles outside of the domestic sphere, and the contributions of the sexes are quite equitable.

O'Laughlin now turns from the sexual division of labour in the various work processes to sexual inequality in the *social relations of production.* She examines the different units of labour co-operation and resource pooling such as the household, the granary group, and the lineage, and finds that within the household, men control the cash revenues of wives and unmarried sons; within the granary group, authority over both resources and products belongs to the senior male; within the lineage, elders control bride-wealth, medicines, nets and musical instruments and supervise co-operative work (1974, p. 306). Though access to the basic means of production, nets, axes and breeding animals, is not juridically sexually defined, the *actual* distribution is skewed in favour of men, and women rarely inherit from their fathers (1974, p. 307). Egalitarian rules, therefore, do not reflect real social relations of production, which are marked by considerable sex (and age) asymmetry (1974, p. 308).

What is impressive so far in O'Laughlin's account is, firstly, the distinction between male and female access to the means of production (a distinction wholly absent from orthodox marxist accounts of relations of production). Secondly, she is always careful to indicate which category of males benefits from any particular practice involving sexual asymmetry. For example, as with distribution, *control* of labour differs according to both sex and age criteria. 'Control of labour in the process of production, like control of the means of production, belongs pre-eminently to men' (1974, 308). A husband can recruit more un-reciprocated labour from junior patrilineal kin than women can, and senior men may recruit more days of surplus labour than do women. So, because of the simple technology of the Mbum Kpau:

> The primary determinant of variation in the levels of production and possible accumulation is consequently the input of labour. Sexual asymmetry in the appropriation of surplus labour is therefore the strongest indication thus far of the subordinate status of women.
>
> O'Laughlin (1974, p. 309)

O'Laughlin sees a contradiction arising between 'the technical and social relations of production'; in the former there is a rough equality, and in the latter, male control of the surplus products and labour of wives, daughters, and sons:

> An analysis of sexual asymmetry in relations of production thus leads inevitably in this case to a close consideration of two problems – rules of marriage and accumulation of surplus.

> A discussion of the organisation of production among the Mbum Kpau is . . . incomplete without a description of the organisation of reproduction. A number of anthropologists working in the Marxist tradition inspired by Althusser, have in fact suggested that the dominance of male elders in African societies may usually be based on their control of the forces of reproduction - surplus labour and product, rights in women and bridewealth. Structures of reproduction thus provide the link between economic infrastructure and politico-juridical superstructures.
>
> (1974, p. 309)

Acknowledging Marx's formulation that a mode of production must 'provide' a set of productive processes and the conditions of its reproduction, O'Laughlin, like Althusser, makes an analytical distinction between three aspects of reproduction: 1) reproduction of the means of production; 2) reproduction of the labour force; and 3) reproduction of the relations of production (1974, p. 310). The conditions of reproduction of the means of production consist of an accumulation of surplus by senior males. The reproduction of the labour force (O'Laughlin is here referring to biological reproduction and socialization) is essential to the existence of any economy. Further, given the importance of labour relative to the means of production, in the Mbum economy, *control* over the reproduction of labour entails great authority; indeed, control over reproductive rights in women of the lineage (rights to bridewealth and children), is vested entirely in male elders (1974, p. 311). O'Laughlin argues that this results in a central contradiction for women: though the system by which labour is reproduced is based on women's primary responsibility for biological reproduction and socialization, women have no authority whatsoever over reproductive rights (1974, p. 312):

> This lack of authority must be related to rules of exogamy, virilocal residence, and patrilineal descent, through which women bear children for groups other than their own. The prerequisite of biological reproduction therefore becomes the alienation of women from their own reproduction: reproductive rights in women must be exchanged between patrilineal groups invariably controlled by senior males.

The control of bride-wealth by the elders consolidates their authority over sons and junior siblings, who are dependent on their elders for the payment of bride-wealth. In emergencies bride-wealth can be exchanged for the means of production, tools, livestock, and seeds:

> It is control of bride-wealth, the first expression of the power of the elders, that merges superstructures of lineage authority with infrastructural relations of production.
>
> The alienation of women from aspects of their own powers of reproduction in the Mbum system of bride-wealth exchange is therefore a precondition of the basic infrastructural contradiction - the alienation of women and juniors from their own surplus product.
>
> (1974, p. 313)

Finally, O'Laughlin turns to reproduction of the relations of production. She insists that:

In order to reproduce a system of social relations of production that either contains or is grounded in contradiction, the society must mediate these contradictions within politico-juridical superstructures and/or ideological representations.

(1974, p. 314)

O'Laughlin indicates that, though there are few politico-juridical superstructures that exclude or inferiorize women, at the ideological level there are numerous expressions of sexual distinction and affirmation of male dominance, one of these being the prohibition on the consumption of goats and chickens by women. Here she suggests (1974, p. 315) that there is a structural equivalence between women and livestock; both are kept by men, primarily for reproduction, to bring wealth to their owners through exchange:

As a form of surplus product, by definition not intended for subsistence, livestock are linked to the process of reproduction of the means of production, just as women are linked to the process of reproduction of labour.

The means of reinforcement of the prohibition is through the threat of sterility, of reproductive failure, and of pain and death in childbirth. Thus, there is a *moral* linking of an arbitrary cultural practice (food taboos) to that which is biologically necessary: that women bear children (1974, p. 316).

In conclusion, O'Laughlin maintains that marriage and economy are part of a 'single system of social production'. They can be seen as 'two systems' whose functional interdependence supports structures of social asymmetry in the dominance of senior males, but this is not to say that the structure is therefore either harmonic and free of contradiction, or a direct reflection of the division of labour (1974, p. 317). Ideology, since it is 'allusion to underlying reality as well as illusion . . . may provide clues . . . to the rooting of the basic social relations of production in the bride-wealth system' (1974, p. 318).

O'Laughlin has analysed the material basis of sexual asymmetry in one African society. She has argued that the 'dominance of men is based primarily on their control of women and surplus, rather than on any technologically defined or natural division of labour' (1974, p. 301). The real usefulness of her analysis lies in her attempt to provide the basis of a materialist analysis of women's subordination, through an account of the sexual skewing of the social relations of production. There are two areas however in which we would see the need for theoretical development.

Firstly, though O'Laughlin's methodological precision in the use and application of concepts allows her to explain a particular ideology in terms of the particular contradiction it mediates, any notion of political struggle in the maintenance of hegemony is omitted. Women are seen to pass on to their children, to 'live out the representation of their own inferiority and to pass it on to their children'

(1974, p. 317). This would seem to suggest an almost complete alignment between political and ideological practices.

Secondly, by operating primarily within a marxist framework, O'Laughlin does not attempt to bring into her analysis the feminist question of the control of female sexuality, as it relates to the particular relations of reproduction in the Mbum society she describes. Though a marxist framework can more easily accommodate an examination of the reproduction of the labour force, the control of sexuality must be regarded as a vital aspect of an analysis of women's subordination. A full examination of this subordination would have to take into account the triple material appropriation practised on women, of their capacity to labour, of their capacity to procreate, and their sexuality: each appropriation being seen in terms of the ideological, political and economic mechanisms employed. As Aaby (1977, p. 36) argues, the very act of exchange of women, makes them into objects, and this 'reification' involves absolute control over the person or some of their activities (reproductive potential, labour power, sexuality). The suggestion here is that women are exchanged like commodities, because they have the capacity to increase wealth through their own labour, through their reproductive potential, and as daughters exchanged for bride-wealth (7). Both O'Laughlin and Aaby extend the analysis of the exchange of women begun by Lévi-Strauss. They uncover aspects of exchange that can be seen as political (sexual politics, and the power of the elders), and they attribute to the exchange of women in marriage a fundamental role in the *economic organization* of the society.

O'Laughlin gives little indication of how she thinks certain aspects of her analysis might be applicable to an examination of women's subordination, in the capitalist social formation. In her final sentence, though, she provides a useful point of entry for an analysis of the terms in which specific ideologies of sexuality articulate with forms of social and economic organization. She hints that 'a comparable analysis of competitive rituals of beauty . . . might provide some insight into the place of sexual asymmetry in a society that so tenaciously treats relations between persons as relations between things' (1974, p. 318).

If an attempt were to be made to apply her analysis to women's subordination under capitalism, one of the first modifications would have to be to indicate the differential mechanisms of that subordination by class (see Article 9). In Mbum society all women labour and have access to the means of subsistence, but their access to subsistence is a potential parity in domestic affairs between husband and wife, no more. Further, this is only realizable if domestic tasks are shared or socialized. As O'Laughlin insists, a certain parity with men in the domestic and social labour processes says nothing about inequalities within the wider social relations of production. As in Mbum society, then, the economic subordination of women in capitalist society cannot be regarded as technologically determined.

In Mbum society there are no classes as such, because all males eventually marry, become elders, and take their turn in the organization of the collective appropriation of surplus labour and bride-wealth. Thus there is *age* and *sex* asymmetry in access to the means of production (tools and breeding animals) and surplus labour; in capitalist society there is *class* and *sex* asymmetry in access to ownership of the means of production (machines and raw materials) and surplus labour.

In capitalist society, biological reproduction of the labour force and early socialization are the primary responsibility of most women. A contradiction exists for them, as it does for Mbum women, between this primary responsibility and their 'separation' from the product of their own reproduction, in the sense that most women 'bear children for groups other than their own' (1974, p. 312), not for another patrilineage, but for another class.

Biological differences are also linked in the capitalist social formation to sexual asymmetry in economic relations of production (to productive property and the wage). Now however, there are various ideological mechanisms that mediate sexual asymmetry for women of all classes, for example, romantic love, domesticity and motherhood (8). We would maintain that these ideologies have contributed to securing the subordinate placing of women within the relations of reproduction.

Enter sex-gender relations

We would locate the major absence in O'Laughlin's analysis of sexual asymmetry in Mbum society as the omission of a full consideration of the contradictory nature of the relations of biological reproduction at the ideological and political levels. She does not theorize a relatively autonomous sphere concerned with the acquisition of sexual identity, control of sexual practices and biological reproduction. It is for a full theorization of this area that Gayle Rubin argues in her article, 'The traffic in women: notes on the "political economy" of sex' (1975). Pointing to the absence in Marx of a theorization of what he terms 'the historical and moral elements in the determination of labour power' (Marx 1972, p. 171), Gayle Rubin calls for a separation of the relations of biological *reproduction* from the relations of production. Furthermore, she insists that the ideological relations of sex and gender and their acquisition should not merely be subsumed under the relations which govern biological reproduction. In order to theorize this area of sexuality and procreation, Rubin introduces the concept (1975, p. 149) of 'sex-gender systems' by which she means:

> the set of arrangements by which a society transforms biological sexuality into products of human activity and in which these transformed sexual needs are satisfied.

In the absence of materialist concepts for an analysis of forms of sexuality, Rubin turns to Lévi-Strauss for the basis of a theory of sex-gender systems, which she locates within kinship. The problems with her theorization, which we examine below, arise initially from her narrow definition of kinship. Her position in 'The traffic in women' is to some extent contradictory. She does indicate in principle the important anthropological finding that kinship structures function at a variety of levels within the social formation. Yet in her attempt to delimit what she means by sex-gender systems, she abandons any complex definition of kinship, or by extension, of the function of the nuclear family under capitalism. She defines kinship as merely 'the observable and empirical forms of sex-gender systems' (1975, p. 169). This reduction becomes crucial when Rubin turns her attention to contemporary sexual politics.

As we have seen from our brief look at Marxist approaches to anthropology, kinship is multifunctional within the social formation. It may structure the form of economic production and distribution (Hindess and Hirst), control access to and the exchange of women (Meillassoux and Godelier), and be effective as the material practice within which power relations between the sexes are 'lived' (O'Laughlin). The extension of these analyses of the function of kinship to include the structure of the nuclear family under capitalism would need to centre on the way in which these functions have been structurally modified (see below).

In posing Lévi-Straussian concepts in a critical way, as the starting point for the development of a materialist theory of sex-gender relations, Gayle Rubin provides a useful criticism of Lévi-Strauss's use of the concept of the exchange of women as neutral, 'symbolic' exchange. Within the terms of her limited definition of kinship, she identifies the exchange of women as *one* necessary and useful concept for the understanding of the social relations of kinship, in which men have certain rights in their female kin which women have neither in themselves, nor in their male kin. These rights are exercised through specific material practices which put real constraints on women's sexuality and procreative capacity. Thus the exchange of women cannot be merely symbolic but must involve relations of dominance and subordination.

Developing certain implications of Engels's work *Origin of the Family,* Rubin stresses the more complex nature of sex-gender systems, as distinct from biological reproduction. She sees this as a moment in the circuit of production and reproduction of forms of sexuality and human labour power. In her explanation of the term 'sex-gender system', she provides useful illustrations of the culturally specific forms of socially constructed sexual practices, and of the sexual division of labour. She shows that sexual systems do indeed vary so as to include, for example, socially approved forms of transvestitism and homosexuality. Yet if we are to move beyond elaborations of sex-gender systems, to a position from which we can use anthropological material, at least initially, to generate a political understanding of current sex-gender systems, we must ask *why* such forms of sexual identity are approved and reproduced, i.e. we must look for the material base of sex-gender systems. This involves asking what the economic base of the form of social organization is, together with the demographic and ecological constraints on which these sexual systems are predicated. That is we must pose the nature of the relationship between economic production and the reproduction of sex-gender systems. However, Rubin's failure to integrate kinship as the site of sex-gender systems into the social formation leads inevitably to a politically unviable dualism between kinship/nuclear family and the mode of production.

Yet to locate theoretically the positioning and functioning of sex-gender within a social formation is still not to move towards a conceptualization of the *acquisition* of sexuality, i.e. the terms under which the individual is interpellated into a structured set of sexual relations, located in material practices, which are effective in the construction of sexual identity. In response to this absence, Rubin attempts to negotiate the problems of Freudian psychoanalysis in its Lacanian form. She sees it as the most fully developed theoretical system with which to explain the 'acquisition' of sexuality. However, this theory relies on a non-neutral, phallocentric system of concepts which Rubin fails to problematize. In fact, the uncritical use of Lacanian concepts (posed, and seemingly accepted by Rubin, as the ever pre-given structure for the entry into all culture) can be traced to her initial, restricted definition of kinship as concerned solely with the construction of sex-gender identity. In the terms of that analysis, no attempt is made to trace the effectivity of sex-gender systems with the political and economic functions of kinship. It is precisely the absence of that type of interrelated analysis which prevents any development of a *historical* and *materialist* analysis of the patriarchal structure of the unconscious (see Article 6).

The ultimate political conclusion to be drawn from Rubin's argument is similar to that of Juliet Mitchell in *Psychoanalysis and Feminism;* i.e. that the contemporary organization of sex and gender is anachronistic and bears no relation to economic, political and other ideological structures (Mitchell 1975, pp. 409–11). Rubin insists (1975, p. 199):

The organization of sex and gender once had functions other than itself – it organized society. Now it only organizes and reproduces itself . . . relationships of sexuality . . . lack the functional load they once carried.

Contemporary forms of kinship/familial organization are seen as redundant in Rubin's analysis. This is the point at which one feels the need to insist on the analysis of women's role as domestic labourers and biological reproducers in the circuit of capitalist production and reproduction. That is *again* to move beyond the particularized definition of the structure and function of the family, and to insist on its multifunctional and inter-related roles at all levels within the social formation.

Relations of biological reproduction

One of the problems with attempting a theorization of the relations of reproduction is that an uncritical use of the term 'reproduction' not only leads to confusions and conflations between different meanings of reproduction, but also as O'Laughlin (1977, p. 4) points out, it is loaded with the functionalist and teleological implication that social systems exist merely in order to reproduce themselves over time. If the concept is to be of use in furthering our understanding of women's subordination, it is important to 'isolate' levels and sites of reproduction; in particular, social reproduction (the reproduction of relations and forces of production) must be differentiated from the specificities of both reproduction of the labour force/(power) (9) and biological reproduction.

We should like to concentrate here on biological reproduction, and would agree with Maureen Mackintosh (1977) in her important review of Meillassoux's *Femmes, greniers et capitaux* that it is crucial to theorize the nature and form of the *relations* through which biological reproduction (10) takes place, admitting to these relations some autonomy. She characterizes these relations as patriarchal, giving a definition in terms of 'control of women, especially of their sexuality and fertility, by men' (1977, p. 122). We would like to extend the notion of fertility to include not simply control over the rate of procreation, but also control over women's procreative capacity (11). We would also argue the need to extend Mackintosh's definition to include the recognition that the sexing of subjects is integral to the relations of biological reproduction.

Mackintosh stresses that if we are to confront theoretically the feminist problematic, 'the fact and implication of women's subordination to men and of women's struggle against that subordination' (1977, p. 199), these relations of biological reproduction should be a primary area of investigation. She poses the essential problem of investigating the differing forms of these relations and their inter-relation with social relations of production, and raises the issue of how changing modes of production alter *forms* of relations of biological reproduction without destroying their patriarchal nature. However, perhaps due to her correct stress on the futility of searching for original sources of women's subordination, she appears to avoid the question of *why* the relations of biological reproduction should take a certain form in a particular social formation.

Importantly, this indicates the need to understand women's subordination at the point of articulation between relations of production and reproduction. A central aspect of this specificity lies in the relation between, on the one hand, women's location within relations of human reproduction and, on the other, their contribution to the reproduction of the labour force. In defining the reproduction of the labour force, it is important to distinguish day-to-day reproduction, which includes tasks of domestic labour and 'caring', from generational reproduction, which includes procreation, regulation of sexuality, socialization, especially the social construction of sex-gender identity (cf. Beechey 1977; and Edholm *et al.* 1977). Although O'Laughlin (1977, pp. 6-7) is correct in arguing that the quantity, quality, and value of labour power employed in capitalist production constantly alter with changes in the technical conditions of production and the class struggle, we would stress that relations of biological reproduction partially structure the reproduction of the labour force. We would also maintain that reproduction of *sexed subjects,* while having a basis in the reproduction of the labour force (or a necessary mode of articulation with that process of reproduction), also involves altogether more contingent processes at the ideological and political levels.

Mackintosh (1977, p. 124) implicitly makes a central connection between the relations of biological reproduction and the reproduction of the labour force, through viewing relations of biological reproduction as the means by which reproduction of labour power and the insertion of individuals into the class structure are controlled under capitalism. It is certainly true that control over women's procreative capacity and the rate of procreation are likely to be an essential part of the organization and reproduction of the labour force, and further, as Edholm *et al.* (1977, p. 108) point out, 'in pre-capitalist formations, labour is not generally "free" in the same way that it is under capitalism', and thus 'access to labour is controlled by quite other mechanisms than that of the capitalist labour market'. This has the corollary, or so argue Edholm *et al.*, that the relations of biological reproduction, as a means by which labour is controlled and allocated, becomes critically important.

However, this should not lead us to equate a control of women's procreative capacity with control of differential allocation of labour, for, as Edholm *et al.* stress (1977, p. 111), there is no necessary relation between the two:

... even where kinship systems typically order both human reproduction and the allocation of labour, the determinations of these activities may be quite distinct, though correlated. What has to be born in mind is that the production of new human beings is a distinct labour process.

The danger of assuming that regulation of biological reproduction (population control) will *inevitably* parallel demands for a particular level of labour force is of no less relevance in relation to understanding women's subordination in the present conjuncture (12).

If we take the question of abortion, for example, analyses which view abortion purely in terms of capitalist population control lead to a distortion and a reduction of the complexity of the issue. The whole question of abortion is deeply embedded within a set of sexual ideologies concerning the defining of femininity and of a 'woman's place' (13). The demands for free abortion and contraception should not be simply *economic* demands, but must challenge the underlying *ideologies* on which the debate is predicated, crucially the harnessing of women's sexuality to procreation. Thus, with the recognition that abortion and contraception provide the material basis for the divorce of sexuality from biological reproduction, the demand for abortion and contraception must be centrally linked to the demand for women to define their own sexuality.

Relations of biological reproduction: the determinants of sexual ideologies

In the exposition of the various anthropological approaches considered in this article, we have attempted to locate the particular forms of women's subordination in primitive societies around the central concept of biological reproduction and its specific relations. Our critique of particular analyses has, in a general sense, been directed at either the absence of the feminist problematic (characteristic of Hindess and Hirst), or the failure to outline the specific sites and forms of women's subordination within an overall conceptualization of the social formation (characteristic of Rubin). Thus, what we would now insist, for any theorization of biological reproduction and its relations, is the necessity of articulating those concepts with an analysis of the mode of production itself. Furthermore, what our examination of particular forms of sexual ideology in primitive societies has indicated is that the maintenance and reproduction of the relations of biological reproduction are crucially linked to the terms in which ideologies of sexuality are constructed.

In an extension of the logic of Althusser's argument (1971a), we would maintain that relations of biological reproduction cannot be secured solely at the economic level, but require as a condition of their existence, the continual work of ideology (14). That is, that the subordination of women in the reproductive sphere requires the massive dissemination of specific forms of sexual ideology (myths of masculinity, of motherhood, of maternal deprivation, of the primacy of heterosexual genital sex, etc.) in order to secure and maintain those unequal relations of reproduction. The continuation of those relations is dependent on the work performed by the dominant sexual ideology, that is the process whereby individuals live out the various ideological forms of masculinity and femininity (the particular historical forms of sex and gender) 'all by themselves' within material practices. In terms of an overall theoretical programme, it is now urgent that, as feminists, we begin to think through the specific *ideological* forms of the patriarchal structures of sexuality, in articulation with the form of the relations of human reproduction, and ultimately with the capitalist mode of production itself.

In the context of the work on anthropology considered in this article, Gayle Rubin's insistence on the specificity of the ideologies of sex and gender provides one of the most useful points of departure for that type of articulation. Her use of anthropological data effectively demonstrates the extreme nature of the variability of sexual ideologies across trans-historical and trans-cultural perspectives (15). Anthropological analysis of the functioning of sexuality in pre-class societies can serve the useful political task of demonstrating that the present form of monogamous heterosexuality is neither natural nor innate, but socially learned and controlled. And we should hold strongly to that ideological moment of sexual subordination in the investigation of the structure of sex and gender, as the corollary to the form of analysis performed by Hindess and Hirst, Godelier and Meillassoux. As we have indicated, those Marxist developments of anthropological categories, while usefully moving toward an analysis of kinship structures as multifunctional effects within the social formation, fail almost entirely to preserve the specificity of relations of sex and gender.

But, we would maintain that to insist on the inclusion of the ideological structures of sexuality and sexual practice in the focus of analysis should not be to relegate those structures to a *separate* system of patriarchal relations, or to label them as merely archaic or obsolescent. It is, we would argue, precisely because ideologies of sex and gender are inextricably linked to the maintenance and reproduction of relations of sexual asymmetry at the political and economic levels that *ideological struggle* must form an integral part of the terms on which gender politics are conducted.

Again, the investigation of primitive societies can reveal, at that low level of development of the productive forces, the multiple and interrelated functions of kinship, to include the structural organization of sex-gender systems. It is that specific type of analysis which can provide the *framework* for the examination of kinship/familial structures under capitalist relations. As much of the work in this book has attempted to demonstrate, it is precisely the economic and ideological effectivity of the family in the circuit of capitalist production and reproduction that is masked under capitalist relations, and *represented* as unrelated to the specific demands of the capitalist mode of production. Anthropological studies can effectively demonstrate the terms under which kinship structures function at a variety of related sites in pre-class societies; and in a way that can usefully provide a methodology for the investigation of the functioning of familial relations under capitalism. But let it be clear what is *not* being insisted here: it is not that we can trace in any evolutionist manner the structures of kinship from their function in primitive societies to their development under capitalism. It is rather that *structurally* (in terms of the articulation of levels within specific social formations), we can locate some 'continuity' between kinship patterns of organization in primitive societies and the forms of the family under capitalism. For in an analysis of the position of women in primitive societies, and its relevance for similar analyses of the capitalist social formation, we would hold to Marx's own notion of *structural development* (conceptually, and in the real concrete), outlined in the 1857 introduction to the *Grundrisse* (Marx 1973, pp. 102-8). It is in that sense that we would see the primary theoretical/political relevance of a specifically marxist anthropology for present analyses.

However, many feminist analyses of the position of women under capitalist relations still tend to separate out analytically the economic and ideological functions of the family. There has as yet been little attempt to trace concretely the relationship between the specific structures of sexual *ideologies* and the *economic* position of women, both in the reproductive sphere of the family, and as wage labourers. Veronica Beechey for example, in her valuable analysis of female wage labour under capitalism (1977), while acknowledging the effectivity of ideology in securing certain of the terms of women's subordination at the economic level, only frames her specifically *economic* analysis with the proviso statement that:

> It is not directly concerned with the important question of the role of the State in reproducing a particular form of family and role for women, *and the ideology of domesticity*. [our italics]
>
> Beechey (1977, p. 60)

What we would maintain is that there are crucial points in the economic analysis of women's subordination that cannot be fully developed without *simultaneous* attention to the structure of particular forms of sexual ideology, as they maintain and reproduce relations of domination and subordination in the productive and reproductive sphere. The problem cannot simply be resolved by a division of labour *between* those analyses which locate the *economic* structures of women's subordination, and those which attend to the *ideological* 'effects'; for there are vital points in present conjunctural analysis where we need to trace the precise terms of articulation and inter-relationship between levels (16). Furthermore, it is a task which we believe would have pertinent political effects in clarifying theoretically the terms on which economic and ideological struggles could be inter-related.

In a more general sense we should, as feminists, begin to recognize the structure of our own recent history as it determines the terms of our theoretical development. The forms and structures utilized within the Women's Movement for the understanding of the ideological level of women's subordination were not originally developed in interrelation with the various forms of economic analysis (e.g. the 'domestic labour debate', the analysis of female wage labour, etc.). Rather, work on the ideologies of sexuality and sex-oppression were developed in contradistinction, and in some senses in antagonism, to analysis of the economic level, and with concepts that were, for good reason, in no sense, 'orthodoxly' Marxist. It is the terrain of that dualism which we now inherit, theoretically and politically. The work of feminist analysis which attempts to develop particular Marxist concepts (specifically for our work here, the mode of production in articulation with the mode of reproduction) must hold hard to interrelated developments at the level of ideology. Again, what our examination of Bridget O'Laughlin's analysis has demonstrated is the crucial articulation between specific ideologies of sexuality, and economic and political determinants in primitive societies.

As a precondition for theoretical work on the analysis of sexual ideologies, we would emphasize the necessity of articulating those structures with the structured relations of production and reproduction. It provides one specific framework for thinking through ideologies of sex and gender, without the complete separation (in the form of total autonomy) of the patriarchal structure of those ideologies from the relations of sexual asymmetry at the political and economic levels. Conversely, we should be aware of the dangers implicit in such an analysis, in the tendency towards functionalism and reductionism. Yet it is politically because, at the point of departure, we feel the need to err in that direction (rather than in terms of any *separate* structure of patriarchal relations) that we initially choose to construct our object of analysis in those terms.

Acknowledgements

We would like to thank the following people for their helpful comments: Erica Flegg, the Feminist Research Workshop (West Midlands), Richard Johnson, Andy Lowe, and Greg McLennan.

Notes and references

1   For a useful example of the approach to *Capital* which holds, consistently and exclusively, to a position that individuals are theorized by Marx only in so far as they appear as *economic* bearers or agents, see Victor Molina (1977).

2   With regard to the analysis in *Capital* itself, we would necessarily feel the need to hold to a greater sense of complexity in the consideration of what is held by Marx as 'natural', in his theorization of the capitalist mode of production. Certainly, in the most general sense, to categorically insist that Marx has an 'extra-social' account or assumption about sexual relations would appear to contradict his whole system of thought in some very central ways. What we take issue with here is those *readings of Marx* which quite specifically relegate sexual relations to the 'natural' or non-social sphere. For Marx himself, we feel that a thorough re-examination of the terms of his mode of working in *Capital* (i.e. what is held as *theoretically constant,* and what is considered through specific *historical* analyses) would serve as a point of departure for an investigation of his own position regarding sexuality and sexual relations.

3   See, for example, Ernestine Friedl (1975), Rayna Reiter (1975), and Michele Rosaldo and Louise Lamphere (1974).

4   In that the focus of our analysis here concerns the position of women in primitive societies, we do not consider those anthropological analyses which consider the variety of *specific* modes of production which exist in those societies. Nor do we deal with debates which attempt to locate the differences between pre-class and pre-capitalist societies. For discussion of those issues, see: C. Coqnery-Vidrovitch (1975); P. Rey (1975); and E. Terray (1972).

5   We would maintain that the question of the primacy of the *relations* over the *forces* of production is a matter of historical-empirical investigation, and cannot be asserted solely at the level of general concepts. For example, in the initial transition from feudalism to capitalism it is the relations that are decisive; pre-existing forms of the labour process are subsumed under capitalist relations. But in the industrial revolution, at the point of transition to machinofacture and to the real subsumption of labour, it is the movement of the productive *forces* that is decisive in defining the nature of that point of transition.

6   In this respect the Mbum can be seen to fall within what Hindess and Hirst have referred to as the 'complex redistribution' form of the primitive communist mode of production, in which the distribution of the surplus follows the structural patterns of kinship. But the Mbum economy also illustrates the difficulty of *labelling* social formations in which different forms of the labour process co-exist. See Taylor (1976). The existence of cash revenues adds a further complication to the use of primitive communist mode of production with respect to the Mbum.

7   O'Laughlin's analysis can be seen to support Aaby's contention (1977, p. 50) that the control of women is an essential condition of the accumulation of surplus in societies in which land is the instrument of labour.

8   The ideology of romance is the subject of a forthcoming thesis by Rachel Harrison and work is being done by Catherine Hall on the ideology of domesticity.

9   Only under the capitalist mode of production is the labourer separated from her/his capacity to labour (labour power). Thus, to permit applicability to pre-capitalist social formations, we use the notion of reproduction of the labour *force*.

10 Mackintosh uses the concept of *human* reproduction, but her usage appears to be synonymous with *biological* reproduction.

11 Edholm, Harris and Young (1977) define the social relations of human reproduction as 'the conditions of possession of both the means of (re)-production and of control over the product'. Thus, this definition has the additional element of control over the product, presumably meaning control over offspring. While this is definitely of importance in relation to women's subordination, we have not had the space to address this question here.

12 This is not to deny that population control may play a central role in certain planned economies. For example, Albania's and Rumania's concern with increasing their small populations has meant that abortion and contraception are generally unavailable in both countries.

13 Val Amos looks at the question of abortion in relation to black women in Britain in her unpublished dissertation *Black Women and Employment* (1977). Also see Victoria Greenwood and Jock Young (1976) for a discussion of the relation between the question of abortion and social democratic ideology.

14 While recognizing those critiques of Althusser which point to an implicit functionalism in the essay, 'Ideology and ideological state apparatuses', what we would insist in this context is that Althusser's theorization does provide the most useful point of departure for our analysis on the work of sexual ideologies. Furthermore, Althusser's own position in the essay does maintain (however ambiguously) that ideologies are imposed through a process which involves struggle (specifically *class* struggle, but in terms of our insistence here, also *sexual* struggle). Generally, what we would argue is that relations of biological reproduction are intrinsically contradictory, and therefore require for their maintenance and reproduction the intervention of the state, and the work of specific forms of sexual ideology.

15 For example here see Margaret Mead, *Sex and Temperament in Three Primitive Societies* (1935) and Ann Foreman, *Femininity as Alienation* (1977, p. 21).

16 For discussion of the articulation of economic and ideological structures within a particular conjuncture, see the section on the welfare state and the Beveridge Report in Article 3 (pp. 46-52).

9 'Shirley': relations of reproduction and the ideology of romance

Rachel Harrison

Shirley (Brontë 1974) was first published in 1849. By taking relations between the sexes as its main object, it apparently fits the romantic genre. Yet it is also the only Brontë novel to deal directly with the capitalist mode of production. The mill, the means of production, is the central focus for the entire range of class and sex relations that compose the plot. For this reason it can be seen as one route into marxist-feminist historical analysis which, as Sally Alexander points out, must consider the terms of the articulation of the capitalist mode of production 'through a patriarchal family structure – even at the most volatile moments of industrial upheaval' (Alexander 1976, p. 111). Though she is speaking here of the formation of a 'male dominated hierarchy of labour powers in trade after trade', the formulation holds with respect to family structure in all social classes.

The 'method' adopted here must be seen as a distinctive form of analysis (1). However, it is one which should perhaps be used in conjunction with more literary treatments of *Shirley* (2). The 'method' is to use a particular text to relate a specific historical content of bourgeois ideology, the ideology of romantic love in the second quarter of the nineteenth century, to two material processes – those of production and its relations, and those of (biological) reproduction and its (class-specific) relations. It assumes the need to uncover the way that romantic ideology operates to secure the contradictory subordination of a particular class of women within the relations of biological reproduction (3).

Althusser wrote of the reproductive nature of ideology in the following way (1971a, p. 170).

> The reality . . . which is necessarily ignored . . . is indeed, in the last resort, the reproduction of the relations of production and of the relations deriving from them.

If the relations of biological reproduction are regarded as one of 'the relations deriving from them', then the task of analysis is to understand the interrelation between these two relations – in this case, between the relations of production and the relations of biological reproduction, in a particular conjuncture.

Before turning to the text of *Shirley* itself, I look briefly at the social relations of novel production, and conclude with a discussion of some of the theoretical issues that arise from this type of marxist-feminist analysis.

The social relations of novel production

In this section, I examine very briefly, four aspects of novel production and its social relations: 1) the position of the female author in the domestic writing process; 2) the position of the female author in relation to the process of distribution; 3) the use of female labour in the production of paper and in the printing industry; 4) the consumption of novels, leisure, and domestic labour.

1) One of the problems with analysing the subordination of women in relation to the social relations of production is the fact that women cannot be unproblematically located in particular classes. Their economic relation to production is generally mediated through their father's or their husband's class relation. As the daughter of a clergyman, whose 'living' was only for his lifetime, Charlotte would have lost this mediation if she had outlived him. For particular historical reasons, one of these being male emigration to the colonies, there were 'surplus women' in the first half of the nineteenth century. An increasing number of women, therefore, had a 'degrading wait for a husband, expected to provide her with board, lodging and a purpose in life thrown in' (Basch 1974, p. 102).

As one of these so-called 'redundant women', by implication a woman whose reproductive function was unfulfilled, a daughter of the genteel poor like Charlotte Brontë was particularly unlikely to marry, because she was dowryless. She wrote, therefore, from moral indignation at the plight of 'redundant women' and from financial necessity (4).

Because novels were written at home does not mean that they cannot be seen as a particular form of labour process, the domestic writing process. The conditions under which women wrote were circumscribed by the prevailing views of women's place and by legal and economic constraints which secured them in a subordinate relation to the male head of the household. They were subordinated *as women* and as novelists.

Though many female novelists were not married, if they were, writing was considered a 'harmless occupation' and paper, the material requirement of writing, was cheap (Virginia Woolf, quoted in Miles 1974, p. 26). The domestic writing process need not disturb the routines of domestic life, and its private nature meant that the wife's gentility, her morals, her 'virtue', were not endangered. Nevertheless, it was considered that writing should not be 'the business of a woman's life' (Basch 1974, p. 9). Not only was a married woman's relation to writing ideologically mediated, but by law its proceeds belonged to her husband (Basch 1974, p. 19). They were not a source of economic independence for a wife.

2) The social relations of novel production were not neutral with respect to gender, either in the domestic writing process or in relation to the exchange of the finished object. Novel writing, like seamstressing, was becoming an increasingly overcrowded profession (Basch 1974, p. 109). Sexual discrimination was practised against women by male-run publishing houses. Women writers, like their male counterparts,

produced a manuscript, a use value, for exchange on the market. The selection and censorship of manuscripts lay in the hands of publishing houses (booksellers) and circulating libraries (Griest 1970). They monopolized the tastes, to a great extent, of the predominantly female consumer. So like all authors, women suffered from the problem of the increasing anonymity of capitalist market relations, a distant publisher and an even more distant audience (consumer). But *women* wrote in a male-dominated world that affected the conditions of domestic production of manuscripts, the content of the manuscript itself (selection and censorship) and required them to simulate masculinity, by taking on male pseudonyms.

3) In the printing trade itself, technological changes had allowed the substitution of the unskilled labour of women and children for skilled male labour.

... certain London firms where newspapers and books are printed have gained for themselves the honourable names of 'slaughter-houses'. Similar excesses occur in book-binding, where the victims are chiefly women, girls and children.

Marx (1976, p. 592)

Worse still were the conditions endured in the first stage of paper production, the process of sorting the rags which were the raw material of paper. As late as 1866, a Public Health report examined the spread of smallpox in the London rag trade, and notes:

One of the most shameful, dirtiest and worst paid jobs, a kind of labour on which women and young girls are by preference employed, is the sorting of rags. ... they themselves are the first victims [of smallpox] ...

Marx (1976, pp. 592-3)

In both these instances the employment of cheap female labour was made possible by the fact that their labour, being mediated through their father's or husband's relation to production, was not expected to cover the costs of its reproduction (5).

4) The last factor to be considered in the production, distribution and consumption of the novel is the increase in domestic service that accompanied the 'more extensive and more intense exploitation of labour power' (Marx 1976, p. 574). The greater volume of profit that resulted from the move from absolute to relative surplus value enabled the employment of a greater number of unproductive workers, not only in industrial production (where unproductive services were necessary for the realization of profit), but also in the home, where unproductive services were necessary to ensure the leisure and seclusion of the wives of the bourgeoisie.

Marx noted that between 1838-50 the wealth of the manufacturers based on the increasing exploitation of labour power increased by an average of 32 per cent (Marx 1976, pp. 540-1). Machinery 'augments' surplus value, and the 'mass of products in which surplus value is embodied' (Marx 1976, pp. 572-3). A larger portion of the produce of society is changed into surplus produce or luxuries, which are consumed by an increasingly wealthy capitalist class and their dependants. This in turn allows for the unproductive employment of the working class as servants (Marx 1976, p. 574). Even in the 1860s 'modern domestic slaves' actually outnumbered the total number of workers employed in production. 'What a splendid result', Marx wrote, 'of the capitalist exploitation of machinery!' (Marx 1970, p. 447).

The production and consumption of novels rested then on a fourfold, class-specific subordination of women; firstly the subordination of female novelists, secondly the subordination and exploitation of female labourers in printing and paper making; thirdly, the subordination of domestic servants and fourthly, the subordination of female consumers. This fourfold subordination will be considered further in the conclusion, in the light of the examination of *Shirley*.

'Shirley'

Shirley was published in 1849, just after the defeat of Chartism. Eagleton maintains that Chartism was the 'unspoken subject' of *Shirley*, though for reasons of expediency, it was back-dated to the Luddite events of 1812 (Eagleton 1975, p. 45).

In their introduction to the Penguin edition, Judith and Andrew Hook suggest that Charlotte Brontë must be seen as more than a novelist of private life, for *Shirley* stands with the 'condition of England' novels of Mrs Gaskell, Dickens, Disraeli and Kingsley, all novelists who tried to deal directly with the major social issues arising from rapid industrialization.

Shirley is set retrospectively in the early decades of the nineteenth century. The Napoleonic wars, the bad harvest of 1811-12, the Luddite riots (6) and the British government's Orders in Council, converged to highlight the antagonistic relation between capital and labour. Charlotte Brontë explains that the Orders in Council forbad trade with France, and this 'by offending America, cut off the principal market of the Yorkshire woollen trade, and brought it consequently to the verge of ruin' (Brontë 1974, p. 62; all subsequent undated references refer to this edition).

Within this context, a particular, carefully observed account of two interrelated love-and-marriage themes takes place.

The first concerns the love of Caroline Helstone for Robert Moore, a manufacturer fallen on hard times. His ambition is again to own the mill and the cottage which he is now forced to rent. The novel opens with Robert Moore's attempt to introduce new power looms into 'his' woollen mill, but these are intercepted during delivery and smashed by machine breakers. Cloth is stockpiling in the storehouse and the mill workers are on short time (p. 162). The need to be poised to increase productivity when the Orders in Council are repealed means that manufacturers are competing to invest more capital in machinery (in constant capital), than in labour (in variable capital). Robert Moore's harshness to his employees is partly excused on the grounds of his foreign (Belgian) ancestry, though in his harshness, 'he only resembled thousands besides, on whom the starving poor of Yorkshire seemed to have a closer claim' (p. 61).

As to the sufferers, whose sole inheritance was labour,

... and who had lost that inheritance – who could not get work, and consequently could not get wages, and consequently could not get bread – they were left to suffer on; perhaps inevitably left: it would not do to stop the progress of invention, to damage science by discouraging its improvements; the war could not be terminated, efficient relief could not be raised; there was no help then; so the unemployed underwent their destiny . . . .

(p. 62)

This misery generated hatred of the machines, the buildings, and the manufacturers, in particular hatred of Hollow's mill and Robert Moore.

Caroline Helstone is the eighteen-year-old niece of the Rector of Briarfield, under whose joyless protection she has lived since her mother deserted her. In this respect, she is unlike Jane Eyre (Brontë 1847) and many 'typical' heroines of the period, who are absolute orphans, that is, totally devoid of the protection of a male relative and, therefore, sole protectors of their own virginity and sellers of their labour power. In other respects she can be seen as a typical Charlotte Brontë heroine.

Because Robert is too immersed in the production of a surplus to return Caroline's love, she is denied the primary definition of feminine fulfilment, of non-working-class women of the time, the role of wife and mother. She therefore rebels against the fetters imposed on the young single middle-class woman. She wishes either to have a profession, or to help Robert in the counting house. The nursery rhyme imagery of Robert 'in the counting house' and Caroline 'in the parlour', vividly catches the increasingly rigid sexual division of labour of the early nineteenth century. When later, Caroline falls into a psychosomatic decline from frustrated love, she does not, like Catherine in *Wuthering Heights* (E. Brontë 1965, first published 1847), dream of the freedom of the moors and Heathcliffe's love, that is outside social relations, but being with Robert in the counting house (Brontë 1974, p. 405).

Though she pines passively for Robert to return her love, her own love is not wholly uncritical. It founders on a particular contradiction between the values of Christianity on which she has been raised, and the practices involved in capitalist productive relations. Though she loves Robert as a 'person', she cannot love him as an agent of capital – a callous capitalist hated by the work-force. Her reservations are compounded by the practical problem of attracting a man whose sole interest is engaged in production.

As an educated woman, Caroline is capable of becoming a governess. Though she wishes to take this initiative, her uncle refuses his consent (p. 204). Because she is denied the right to sell her labour, Caroline channels her energies into charitable work, but she does this reluctantly. The customary use of the labour of spinsters by the clergy, that is, the associations of charitable work with spinsterhood, was more than Caroline could bear. Though there was no room in the professions for women, Caroline sees clearly the unfairness of the differential access of the sexes to the professional labour market (p. 377):

Old maids, like the houseless and unemployed poor, should not ask for a place and an occupation in the world; the demand disturbs the happy and the rich: it disturbs parents. . . . The brothers of these girls are every one in business or in professions.

Her 'feminism' then, was of a limited kind; like the 'feminism' of the period in general, it aimed at remedying certain injustices, especially the injustices experienced by spinsters (Basch 1974, p. 10). Caroline asserts that though the sole aim of spinsters is to marry, they become objects of ridicule, because 'the matrimonial market is overstocked' (p. 377). Charlotte Brontë, in a direct address to the reader, argues for more opportunities for daughters on the grounds that they would then be of greater service to men (p. 778).

The matrimonial market is not, however, overstocked with heiresses, the position of the second heroine of the novel; but it is not until almost halfway through the novel that Shirley Keeldar is introduced. At twenty-one years old, she has come into her inheritance, 'a property of a thousand a year . . . which had descended, for lack of male heirs on a female' (p. 208). Within the prevailing definitions of femininity, Shirley, as a woman, is in an ideologically 'incorrect' relation to the means of production – in this case both Hollow's mill and the estate on which it stands – because her relation is direct, unmediated through a male (either a guardian with rights to the appropriation of surplus labour) or a father or husband.

As an aristocrat (7), Shirley performs aristocratic duties, riding round the estate, supervising production, extracting rent, and paying the wages of the agricultural workers.

As a bourgeois woman (8), as the owner of the mill, she is never directly involved in its management, though 'half her income comes from that works in the hollow' (p. 215). She does not venture beyond the counting house where financial matters are discussed with Robert Moore. Nor is she concerned that all the hatred of the work-force falls on him. It is as though, as a woman, she is allowed to cope with what is idealized in the novel as the deferential 'feudal' relations of production, with the manor house and the land, but *not* with the explicitly antagonistic relations of capitalist production. It is Robert as manager who confronts the work-force with his pistol, who forces through the new frames. In the manufacture of 'my cloth' he claims, 'I will employ what *means* I choose' (p. 156, my italics). When machine breakers march on the mill at night, it is Robert who organizes its defence, while Shirley (though armed) recognizes the limits imposed on her intervention by her gender. When Caroline wishes to rush to

Robert's side, Shirley argues that the days of chivalry, of inspiring men with heroism are past. This is 'a struggle about money, and food and life' (p. 329). The soldiers (p. 334), the clergy (p. 354) and local property owners are perfectly able to defend Moore's machines, 'his metal darlings' (p. 375). Though Eagleton indicates that Shirley is politically ambiguous towards helping the poor and shooting them (Eagleton 1975, p. 53), she has no doubts as to where her loyalties lie, in the long run: 'If the poor gather and rise in the form of the mob, I shall turn against them as an aristocrat' (p. 268). Though she feels a 'womanly sympathy' for the sufferings of the poor, it is her structural position as aristocrat that informs her charitable projects. With the help of the 'old maids' of the district, deserving poor are distinguished from the undeserving poor, and the clergy are beguiled by Shirley into contributing and organizing the relief of the workless poor. While Robert Moore, the callous capitalist, introduces the new machinery which contributes to unemployment, Shirley as compassionate capitalist organizes the channelling of 'surplus profit' towards the costs of reproduction of the unemployed labour force. While Robert was well aware of the 'humiliating nature' of this relief, it had the desired tranquillizing effect:

> The neighbourhood seemed to grow calmer: for a fortnight past no cloth had been destroyed: no outrage on mill or mansion had been committed.
>
> (p. 288)

Needless to say, the presence of a beautiful rich single woman in Briarfield raises the expectations of a doting young baronet, whose 'lineage and wealth', are 'far beyond her claims' (p. 248). To her uncle's dismay Shirley refuses the baronet on the grounds that though he is amiable, he is 'not my master'. She argues that her uncle's standards are those of the decaying European aristrocracy. He accuses her of poisoning her mind with French novels (p. 412).

Shirley has a 'progressive' understanding of marriage for love (9) which contradicts the actual juridical practices with respect to the sexual division of property between man and wife in the nineteenth century. Because legally her productive property must pass to her husband on marriage, any marriage must be 'regressive' for her. Robert predicts that '. . . she will never marry: I imagine her jealous of compromising her pride, of relinquishing her power, of sharing her property' (p. 561). Shirley's ambiguous status as a female man is frequently jokingly defused by referring to her as 'he' or 'Captain Keeldar' (p. 273).

Charlotte Brontë, as one might expect, chooses to allow Shirley neither to marry into a 'higher lineage' nor to remain single. It appears that for some time Shirley has loved Robert's younger brother Louis. He had 'sunk' in the world like Robert, because of their father's merchandising misfortunes, but to a far more painful position than that of tenant of a mill. His position was that of tutor to Shirley's young cousin – a position similar, except in respect of gender, to that of Jane Eyre, a dependent employee, a satellite on the fringes of the family circle, a member of the gentry but treated as a servant. Of course, while Jane Eyre suffered from class inferiority and sexual subordination, Louis experienced only the former.

In spite of Shirley's 'masculine' position with respect to the social relations of production, she feels that she cannot, any more than Caroline, be the first to declare her love. The conventions of what they see as feminine honour prevent this. Sexual custom overrides even Shirley's class position in courtship etiquette. As a suitor, who is of inferior class, Louis, though 'trembling with devotion' is also unable to speak of marriage. Like a feudal knight, he is consumed with 'secret ecstasy' for his 'mistress' (p. 473). He writes in his notebook: 'Her hand I never touched, never underwent the test' (p. 576). Yet at the same time, he has the sorts of characteristics demanded of a lover by Shirley. He regards Shirley like a horse to be tamed and broken in, which avoids the understanding that it is her property which makes her spirited and independent. Eagleton writes that, as in *Jane Eyre*.

The lower character is able to exercise power because of a 'weakness' in the 'higher' character: Rochester is a cripple, Shirley is a woman.

Eagleton (1975, p. 58)

To gain love, fulfilment as a woman, Shirley must be made to understand the inevitable closing in of the ideological, legal and economic practices of patriarchal family structures. Louis explains:

First tutor, then husband, I would teach her my language, my habits, and my principles, and then I would reward her with my love.

Brontë (1974, p. 576)

However, it is through the relationship that develops between Shirley and Caroline that Charlotte Brontë discusses questions of marriage and sexual inequality. In spite of the fact that 'the heiress was very rich', and Caroline 'had not a penny', Charlotte Brontë insists that there was 'a sense of equality between them' (p. 230). Yet their self-consciousness of themselves as women was necessarily of a different kind. Caroline, failing to find love, wishes for sexual equality in a profession. Shirley was aware of the stigma attached to being a governess, when the criterion of female gentility was leisure. Caroline cannot love Robert completely without compromising her Christian principles. Shirley cannot love without losing her independence, abdicating her ownership of the means of production. How is this double romantic impasse resolved?

The resolution

By using a literary device that occurs in several of her novels, Charlotte Brontë resolves the stalemate in the love affairs through the calamity of physical infirmity (10).

Firstly, Shirley believes herself to be dying from a dog bite. Driven to confide in Louis, through anxiety over making a will, she becomes dependent on him for advice. Though Shirley agrees to marry Louis, Charlotte Brontë does not depict this marriage as a happy solution. Shirley pines after her previous independence, for 'her virgin freedom' (p. 584). Like a legendary feudal lady, she prevaricates and hesitates over the final settlement, putting off 'her marriage day by day, week by week, month by month', until Louis 'fettered her to a fixed day'. 'Vanquished and restricted,' she '. . . abdicated without a word of struggle' (p. 592).

After her marriage, Shirley takes on the lifeless characteristics of the subordinate partner. When she asks Louis, 'Are we equal then, sir? Are we equal at last?' Louis replies, 'You are younger, frailer, feebler, more ignorant than I' (p. 578).

Shirley's unmanning through love, her voluntary subordination, legitimates not only the transfer of property rights (a transfer peculiar to the unusual relation of penniless suitor to heiress), but also the general breaking in for the performance of wifely functions. Prior to revealing his love, Louis describes to Shirley with remarkable explicitness (p. 576) what marriage to an imaginary orphan girl would hold: 'Perhaps, eventually, when her training was accomplished to behold her the exemplary and patient mother of about a dozen children.'

Thus, when Louis says 'you are mine' he is claiming his right to all the (productive) property that was previously hers, and also to her procreative capacity and sexuality.

Charlotte Brontë operates with an ambivalent acceptance of the ideology that a woman's destiny and her fulfillment lies in marriage. She hardly questions the sexual division of property inside marriage, or examines the material basis on which these practices rest. She resolves the contradiction for Shirley by a resort to an explanation of relations between the sexes that is grounded in a notion of personal power relations (11). The whole of the courtship of Shirley and Louis is framed in the language of feudality; 'Shirley is a bondswoman . . . she has found her captor' (p. 562).

The second physical calamity is that Robert is shot at as he returns from London. Temporarily 'unmanned' by this, he allows Caroline to visit him, and eventually proposes marriage 'to bring me solace, a charity, a purity, to which, of myself, I am a stranger' (p. 595).

So Caroline's prayers for the soul of her callous capitalist are answered. Her continuing presence is required however, for only the presence of the 'angel in the house' ensures that the new man, sensitive now to true love, can remain transfigured by that love into the form of a benevolent capitalist, that is, the characteristic form of the *bourgeois* relations of reproduction are now secured.

As Robert outlines his plans for the future, we see the magnitude of the ideological resolution of what remain real contradictions.

Shirley begins and ends with an account of particular capitalist relations of production. Those relations begin as overtly antagonistic, and are transformed during the course of the novel into seemingly non-antagonistic relations. In fairness though, this is not entirely accomplished through the mediation of Caroline's love. The repeal of the Orders in Council, in the final pages, provides the necessary economic conditions for the re-expansion of cloth production, Robert is saved from bankruptcy, and unemployment is reduced. In other words: 'The rising surplus makes it possible for the capitalist class to exchange its tyranny for a benevolent despotism (Nicholaus 1967, p. 271).

In the final chapter, Louis has become a man of property, and is to be made a magistrate. With production picking up, Robert promises Caroline that within ten years,

> [Louis and I] will divide Briarfield parish between us. My success will add to his and Shirley's income: I can double the value of their mill property . . . there will be cottages in the dark ravine. . . . I will get an act for enclosing Nunnely common. . . . Caroline, the houseless, the starving, the unemployed shall come to Hollow's mill from far and near . . . .
>
> C. Brontë (1974, p. 598)

Mrs Moore 'smiled up in his face', the acceptable face of capitalism; 'she mutely offered a kiss' (p. 598). Except that the two heroines have been rendered speechless, all in the parish of Briarfield appears resolved. The two brothers now either own or control the two prevailing means of production. Louis Moore, aristocrat, owns the land. He is saved economically from the servitude of tutoring by the prevailing patriarchal relations of biological reproduction, in which property is vested entirely in the hands of the husband. Robert Moore controls the mill in the family name if not his own. He has been saved spiritually by Caroline's love, and economically by the repeal of the Orders in Council.

Caroline has gained what she has been brought up to want. Her victory is marriage, and the modification of her husband's heart. She has solved the contradiction of loving a hated man.

Shirley has gained what she thought she wanted, 'a master'. She has exchanged the means of production and given access to her procreative capacity, for the 'benefit' of loving male protection. She and Caroline are now equally subordinate, reduced to the common denominator of the procreative function, and equally dependent on their husbands for the means of subsistence.

In the early part of *Shirley*, the four main protagonists are unmarried. Shirley is the only one with *economic,* but not ideological, security. Caroline, Robert and Louis are all in equally precarious economic positions. By the end of the novel, with all the protagonists married, a resolution has been achieved at Shirley's expense. The 'correct' formula for the sexual division of property has been affirmed. Furthermore, not only the two wives, but all the labour in the valley is now dependent on the Moores' 'benevolence' for its reproduction. The ownership and control of land and capital are united in one family, so that together the two brothers are in a position to appropriate the labour power of a 'docile' work-force, and the procreative capacity of their own docile wives. This is a resolution indeed (12). But *Shirley* is more than a recreation and celebration of the 'class consolidation between squire and mill-owner, achieved by the catalyst of working-class militancy' (Eagleton 1975, p. 45); it is also a recreation of patriarchal family relations even in *extreme* cases, the case of the heiress.

In *Shirley*, Charlotte Brontë is working with a necessarily descriptive account of the changing forces and relations of production. She describes the conditions of competition leading to the introduction of new machinery, and the harsh effects of this on the labour force. She describes the crisis of unemployment, which is, in this historical conjuncture, a crisis in the reproduction of labour power, and its management and containment through voluntary charitable effort. She describes the antagonistic social relations of production, the machine breaking and the attack on individual capitalists that resulted from the introduction of machinery and was exacerbated by the Orders in Council.

However, because *Shirley* takes the characteristic form of a novel, it has as its focus certain personal relationships between the sexes. It is the combination of the 'apparent' conventional focus, together with its 'condition of England' aspect, (its framing of the love story in the industrial upheavals of a Yorkshire mill valley in a particular period), that allows the novel to 'deliver' an important articulation. The articulation it delivers is that between a particular ideology, that of romantic love, and of particular economic relations between the sexes, secured through the mediation of that love. *Shirley* exposes the ideological and economic conditions of aristocratic and bourgeois relations of (biological) reproduction.

It is suggested then, that because *Shirley* is in the form of a novel depicting relations between the sexes, Charlotte Brontë has, necessarily, to work with an 'expanded' version of the 'social formation', i.e. her version has to include not only the economic, political and ideological relations between owners of property and the 'labouring poor', but also the subordination of women in relation to these productive relations. So Charlotte Brontë operates, with two interrelated levels, a level which is concerned with the protracted courtships of the two couples, and a level concerned with the relation of the protagonists to productive property. To specify the relation between these two relatively autonomous spheres, Charlotte Brontë uses an 'extreme' case, (a gender 'accident' of birth) to indicate that it is not only men of different classes who participate in the social relations of production, but women too. They do so however on gender-specific terms. Shirley's unmarried relation is contradictory because it is not mediated through a man. This means that her ideologically correct gender identity, her feminine virtues, contradict her situation in a structurally determined class place generally reserved for men.

Caroline, in contrast, is located, as are most women, in a mediated relation to production, (through a male relative, father, husband, or guardian). In *Shirley*, therefore, it is generally not so much individual men who are related to production, but families of different classes, land-owning families, poor families, etc. While Brontë upholds this family construct morally, she understands the way that it shapes the subordination of women of particular classes, in relation to the family.

As an heiress, Shirley is an anomaly in a world in which productive property is generally owned by men (13). Her economic independence as a single woman is legally permissible, however. But as a married woman Shirley has to submit to, or become 'engendered' into a relation constructed ideologically, legally and economically on a patriarchal basis of male domination and female dependence. On marriage, Basch writes, a woman becomes a minor, she loses her legal existence (Basch 1974, p. 16). We have seen that *Shirley* reveals the economic mechanisms of subordination of the bourgeois-aristocratic woman (Shirley) and the middle class woman (Caroline). The former mechanism is the sexual division of property, the latter the sexual division of access to middle class occupations. As we have seen, romantic love mediates these specific contradictions in different ways, depending on the class position and marital status of the women concerned. Though the subordination of the working class, and within this the working class woman, is taken for granted in *Shirley*, the subordination of aristocratic, bourgeois, and middle class woman is not. Caroline and Shirley are made to negotiate a tension between what Brontë regards as 'natural', the passage from love to marriage, and what she regards as unfair, the sexual division of property, and the sexual division of labour.

In *Shirley* there are two relations of (biological) reproduction, an aristocratic and a bourgeois, taking shape through the mechanisms of gender-differentiated economic structures which are mediated and secured through discriminatory legal practices and romantic ideology. In the process of entering the aristocratic relation of (biological) reproduction, Shirley gives up her productive property and 'sinks' from privileged owner to dutiful procreator. In the process of entering the bourgeois relation of biological reproduction Caroline 'rises' from middle class gentility to become an honorary member of the bourgeoisie, in the only way possible for a woman, by marriage. Shirley too, is, after her marriage, only an honorary member of her husband's class, without its defining characteristic, the right to the extraction of surplus labour.

Charlotte Brontë produces an advanced descriptive formulation of women's subordination in articulation with class/property relations. But the contradictions of the text can only be understood through later theoretical developments. For though Charlotte Brontë examined the distribution of property between classes and sexes, she could not be aware of the internal mechanisms that its ownership involved, the right to the appropriation of surplus labour, and the accompanying process of capital accumulation.

It follows from this that her resolution was necessarily a false one, in both its 'solution' of the antagonistic relations between capital and labour, and in her 'solution' to the impasse reached in the relations between the sexes. There could be no solution to the fact that behind the appearance of the capitalist and the aristocrat at the site of production, there lie two relations of biological reproduction.

Both of these relations of biological reproduction occur within socially constructed relations which secure the sexual subordination of aristocratic and bourgeois women (14) in the interests of the production of a fresh generation of heirs to the means of production.

Relations of reproduction

I would argue that, in order to understand women's subordination, we must expose the ways in which women's procreative capacity is appropriated in different historical conjunctures, and with respect to different classes. Like different forms of appropriation of labour capacity, the general concept of the appropriation of labour capacity can only be seen as a tool to examine the way that actual appropriation has always to exist in a particular historical form, or forms. I would suggest that it is this aspect of the relations of (biological) reproduction, the appropriation of women's procreative capacity, that underlies the way in which her other capacity, her capacity to labour, is appropriated or not appropriated, according to her husband's or father's relation to production. In other words, the historical form of appropriation of a woman's procreative capacity is mediated by her husband's relation to production, that is, by whether the 'product' of her reproduction is an agent of capital or an agent of labour.

Marx insisted that the social relations of production are generated and reproduced at the site of production itself:

> Capitalist production . . . also produces and reproduces the capitalist relation; on the one side the capitalist, on the other the wage-labourer.
>
> Marx (1976, p. 724)

The family, then, does not *generate* the social relations of production. Rather, families of different classes perform the task of *distribution* of a fresh generation of agents to their places in relation to production. The aristocrat and the capitalist transmit to their legitimate sons and heirs their positions within the relations of production. The legitimacy of the heir is a biological legitimacy, based on the husband's monopoly of genital access to the procreative capacity of his wife, and his right to regulate her sexuality. The law upholds the *transmission* of the right to the ownership of the means of production, through the family. Thus, like ideology, it sanctifies the family.

In *Shirley*, the repression of sexuality is an obvious consequence of the impasse reached in the two courtships. Though its sublimation in dreams and charitable works is carefully described, Charlotte Brontë does not question the prevailing rigid sexual morality. The force of passion in her work is wholly directed towards marriage.

In *Woman's Estate*, Juliet Mitchell writes of four key structures involved in women's subordination: these are production, reproduction (of children), socialization and sexuality (Mitchell 1971, p. 101). Of sexuality, she says: 'Throughout history women have been appropriated as sexual objects, as much as progenitors or producers (1971, p. 110). However, because she is attempting to formulate a *general* theory of women's subordination, she does not specify the particular forms that this appropriation of sexuality takes at different historical moments. It must be stressed that the many 'social accretions around our biological distinctness' (Rowbotham 1973, p. 117) are invariably class-specific accretions.

Capitalist Mode of Production : Relations of Reproduction

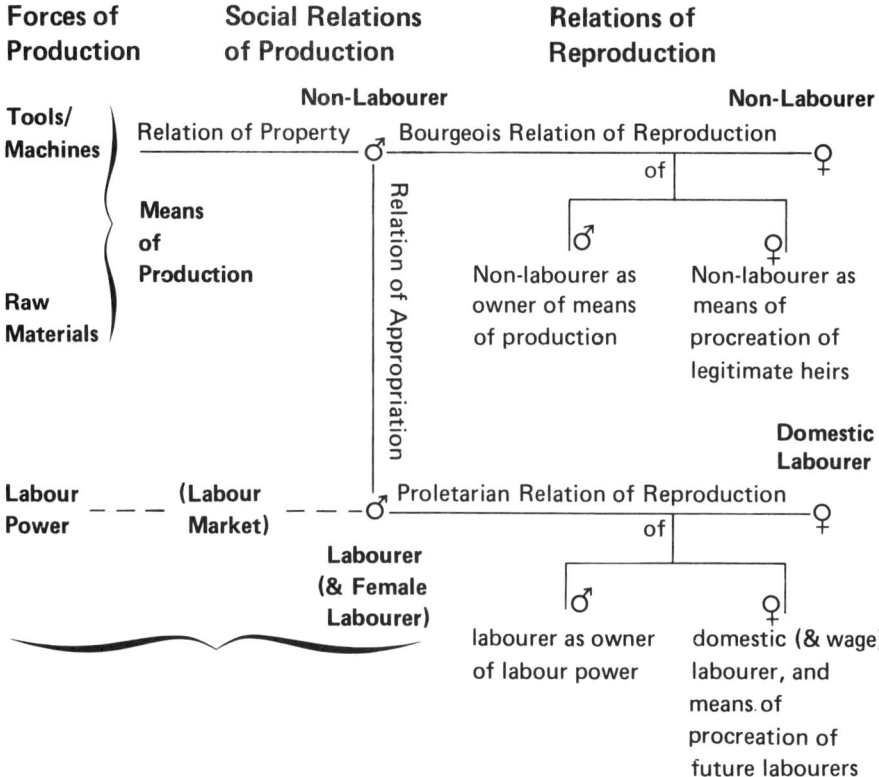

For example, aristocratic and bourgeois (and middle class) men appropriated the procreative capacity of their wives, regulated their sexuality, and circumscribed their capacity to labour. However, as Engels (1970) indicated, and Stephen Marcus (1964) charted, they appropriated the sexuality of prostitutes. Thus the overarching Victorian morality of virginity, chastity, and monogamy was held to be class-specific in practice; it involved the repression of the sexuality of one class of woman, and the buying of the sexuality of the other.

Shirley has provided a certain understanding of the way that particular classes of women live their subordination. This understanding must be seen as incomplete, however, because of the absence of working class women from the test. This is not to accuse Brontë of failing to accomplish what she did not set out to do; it is only to indicate that the text cannot be regarded as a description of the social formation as a whole.

Because Charlotte Brontë does not deal with the subordination of working class women, she does not confront the problem of how it is that the subordination of women of all classes serves the same system, but differently.

Working class women are also placed in particular class-specific relations of (biological) reproduction (15). They are tied by the bonds of marriage to the generational reproduction of fresh labour, both social and domestic (female), and the day-to-day tasks of domestic labour. For this reason, working class women do not fall unproblematically into Marx's category of 'free labour': they are bonded to their husbands in a particular form of subordination, and are therefore not the 'untrammelled owners of their capacity to labour, of [their] person[s] (Marx 1970, p. 168). Though Marx and Engels were right to indicate that the employment of women in social production is progressive in the sense that it lessens their dependence on their husbands, they did not take into account the fact that women are always placed in a relation both to production and to (biological) reproduction (16). Historically, capitalist production utilized and transformed a particular form of the family as an 'economic unit', (meaning a unit composed of a male head of the household and a number of dependants). It benefitted from the cheaper cost of female labour power that was the result of this already constituted dependence. This mediated relation of working class women (17) benefited the process of capital accumulation in two ways, as Veronica Beechey has suggested. Firstly, it enabled the employment of female labour at a low wage, because the female wage was not expected to cover the costs of reproduction (of the whole family). Secondly, it enabled the cheap reproduction of labour power through the use of unpaid domestic labour (Beechey 1977). The working wife was therefore situated in a kind of permanent transition between two modes of labouring, the capitalist mode and the family mode. Coulson *et al.* (1974) are right to stress the 'concrete contradiction' involved here:

The separation of domestic and wage labour has had the twin effect of both ascribing to women a dependent legal and economic status (as wife), *and* the possibility of material and social existence independent of men and the family.

(See *State* section in Article 3, pp. 46-54, for a discussion of state management of this contradiction.)

Ann Foreman (1977, p. 91) notes how the introduction of power looms enabled employers to use this cheap female labour:

The result was violent as Charlotte Brontë described in *Shirley*, . . . [it made] skill redundant and drove down the level of real wages, [and it] threatened the tradition based division of labour between men and women.

However, the Factory Acts (see pp. 48-50) had the effect of resecuring the *tradition* based division of labour between men and women. They ensured that the reproduction of the labour force would retain a patriarchal character.

Thus, the appropriation of the procreative capacity of women of different classes to ensure, on the one hand, the procreation of fresh heirs and, on the other, the procreation of fresh labour for exploitation, are two forms of (biological) reproduction that have been secured, historically, through particular relations of ideological, legal, and economic coercion. The economic mechanisms of coercion described in *Shirley* were those of differential female access (on marriage) to the means of production, and to middle class occupations. The economic mechanism of coercion for working class women was that of differential female access to the means of subsistence, the wage. The subordination of all wives, which was immediately advantageous to all husbands, functioned ultimately in the interests of the ruling class male. It supplied him with legitimate heirs and middle class functionaries, and provided for the cheap reproduction of fresh labour. The implications of this analysis would suggest that though women of the ruling class and middle class women may have a lot to lose with their chains, it is in their interests ultimately to unite with all other women to oppose the social relations of capitalist production, and hence the coercive patriarchal relations of (biological) reproduction that it maintains.

Summary and conclusion

This article began by examining the social relations of novel production. It included a brief account of the chain from author, through the ideological censorship of the booksellers and lending libraries, to an audience of increasingly leisured bourgeois and middle class women. There was an outline of how the production 'moment' in the circuit of production of the novel rested on the subordination of female authors in the domestic writing process, and on the exploitation of working class women and children in the printing industry and the production of paper. At the consumption 'moment' in the circuit, it was shown how an increasing army of servants enabled the bourgeois and middle class women to have time to read and of course to write (18).

Having examined the novel itself it is easier to see more clearly the relation between this activity in the productive sphere and the sexual subordination of women who did not belong to the working class. The exploitation of female wage labour by the male owners of publishing firms coincided with the interests of a new appropriating class, the industrial bourgeoisie as a whole, for the ideological legitimation of certain corresponding sexual practices. These practices, of premarital virginity and lifelong monogamy, were those required by the new appropriating class, of its women.

Thus, the ideology of love and marriage, with its corollary of virginity and monogamy, bore not only the fruit of dutiful daughters and chaste wives, but was itself a source of profit. As Marx observed:

> The description of the workshops, more especially those of the London printers and tailors, surpasses the most loathsome fantasies of our romance writers.
>
> Marx (1970, p. 465)

The emphasis of this analysis has rested on the articulation of a specific ideology with a specific relation between the sexes, which is shaped in turn by the social relations of production. The ideology of romantic love placed women as sexed subjects in a particular class-specific form of the relation of biological reproduction, and it mediated the contradictory economic mechanisms of women's subordination (differential access to the means of production, and to professional occupations). The overarching ideology of romance placed women in the *relation* of biological reproduction itself. It provided the framework, the legitimation and the affective bonding for other ideologies that compose the matrix of patriarchal ideology, those of femininity, domesticity and motherhood. The ideology of romance can be seen as a particular form of patriarchal ideology, that is, one means of securing patriarchal relations of reproduction.

Finally, as Basch writes, 'the work of a novelist comes from deep within the culture and ideology of the period; and the ideology is in part determined by economic and social infrastructure' (Basch 1974, p. xviii). Millet too sees that 'Charlotte Brontë has her public censor as well as her private one to deal with' (Millet 1971, p. 146). In addition, Brontë felt particularly acutely a more general contradiction experienced by 'superfluous women' in the nineteenth century, between the idealization and the structural subordination of particular classes of women. For this reason *Shirley* is both an exemplary text, and a cry from the heart. On the one hand, it is part of a range of literature (19), ideologically orchestrated by the publishing bourgeoisie, on the other, it is an indication of the way that this work of inculcation of female dependency provoked a resistance to the contradictions it set up.

Acknowledgements

I would like to thank Michael Green, Catherine Hall, Richard Johnson and Andrew Tolson for their helpful comments.

Notes and references

1. This article is only a small part of work towards a thesis which examines romance in three different conjunctures, the aristocratic feudal romance, the bourgeois romance of the second quarter of the nineteenth century, and the popular romance of the 1950s. Much has had to be omitted from this analysis, leaving only the skeleton of a novel which exposes many layers of contradiction, and missing out entirely its relation to previous forms of romantic literature, e.g. the domestic and Gothic literature of the eighteenth century.

2. I am thinking here of Terry Eagleton's marxist analysis (1975), a certain type of feminist criticism reading for feminist consciousness (Millet 1971), and feminist historical analyses which juxtapose textual detail with 'real' empirical data of the period (Basch 1974).

3. The term relation of (biological) reproduction is used here to designate class-specific relations of reproduction which have historically taken a patriarchal form, i.e. a form in which the wife is subordinated to the husband, and in

which the husband is legally entitled to appropriate his wife's procreative capacity, her capacity to labour, and her sexuality (in certain instances her property and income too, and the right to control the necessary labour of their children). Because the subordination of the wife is regarded as contradictory, it is seen to require securing through particular ideological, legal-political, and economic mechanisms of coercion, which vary according to class.

4 Catherine Hall has made a similar point in an unpublished paper entitled 'Sex and Class in *Shirley*'.

5 This argument is made by Veronica Beechey (1977).

6 These events are charted by Edward Thompson (1970) in *The Making of the English Working Class*, especially Chapter 14.

7 I am adopting Charlotte Brontë's designation of Shirley as an aristocrat, although the aristocracy is an ideological category at work in the novel. Romanticized 'feudal' relations of agrarian production are made to contrast with the 'masculine' nature of capitalist relations, whereas agricultural production in this period should probably more accurately be seen as agrarian capitalist in form.

8 In this analysis I use the term 'bourgeois' in a strict sense. The term *bourgeois woman* is used to indicate a woman who owns the means of production, as Shirley owns the mill before she is married. The term *bourgeois wife* is used to indicate a woman whose husband owns the means of production. The term middle class also refers strictly to women who are daughters of wives of middle class men – that is, men who are engaged in middle class occupations, but who do *not* own the means of production. (Only as governesses or novelists, for example, could women be middle class in their own right.)

9 C. James (1964) notes in his analysis of popular *Fiction for the Working Man* that because a woman's love must be pure and holy, any marriage contrary to these affections is 'moral adultery'.

10 Raymond Williams (1961) discusses this in *The Long Revolution*, Chapter 2.

11 In *Sexual Politics*, Kate Millet (1970) also understands women's subordination in terms of power relations between the sexes. She bases this on notions of political status, sociological role and psychological temperament, and falls short of a theory of women's subordination in relation to modes of production. As Charnie Guettel writes: 'Millet accurately points out the relevance of Engels' assertion that patriarchal authority rests on economic dependence of members of the family. But Engels goes further in stating that patriarchy itself as a form of authority is a result of a mode of production' (Guettel 1974, p. 27).

12   The subordination of wives of workers plays no part in Charlotte Brontë's scheme of things.

13   This is not to suggest that the heiress is an anomaly *in literature.*

14   Elizabeth Wilson quotes the *Finer Report* (1974, vol. 2, p. 117): 'Middle class families handled their accumulating industrial wealth within a system of partible inheritance which demanded a more severe morality imposing higher standards upon women than ever. An adulterous wife might be the means of planting a fraudulent claimant upon its property in the heart of the family; to avoid this ultimate catastrophe, middle class women were required to observe an inviolable rule of chastity' (Wilson 1977, p. 24). Note: his use of middle class is equivalent to my use of bourgeois.

15   For reasons of clarity, a two-class model is used in this diagram. Though the term non-labourer can be used to designate both the aristocratic class and the capitalist class, in this diagram it represents only the capitalist class, the bourgeoisie proper. The term non-labourer is one used by Hindess and Hirst in *Pre-capitalist Modes of Production* to refer to a class which does not perform productive labour. They argue that in feudalism and capitalism surplus labour is appropriated by a class of non-labourers, and that this constitutes antagonistic relations between a class of labourers (wage labourers, peasants, etc.) and a class of non-labourers (capitalists, feudal lords, etc) (Hindess and Hirst 1975, p. 10). It is important to remember that they operate at a particular level of theoretical analysis which does not deny the fact that, empirically, capitalists are frequently very busy, as Robert Moore was, for example, in the counting house!

16   Roisin McDonough and I discuss this in greater detail in an article in *Feminism and Materialism,* to be published by Routledge & Kegan Paul in Spring 1978.

17   The marriage relation which mediates the sale of her own labour power, also mediates the relation between her domestic labour and the sale of her husband's labour power. 'The working class housewife contributes to the production of a commodity – labour power – the sale of which guarantees their existence (this she has in common with other proletarians). . . . What mediates this . . . is not the market but the marriage contract: it is on the basis of the social relations of marriage and parenthood that the wife's labour is related to social labour' (Magas *et al.* 1975, p. 63).

18   Servants were often avid consumers of bourgeois romantic literature, and cheap popularized versions were available (Freist 1970).

19   For example, with reference to magazines, Cynthia White comments: 'The Victorian age gave birth to the 'Feminine Illusion' by which is meant the glorification of Womanhood and the worship of female purity as the antithesis of, and the antidote for, the corruption of Man' (White 1970, p. 42).

And Mirabel Cecil notes that in a period of 'exceptional subordination', writers' idealization of their heroines reached greater lengths than ever before – asexual, spiritual, good angels purifying men, and dressed in white of course (Cecil 1974, p. 90).

Bibliography

Aaby, P. (1977), 'Engels and women', *Critique of Anthropology*, vol. 3, no. 9/10

Adamson, O., Brown, C., Harrison, J., and Price, J. (1976), 'Women's oppression under capitalism', *Revolutionary Communist*, vol. 5

Adlam, D., *et al.* (1977), 'Psychology, ideology and the human subject', *Ideology and Consciousness*, no. 1

Alexander, S. (1976), 'Women's work in nineteenth century London; a study of the years 1820-50', in J. Mitchell and A. Oakley (ed.), *The Rights and Wrongs of Women*, Penguin

Althusser, L. (1969), *For Marx*, Penguin

Althusser, L. (1971), *Lenin and Philosophy and Other Essays*, New Left Books

Althusser, L. (1971a), 'Ideology and ideological state apparatuses', in L. Althusser, *Lenin and Philosophy and Other Essays*, New Left Books

Althusser, L. (1971b), 'Freud and Lacan', in L. Althusser, *Lenin and Philosophy and Other Essays*, New Left Books

Amos, V. (1977), *Black Women and Employment*, MA dissertation, Birmingham University (unpublished)

Anderson, P. (1969), 'Components of the national culture', in R. Blackburn and A. Cockburn (ed.), *Student Power*, Penguin

Barker, D. L., and Allen, S. (1976a), (ed.), *Sexual Division and Society: Process and Change*, Tavistock

Barker, D. L., and Allen, S. (1976b), (ed.), *Dependence and Exploitation in Work and Marriage*, Longmans

Barthes, R. (1970), *S/Z*, Jonathan Cape

Barthes, R. (1972a), *Mythologies*, Jonathan Cape

Barthes, R. (1972b), 'Rhetoric of the image', in *Working Papers in Cultural Studies*, Centre for Contemporary Cultural Studies, Birmingham

Basch, F. (1974), *Relative Creatures: Victorian Women in Society and the Novel 1837-67*, Allen Lane

Bachelli, A., Twort, H., and Williams, J. (1970), 'Peckham Rye Women's Liberation', in M. Wandor (ed.), *The Body Politic,* Stage 1, London

Baxandell, R., Ewen, E., and Gordon, L. (1976), 'The working class has two sexes', *Monthly Review*, vol. 28, no. 3

Beardons, S., and Stevenson, E. (1974), *Women's Studies*, National Union of Students, London

Beechey, V. (1977), 'Some notes on female wage labour in capitalist production', *Capital and Class*, no. 3
Bellotti, E. G. (1975), *Little Girls*, Writers and Readers Publishing Co-operative
Benét, M. K. (1972), *Secretary, Enquiry into the Female Ghetto*, Sidgwick & Jackson
Benston, M. (1969), 'The political economy of women's liberation', *Monthly Review*, vol. 21, no. 4
Berger, J. (1972), *Ways of Seeing*, Penguin
Beveridge, Sir W., (1942), *Social Insurance and Allied Services*, reprinted 1974, HMSO
Bowlby, J. (1951), *Mental Care and Mental Health*, World Health Organization
Braverman, H. (1974), *Labour and Monopoly Capital: The Degradation of Work in the 20th Century*, Monthly Review Press, New York
Braverman, H. (1976), 'Two comments', *Monthly Review*, vol. 28, no. 3
Brontë, C. (1974), *Shirley*, Penguin
Brontë, E. (1976), *Wuthering Heights*, Penguin
Bruley, S. (1976), *Women Awake, the Experience of Consciousness Raising*, S. Bruley, London
Butcher, H., Coward, R., et al. (1974), *Images of Women in the Media*, Stencilled occasional paper, Centre for Contemporary Cultural Studies, Birmingham

Campaign notes (1975), *The Women's Liberation Campaign for Legal and Financial Independence*
Cecil, M. (1974), *Heroines in Love 1750-1974*, Michael Joseph
Cliff, T. (1970), *The Employer's Offensive - Productivity Deals and How to Fight Them*, Pluto
Cohen, R., and Harris, C. (1977), *Migration, Capital and the Labour Process*, Seminar paper, Centre for Contemporary Cultural Studies, Birmingham
Comer, L. (1971), *The Myth of Motherhood*, Spokesman pamphlet no. 21, Russell Press, Nottingham
Comer, L. (1974), *Wedlocked Women*, Feminist Books, Leeds
Conran, S. (1976), *Superwoman*, Penguin
Cooper, D. (1968), (ed.), *The Dialectics of Liberation*, Penguin
Coqnery-Vidrovitch, C. (1975), 'An African mode of production', *Critique of Anthropology*, no. 4/5
Coulson, M., Magas, B., and Wainwright, H. (1974), 'Some critical notes on Wally Seccombe *The Housewife* . . . ', in *Women and Socialism Conference Papers*, vol. 3
Coulson, M., Magas, B., and Wainwright, H. (1975), 'The housewife and her labour under capitalism: a critique', *New Left Review*, no. 89
Counter Information Services (1976), *Women Under Attack*, Counter Information Services, London
Coussins, J. (1977), *The Equality Report*, The National Council for Civil Liberty Rights for Women Unit, London

Coward, R., and Ellis, J. (1977), *Language and Materialism*, Routledge & Kegan Paul
Cowley, J., Kaye, A., Mayo, M., and Thompson, M. (1977), *Community or Class Struggle?*, Stage 1, London

Dalla Costa, M., and James, S. (1972), *The Power of Women and the Subversion of the Community*, Falling Wall Press, Bristol
Dalla Costa, M., and James, S. (1973), *The Power of Women and the Subversion of the Community*, 2nd ed.
Dalston Study Group (1976), 'Was the Patriarchy Conference patriarchal?', in *Papers on Patriarchy*, Women's Publishing Collective, Brighton
Davidoff, L. (1973), *The Best Circles: 'Society', Etiquette and the Season*, Croom Helm
Davidoff, L. (1976), 'The rationalization of housework', in D. L. Barker and S. Allen (ed.), *Dependence and Exploitation in Work and Marriage*, Longmans
Davidoff, L., L'Esperance, J., and Newby, H. (1976), 'Landscape with figures: home and community in English society', in J. Mitchell and A. Oakley (ed.), *The Rights and Wrongs of Women*, Penguin
De Beauvoir, S. (1972), *The Second Sex*, Penguin
Delmar, R. (1972), 'What is feminism?', *Seven Days*, 15 March, reprinted in M. Wandor (ed.), *The Body Politic*, Stage 1, London
Delmar, R. (1976), 'Looking again at Engels's *Origin of the Family, Private Property and the State*', in J. Mitchell and A. Oakley, (ed.), *The Rights and Wrongs of Women*, Penguin
Derrida, J. (1973), *Speech and Phenomenon*, Northwestern University Press
Deutsch, H. (1976), 'Motherhood and sexuality', in P. C. Lee and R. S. Stewart, (ed.), *Sex Differences, Cultural and Developmental Dimensions*, Urizen Books, USA
Diana (1971), 'My view on the aims of the local group', *Shrew*, vol. 3, no. 6
Durkheim, E. (1961), *The Elementary Forms of the Religious Life*, Collier
Durkheim, E., and Mauss, M. (1963), *Primitive Classification*, Cohen & West
Dyer, R. (1976), *Entertainment and Utopia*, Paper given at Society for Education in Film and Television, Weekend school

Eagleton, T. (1975), *Myths of Power: A Marxist Study of the Brontës*, Macmillan
Edholm, F., Harris, O., and Young, K. (1977), 'Conceptualizing women', *Critique of Anthropology*, vol. 3, no. 9/10
Ehrenreich, B., and English, D. (undated), *Witches, Midwives and Nurses*, Glass Mountain Pamphlets, USA
Elyse and Bridget (1971), 'The consumer con-game', *Shrew*, July
Engels, F. (1972), *The Origins of the Family, Private Property and the State*, Pathfinder Press, New York
Equal Opportunity Commission (1977), *Women and Low Incomes: A Report Based on Evidence to the Royal Commission on Income Distribution and Wealth*, EOC

Fanon, F. (1967), *Wretched of the Earth*, Penguin
Faulder, C. (1977), 'Women's magazines', in J. King and M. Stott (ed.), *Is This Your Life? Images of Women in the Media*, Virago
Fell, A. (1974), 'Notes on ideology', *Red Rag*, no. 6
Figes, E. (1972), *Patriarchal Attitudes*, Panther
Firestone, S. (1972), *The Dialectic of Sex: The Case for Feminist Revolution*, Paladin
Fogarty, M. P., Rapoport, R., and Rapoport, R. N. (1971), *Sex, Career and Family*, George Allen & Unwin
Foreman, A. (1977), *Femininity as Alienation: Women and the Family in Marxism and Psychoanalysis*, Pluto
Freeman, C. (1974), 'When is a wage not a wage?', *Red Rag*, no. 6
Freud, S. (1961), 'Totem and taboo', in *Standard Edition of the Complete Psychological Works of Sigmund Freud*, vol. 13, Hogarth Press
Freud, S. (1961a), 'On narcissism: an introduction', in *Standard Edition of the Complete Psychological Works of Sigmund Freud*, vol. 12, Hogarth Press
Freud, S. (1965), *The Interpretation of Dreams*, Discus, New York
Freud, S. (1975), *Introductory Lectures on Psychoanalysis*, Penguin
Freud, S. (1977a), 'Three essays on the theory of sexuality', in S. Freud, *On Sexuality*, Penguin
Freud, S. (1977b), 'Some psychical consequences of the anatomical distinction between the sexes', in S. Freud, *On Sexuality*, Penguin
Freud, S. (1977c), 'Female sexuality', in S. Freud, *On Sexuality*, Penguin

Gagnon, J., and Simon, W. (1973), *Sexual Conduct: The Social Sources of Human Sexuality*
Gail, S. (1968), 'The housewife', in R. Fraser (ed.), *Work*, Penguin
Gardiner, J. (1975a), 'The role of domestic labour', *New Left Review*, no. 89
Gardiner, J. (1975b), 'Women and unemployment', *Red Rag*, no. 10
Gardiner, J. (1976), 'Political economy of domestic labour in capitalist society', in D. L. Barker and S. Allen (ed.), *Dependence and Exploitation in Work and Marriage*, Longmans
Gavron, H. (1966), *The Captive Wife: Conflicts of Housebound Mothers*, Routledge & Kegan Paul
Godelier, M. (1975), 'Modes of production, kinship, and demographic structures', in M. Block (ed.), *Marxist Analysis and Social Anthropology*, ASA Studies, Malaby Press
Gramsci, A. (1971), Q. Hoare, and G. Nowell-Smith (ed.), *Selections from the Prison Notebooks*, Lawrence & Wishart
Greenwood, V., and Young, J. (1976), *Abortion on Demand*, Pluto
Greer, G. (1970), *The Female Eunuch*, MacGibbon & Kee
Griest, G. L. (1970), *Mudies Circulating Library and the Victorian Novel*, David & Charles

Guettel, C. (1974), *Marxism and Feminism*, Canadian Women's Educational Press, Canada

Hall, C. (1974), 'The history of the housewife', *Spare Rib*, no. 26
Hall, S. (1972), 'The determinations of news photographs', in *Working Papers in Cultural Studies*, no. 3, Centre for Contemporary Cultural Studies, Birmingham
Hall, S. (1977), 'The hinterland of science: ideology and the "sociology of knowledge"', in *Working Papers in Cultural Studies*, no. 10, Russell Press, Nottingham
Hall, S., and Jefferson, T. (1976), (ed.), *Resistance Through Rituals*, Hutchinson
Hall, S., Lumley, B., and McLennan, G. (1977), 'Politics and ideology: Gramsci', in *Working Papers in Cultural Studies*, no. 10, Russell Press, Nottingham
Harris, H. (1972), 'Black women and work', in M. Wandor (ed.), *The Body Politic*, Stage 1, London
Harris, N. (1968), *Beliefs in Society*, Penguin
Harrison, J. (1974), 'The political economy of housework', *Bulletin of the Conference of Socialist Economists*
Hartnett, U., and Rendell, M. (1975), *Women's Studies in the UK*, National Union of Students, London
Henderson, R. (1976), 'Consolidating consciousness', *Red Rag*, no. 11
Hindess, B., and Hirst, P. Q. (1975), *Pre-Capitalist Modes of Production*, Routledge & Kegan Paul
Hindess, B., and Hirst, P. Q. (1977), *Mode of Production and Social Formation*, Routledge & Kegan Paul
Hirst, P. Q. (1976), 'Althusser's theory of ideology', in *Economy and Society*, vol. 5, no. 4
Hoggart, R. (1957), *The Uses of Literacy*, Chatto & Windus
Hope, E., Kennedy, M., and De Winter, A. (1976), 'Homeworkers in North London', in D. L. Barker and S. Allen (ed.), *Dependence and Exploitation in Work and Marriage*, Longmans
Horney, K. (1974), 'The flight from womanhood', in J. B. Miller (ed.), *Psychoanalysis and Women*, Penguin
Hunt, A. (1968), *Survey of Women's Employment*, vols. 1 and 2, HMSO
Hussain, A. (1976), 'The economy and the educational system in capitalistic societies', *Economy and Society*, vol. 5, no. 4

Irigaray, L. (1977), 'Women's exile', *Ideology and Consciousness*, no. 1

James, C. (1964), *Fiction for the Working Man 1830-50*, Oxford University Press
Johnson, R. (1969), 'Vaginal deodorants', *Shrew*, November

Kincaid, J. C. (1973), *Poverty and Equality in Britain*, Penguin
Kinnersly, P. (1973), *The Hazards of Work*, Workers Handbook no. 1, Pluto

Koedt, A. (1970), 'The myth of the vaginal orgasm', in L. B. Tanner (ed.), *Voices From Women's Liberation*, New American Library

Korda, M. (1974), *Male Chauvinism: How It Works at Home and in the Office*, Coronet

Kristeva, J. (1974), *La revolution du langage poétique*, Seuil, Paris

Lacan, J. (1972), 'Of structure as an inmixing of an otherness prerequisite to any subject whatever', in R. Macksey and E. Donato (ed.), *The Structuralist Controversy*, Johns Hopkins University Press, Baltimore

Lacan, J. (1977), *Écrits*, Tavistock

Laing, R. D. (1961), *The Self and Others*, Tavistock

Laing, R. D. (1967), *The Politics of Experience*, Penguin

Laing, R. D. (1970), *Knots*, Tavistock

Land, H. (1976), 'Women: supporters or supported?', in D. L. Barker and S. Allen (ed.), *Sexual Divisions and Society: Process and Change*, Longmans

Laplanche, J., and Pontalis, J. B. (1973), *The Language of Psychoanalysis*, Hogarth Press

Larne, R. (1969), 'The most common ailment . . . ', *Shrew*, August

Lefebvre, H. (1971), *Everyday Life in the Modern World*, Allen Lane

Lévi-Strauss, C. (1969), *The Elementary Structures of Kinship*, Eyre & Spottiswoode

Loftus, M. (1974), 'Learning sexism and femininity' in S. Allen, L. Saunders, and J. Wallis (ed.), *Conditions of Illusion*, Feminist Books, Leeds

Mackie, L., and Pattulis, P. (1977), *Women at Work*, Tavistock

Mackintosh, M. (1977), 'Reproduction and patriarchy: a critique of Claude Meillassoux, '*Femmes, greniers et capitaux*', in *Capital and Class*, no. 2

Mackintosh, M., Himmelweit, S., and Taylor, B. (1977), 'Women and unemployment', discussion paper for *What is a Socialist Feminist Practice* day conference, London

McRobbie, A. (1977), *Working Class Girls and the Culture of Femininity*, MA thesis, Birmingham University

Mainardi, P. (1970), 'The politics of housework', printed in 'A woman's work is never done', Agitprop Information, in R. Morgan (ed.), *Sisterhood is Powerful*, Random House, New York

Manpower Studies No. 1 (1964), *The Pattern of the Future*, HMSO

Marcus, S. (1964), *The Other Victorians*, Weidenfeld & Nicolson

Marcuse, H. (1964), *Eros and Civilisation*, Routledge & Kegan Paul

Marcuse, H. (1969), *One Dimensional Man*, Sphere

Marx, K. (1970), *Capital*, vol. 1, Lawrence & Wishart

Marx, K. (1973), *Grundrisse*, Penguin

Marx, K. (1975), *Early Writings*, Penguin

Marx, K. (1976), *Capital*, vol. 1, Penguin

Marx, K., and Engels, F. (1970), *The German Ideology*, Lawrence & Wishart

Mead, M. (1935), *Sex and Temperament in Three Primitive Societies*, Morrow, New York

Meillassoux, C. (1972), 'From reproduction to production: a Marxist approach to economic anthropology', *Economy and Society*, vol. 1, no. 1, Routledge & Kegan Paul

Melville, J. (1944), *New Society*, 28 March

Metz, C. (1975), 'The imaginary signifier', *Screen*, vol. 16, no. 2

Miles, R. (1974), *The Fiction of Sex : Themes and Functions of Sex Difference in the Modern Novel*, Vision Press

Millet, K. (1970), *Sexual Politics*, Doubleday, New York

Millum, T. (1975), *Images of Women: Advertising in Women's Magazines*, Chatto & Windus

Ministry of Labour (1974), Manpower no. 9, *Women and Work, a Statistical Survey*, HMSO

Ministry of Labour (1967), Manpower Studies no. 6, *Occupational Changes 1951-61*, HMSO

Ministry of Labour (1968), Manpower Studies no. 7, *Growth of Office Employment*, HMSO

Mitchell, J. (1971), *Woman's Estate*, Penguin

Mitchell, J. (1975), *Psychoanalysis and Feminism*, Pelican

Molina, V. (1976), 'Notes on Marx and the problem of individuality', in *Working Papers in Cultural Studies*, no. 20, Russell Press, Nottingham

Mungham, G. (1976), 'Youth in pursuit of itself', in Mungham, G., and Pearson, G., (ed.), *Working Class Youth Cultures*, Routledge & Kegan Paul

Myers, N., Mitchell, A., Kay, D., and Charlton, V. (1976), 'Four Sisters', *Red Rag*, no. 11

Myrdal, A., and Klein, V. (1956), *Women's Two Roles: Home and Work*, Routledge & Kegan Paul

Nairn, T. (1972), 'The English working class', in Blackburn, R. (ed.), *Ideology in the Social Sciences*, Fontana

National Women's Studies Conference (1976), *Conference Report*

Newsom, J. (1948), *The Education of Girls*, Faber

Nicholaus, M. (1967), 'Proletariat and middle-class in Marx: Hegelian choreography and the capitalist dialectic', *Studies on the Left*, vol. 7, no. 1

Nichols, T., and Armstrong, P. (1976), *Workers Divided*, Fontana

Oakley, A. (1972), *Sex, Gender and Society*, Temple Smith

Oakley, A. (1974a), *The Sociology of Housework*, Martin Robertson

Oakley, A. (1974b), *Housewife*, Allen Lane

Oakley, A. (1976), 'Wisewoman and medicine man', in J. Mitchell and A. Oakley (ed.), *The Rights and Wrongs of Women*, Penguin

O'Brien, J. (1971), *Women's Liberation in Labour History: A case study from Nottingham*, Spokesman pamphlet no. 24, Russell Press, Nottingham

O'Laughlin, B. (1974), 'Mediation of contradiction: why Mbum women do not eat chicken', in M. Z. Rosaldo, and L. Lampher (ed.), *Women, Culture and Society*, Stanford University Press, Stanford

O'Laughlin, B. (1977), 'Production and reproduction: Meillassoux's *Femmes, greniers et capitaux*', *Critique of Anthropology*, vol. 2, no. 8

Parker, H. J. (1974), *View from the Boys*, David & Charles
Patrick, J. (1973), *A Glasgow Gang Observed*, Eyre Methuen
Pindar, P. (1969), *Women at Work*, vol. 35, Broadsheet 512
Plummer, K. (1975), *Sexual Stigma*, Routledge & Kegan Paul
Political Economy of Women Group (1975), *On the Political Economy of Women*, CSE Pamphlet 2, Stage 1, London

Rapoport, R., and Rapoport, R. N. (1971), *Dual Career Families*, Penguin
Red Collective (1971), *Politics of Sexuality in Capitalism*
Reich, W. (1972), 'Dialectical materialism and psychoanalysis', in *Sex-Pol Essays*, Vintage Books, New York
Rey, P. P. (1975), 'The lineage mode of production', *Critique of Anthropology*, no. 3
Rowbotham, S. (1969), *Women's Liberation and the New Politics*, Spokesman pamphlet no. 17, Russell Press, Nottingham
Rowbotham, S. (1972), 'The beginnings of Women's Liberation in Britain', in M. Wandor (ed.), *The Body Politic*, Stage 1, London
Rowbotham, S. (1973), *Woman's Consciousness, Man's World*, Penguin
Rowbotham, S. (1974), *Hidden from History*, Pluto
Rowbotham, S. (1977), 'Leninism in the lurch', *Red Rag*, no. 12
Rubin, G. (1975), 'The traffic in women: notes on the "political economy" of sex', in R. Reiter (ed.), *Toward an Anthropology of Women*, Monthly Review Press, New York

Sachs, K. (1974), 'Engels revisited: women, the organization of production and private property', in M. Z. Rosaldo and L. Lampher (ed.), *Woman, Culture and Society*, Stanford University Press, Stanford
Scott-James, A. (1971), 'Why women don't have babies', in T. Hopkinson (ed.), *Picture Post 1938-50*, Penguin
Seccombe, W. (1974), 'The housewife and her labour under capitalism', *New Left Review*, no. 83
Seccombe, W. (1975), 'Domestic labour - a reply', *New Left Review*, no. 94
Sharpe, S. (1972), 'The role of the nuclear family in the oppression of women', *New Edinburgh Review*, summer
Sharpe, S. (1976), *Just Like a Girl: How Girls Learn to be Women*, Penguin
Slater, E., and Woodside, M. (1951), *Patterns of Marriage*, Cassel
Smith, Linda (1974), 'Working Women's Charter', in S. Allen, L. Sanders, and J. Wallis (ed.), *Conditions of Illusion*, Feminist Books, Leeds

Solanas, V. (1971), SCUM (Society for Cutting Up Men) *Manifesto*, Olympia, New York

Taylor, J. (1975/76) review of B. Hindess and P. Q. Hirst, *Pre-Capitalist Modes of Production*, in *Critique of Anthropology*, nos. 4/5 and 6
Terray, E. (1972), *Marxism and 'Primitive Societies'*, Monthly Review Press, New York
Thompson, E. P. (1970), *The Making of the English Working Class*, Penguin
Titmuss, R. (1963), 'The position of women, some vital statistics', in R. Titmuss, *Essays on the 'Welfare State'*, Allen & Unwin
Toynbee, P. (1977), 'At the end of the happy ever after trail', *Guardian*, 21 June
Trodd, F. (1974), 'Some facts about equal pay', in S. Allen, L. Sanders, and J. Wallis (ed.), *Conditions of Illusion*, Feminist Books, Leeds
Tufnell Park Group (1971), 'Organising ourselves', in M. Wandor (ed.), *The Body Politic*, Stage 1, London

Venn, C. (1977), 'Women's exile, interview with Luce Irigary', *Ideology and Consciousness*, no. 1

Wandor, M. (1972a), (ed.), *The Body Politic: Women's Liberation in Britain 1969-72*, Stage 1, London
Wandor, M. (1972b), 'The small group', in M. Wandor (ed.), *The Body Politic*, Stage 1, London
Weinbaum, B., and Bridges, A. (1976), 'The other side of the paycheck: monopoly capital and the structure of consumption', *Monthly Review*, vol. 28, no. 3
Weir, A. (1974), 'The family, social work and the welfare state', in S. Allen, L. Sanders and J. Wallis (ed.), *Conditions of Illusion*, Feminist Books, Leeds
White, A. (1977), *Exposition and Critique of Julia Kristeva*, Stencilled occasional paper, Centre for Contemporary Cultural Studies, University of Birmingham
White, C. (1970), *Women's Magazines 1963-1968: A Sociological Study*, Michael Joseph
White, C. (1977), *Royal Commission on the Press: The Women's Periodical Press in Britain 1946-76*, Working Paper no. 4, HMSO
Whiting, P. (1972), 'Female sexuality: its political implications', in M. Wandor (ed.), *The Body Politic*, Stage 1, London
Wilden, A. (1972), *System and Structure*, Tavistock
Williams, J. (1969), 'Peckham Rye Women's Liberation', *Shrew*, August
Williams, R. (1961), *The Long Revolution*, Penguin
Williams, R. (1976), *Keywords*, Fontana
Williamson, J. (1978), *Decoding Advertisements*, Boyars
Willis, P. (1977), *Learning to Labour*, Saxon House
Willmott, P. (1969), *Adolescent Boys of East London*, Penguin

Willmott, P., and Young, M. (1964), *Family and Kinship in East London*, Penguin
Willmott, P., and Young, M. (1973), *The Symmetrical Family*, Routledge & Kegan Paul
Wilson, E. (1974a), 'Gayness and Liberalism', *Red Rag*, no. 6
Wilson, E. (1974b), *Women and the Welfare State, Red Rag*, pamphlet no. 2
Wilson, E. (1977), *Women and the Welfare State*, Tavistock
Wise, A. (1972), *Women and the Struggle for Workers Control*, Spokesman pamphlet no. 33, Russell Press, Nottingham
Wise, A. (1974), 'Trying to stay human', in S. Allen, L. Sanders and J. Wallis (ed.), *Conditions of Illusion*, Feminist Books, Leeds
Wolpe, A. M. (1976), 'The official ideology of education for girls', in J. Alier and M. Flude (ed.), *Educability, Schools and Ideology*,
Women's Liberation Workshop, London (1970), 'Why Miss World?', reprinted as 'Miss World' in M. Wandor (ed.), *The Body Politic*, Stage 1, London
Women's Report Collective (1975), 'Should women study women's studies?', *Women's Report*, vol. 4, no. 2

Young Fabian Pamphlet II (1966), *Womanpower,* Fabian Society
Young, K., and Harris, O. (1976), 'The subordination of women in cross cultural perspectives', in *Papers on Patriarchy*, The Women's Publishing Collective, Brighton

Zaretsky, E. (1976), *Capitalism, the Family and Personal Life*, Pluto

Index

Bold figures indicate pages on which concepts are defined.

abortion, 21, 170, 175
accumulation: of capital, 35, 54, 55, 56-61, 75*n*, 187, 190; of surplus, 162*n*, 174
adolescence, 96-108
advertising, 58, 66, 154*n*
Althusser, L., 80, 109, 120, 126, 128, 135, 137, 163, 171, 175
appropriation: of procreative capacity, 165, 184, 185, **188**, 189; of sexuality, 165, 184, 189; of surplus labour, 157, 162, 163, 165, 181, 187, 194; of surplus product, 157

Beechey, V., 60, 62-3, 77*n*, 169, 172, 190
best friends, 87, 98, 106-7
biologism, 110, 117-18
boyfriends, 98, 106-7
Braverman, H., 75*n*, 77*n*
breadwinners, men as, 64-5
Bruley, S., 33

Capital, 56-7, 62-4, 155, 156, 173, 174
capital: accumulation of, 35, 54, 55, 56-61, 76*n*, 155; capital commodities, 41, 56, 58, 134, 138, 145; circulation of, 56, 58; competition of capital(s), 56, 59; expansion/diversification of, 55-8; labour power, 42 (*see also* labour power); moment of consumption, 61; surplus value, 41 (*see also* surplus value)
capitalism, 67
child-care, 21, 67, 80, 85, 90-1, 134

class: girls and, 96, 99-106; women and, 37, 85, 156*n*, 165, 177, 181, 186, 187, 190, 193
Comer, L., 21
companionship, 82, 84-5, 86, 87
condensation and displacement, 114, 133, 148, 149, 152-3*n*
Conditions of Illusion, 34*n*
consciousness-raising, 12, 28, 30
consumers, women as, 22, 55, 76*n*, 133, 134, 145-6
consumption, 56, 57, 61
contraception, 21, 98, 170
contradiction, 67, 71; mediation of contradiction(s), 161, 192, 193
cosmetics, 22, 104, 133, 134, 146
culture, of femininity, 20, 96-108

Dalla Costa, M., and James, S., 37, 45
Davidoff, L., 20, 44
De Beauvoir, S., 144
demography, 155, 160, 167
dependence, 62; women's on men, 43, 51, 53, 54, 62, 146, 148, 149, 177, 185, 186, 190, 192
de-skilling, 65
discourse, in women's magazines, 139
domestic labour, 36-46, **43**, 55, 87-90, 168, 173, 177, 190, 191 (*see also* housework)
domestic service, 178-9, 191
domestic writing process, 177-9, 191

ecology, 160, 167
Engels, F., 155, 156, 167

entertainment, 138-9
Equal Opportunities Commission, 69
Equal Pay Act, 68-71, 147
equality, 66, 145
everyday life, 29, 136, 141-3, 146
exchange of women, 159, 161, 165, 167

Factory Acts, 49, 190
family, 55, 57, 58, 63, 142, 143-4, 148, 149, 188; economic functions of, 36, 39, 45, 172; girls and, 105-6; ideological functions of, 36, 40, 44, 46, 172; multifunctional role of, 36, 46, 156n; patriarchal structures of, 53, 63, 176; wage, 46, 47, 51, 54, 60, 62, 76n
fantasy/reality, 139-40, 145, 146, 148
fashion, 145
feminine independence, 136
femininity, 55, 64-6, 92, 133-52; in relation to masculinity, 64-6, 111, 116, 129, 134, 136, 137, 148, 149 (*see also* culture of, ideology of)
Figes, E., 117-18
Firestone, S., 72n, 117-18, 144-5
Foreman, A., 41, 46, 47, 119, 175, 190
free individual, 38-9, 136, 137; women as, 145-6, 147, 151-2
Freud, S.: dualism in, 112; on dreams and jokes, 112-14; on language, 112-14; on sexuality, 110n
Friedan, B., 36

Gardiner, J., 37, 38, 40, 73n
Gavron, H., 29, 36
generational reproduction, 80, 90-2 (*see also* child-care)
girls, 96-108
Greer, G., 117, 119
Grundrisse, 59-61

hegemony, 164; Gramsci on, 74n; masculine, 29, 74n, 134, 145, 153n
high-rise flats, 86, 87

Hindess, B., and Hirst, P., 155, 161, 170, 171, 174
home, *see* privatized sphere
home workers, 78n
homosexuality, 167
housewives, and their isolation, 79-95
housework, 38, 42, 87-90 (*see also* domestic labour)
husbands, 177, 178

Ideology and Ideological State Apparatuses, 126ff, 129, 175
ideology, general concepts of, 126ff, **135**, 152n, 164
ideology of domesticity, 24, 39, 47, 57, 67, 136, 166, 172, 175n, 192
ideology of family, 76n
ideology of femininity, 39, 67, 124, 128, 135-52, 192; construction of, 133, 136, 192; subdomains of, 136, 192
ideology of motherhood, 36, 50, 136, 138, 148, 166, 171
ideology of patriarchy, 43, 171, 192
ideology of romantic love, 43, 98, 147-51, 166, 175n, 176, 186, 192
ideology of sexuality, 165, 170, 171, 172, 173
ideology of social democracy, 48, 54, 74
immigration policy, 54-5
industrial reserve army, 47, 52, 56, **60-1**, 61-4
inequality, structures of, 67, 70
Irigaray, L., 124

kinship structures, 121ff, 155, 166-7, 170, 171, 172; economic functions of, 157, 158, 160, 168; ideological functions within, 158, 160
Kristeva, J., 123ff

labour, productive and unproductive, 41-3, 73*n*, 74*n*, 178
labour power, 137, 175; cheap, 58-60, 190; lack of freedom to sell, 65, 180; price of, 60, 63; value of, 42, 59, **60**, 63
labour time, 73*n*
Lacan, J., 114ff, 168
language, 113ff, **115**, 116
laughter, 81, 82
Lefebvre, H., 29
leisure, 88, 95*n*, 146, 147
Lévi-Strauss, C., 115, 121-2, 166, 167

machinofacture, 174
Mackintosh, M., 38, 169
Magus, B., Coulson, M., and Wainwright, H., 39, 41, 43
Marcuse, H., 113
marriage, 92, 105-7, 143, 149, 150-1, 177, 182, 184ff, 194
Marx, K., 38-9, 42, 56-7, 59-64, 65, 79, 80, 172, 173, 174, 178-9, 190
Marxism: and feminism, 109, 123, 127, 155-6; and psychoanalysis, 127ff
masculinity, 64-6, 78*n*, 171
means of subsistence, 60, 191
media, women and, 85-6, 95*n*
Meillassoux, C., 157-61, 167, 169, 171
Millet, K., 118, 192, 193
Millum, T., 20
Mitchell, J., 19, 20, 25, 36, 117ff, 137, 168, 189
motherhood, 20, 50, 90-1, 134, 136, 139, 141, 142, 144, 148, 151, 184 (*see also* generational reproduction)

narcissism, 137-8
nature: arguments from, 18-20; natural, 18-20, 143-4, 146, 154*n*; naturalness, 18-20, 31
non-verbal communication, 81, 82
novel, social relations of production of, 173-9, 191

Oakley, A., 72*n*, 85
O'Laughlin, B., 161-6, 168, 169, 173, 174
oppression, women's experience of, 19, 26-30, 79, 85

patriarchal and capitalist relations, articulation of, 35, 46, 48, 61, 62, 64, 66, 134, 136, 137, 176, 187, 190
personal life, 18, 23-6, 28-31, 39, 79-95, 134, 136, 137, 142, 147
phallocentrism, 117, 122
Political Economy of Women Group, 38, 43, 44, 50, 51, 52-3
political level, 157, 160, 169, 171
Pre-Capitalist Modes of Production, 156ff
privatized sphere, 39, 79-95
production: forces of, 157ff, 163, 172, 174, 185; means of, 163, 185; mode of, 156ff, 173, 174; of commodities, 57, 58, 62; of sexed subjects, 168, 169; social relations of, 135, 136, 153*n*, 156-66, 169, 174, 176, 189; women in, 35, 45, 54-66, 190
psychoanalysis, 109ff, 136; and feminism, 117ff; and Marxism, 126ff; universalism of, 109, 125
Psychoanalysis and Feminism, 120ff, 168
psychoanalytic method, 112

Reich, W., 113
representation of women, 133, 146
reproduction: biological, 47, 54, 155, 156, 159, 163, 164, 166, 168; in relation to production, 35, 39, 45, 166, 168; of capital, 56, 61; of labour force, 38, 46-7, 48, 50, 79, 80, 161, 163, 168, **169**, 170, 175, 182; of labour power, 55, 60, 62; of means of production, 163, 164, 175; of social relations of production, 163, 164, 189; of the

reproduction, *cont.*
   individual, 61, 155; relations of, 56, 63, 128-9, 155, **156**, 166, 167, 168-73, 184, 187-91, 193
Revolutionary Communist Group, 61
Rights and Wrongs of Women, 176
Rowbotham, S., 25, 30, 65, 72*n*, 77*n*, 79, 81, 92, 189
Rubin, G., 161, 166-8, 170, 171

schooling, 99-104
Seccombe, W., 43, 45, 58, 73*n*
self-help health groups, 22-3
Sex Discrimination Act, 67
sex/gender: identity, 20, 31, 62, 160, 161, 171, 173; relations, 109, 122, 128, 157, 166, 168
sexual division of labour, 40, **61**, 62, 65, 159, 161, 162, 167, 181
sexuality, 21-2, 23, 56, 58, 64-6, 91, 92, 136, 137, 148; as attractiveness, 63, 136, 137; control of, 31, 44, 51, 165, 192
Sharpe, S., 101-2
Shirley, 176-95
Shrew, 21
social formation, 16, 136-61, 166-7, 168, 169, 171, 186, 189
socialization, 163, 166
state, 46, 54, 58, 64, 157, 190
subjectivity, construction of, 114ff, 123, 127
subordination: patriarchal, 133, 153*n*
   active, 135
surplus value, 73*n*, 76*n*; absolute, 49, 178; relative, 49, **56**, 58-9, 178

surplus women, 177, 180
symbolic: order, 115; readings, 111; representations, 110, 124, 148
symptomatic reading, 110

trade unions, 60, 65ff, 78
transvestism, 167

unconscious, 112ff; patriarchal structure of, 168

vaginal deodorants, 22

welfare state, 46-54, 58, 175; Beveridge report on, 50-1, 175
White, C., 194
Wilson, E., 50, 52, 194
Women's Estate, 25, 189
Women's Liberation Movement, 8, 11, 12, 20ff, 53, 66, 134, 173; exclusion of men, 27; history of, 173
Women's Report Collective, 9
women's studies, 7-17
work: paid, 54-60, 75*n*, 82-5, 146-7, 148, 149; part-time, 52, 60, 63, 64, 69, 70; shift, 86-7, 95*n*; subjective experience of, 66, 82-5; unpaid, housework, 76*n*, 80, 88-90, 137, 145-6 (*see also* domestic labour, production)

youth clubs, girls and, 108

Zaretsky, E., 129*n*; on the isolation of women, 87-8

praxis 3

A Journal of Radical Perspectives on the Arts

Ten Theses on the Failure of Communication in the Plastic Arts *by Kenneth Coutts-Smith*

A Measure of *The Measures Taken:* Zenchiku, Brecht and Idealist Dialectics *by Roger Howard*

Beneficent Roguery: The Detective in the Capitalist City *by John M. Reilly*

Toward a Theory of the Lyric: Georg Lukács and Christopher Caudwell *by Eileen Sypher*

In the Belly of the Monster: The Filipino Revolt in the U.S. *by E. San Juan, Jr.*

My Education *by Carlos Bulosan*

"Be American" *by Carlos Bulosan*

Ideology as Demiurge in Modern Art *by Ferenc Fehér*

Preliminary Notes on the Prison Writings of Gramsci: The Place of Literature in Marxian Theory *by Jean Thibaudeau*

The Theater of Pirandello *by Antonio Gramsci*

Brecht and the Dynamics of Production *by Marc Zimmerman*

The Marxism of Lucien Goldmann in *The Philosophy of the Enlightenment by Norman Rudich*

Visions of Defiance: Work, Political Commitment and Sisterhood in Twenty-One Works of Fiction, 1898-1925 *by Nan Bauer Maglin*

Painting and Ideology: Picasso and *Guernica by Bram Dijkstra*

Salvation and Wisdom of the Common Man: The Theology of *The Reader's Digest by Ariel Dorfman*

The San Francisco Mime Troupe Commemorates the Bicentennial with *False Promises/Nos Engañaron by Theodore Shank*

Single copies for $3.50 and subscriptions (two issues) for $7.00 (add $1.00 outside North America) are available from *Praxis*, P.O. Box 207, Goleta, California 93017 USA. *Praxis* is distributed in the U.K., Europe and the Commonwealth by Pluto Press, Unit 10 Spencer Court, 7 Chalcot Road, London NW1 8LH, England. Bookshop price: £2.20; subscriptions £4.

Critique of Anthropology

Women's Issue (no. 9 & 10) contains:

R. Reiter	The Search for Origins
P. Aaby	Engels and Women
M. Molyneux	Androcentrism in Marxist Anthropology
J. Moore	The Exploitation of Women in Evolutionary Perspective
F. Edholm	
O. Harris	Conceptualising Women
K. Young	
B. Bradby	Research Note: The Non-Valorisation of Women's Labour
V. Goddard	Research Note: Domestic Industry in Naples
A. Whitehead	Book Review: Jack Goody's *Production and Reproduction*
E. Croll	Book Review: Delia Davin's *Woman-Work*

Subscriptions for nos 9-12 (vol. 3)

Individuals	UK £2.50	Overseas: air $7.50 (£4.20); sea $5.75 (£3.20)
Institutions	UK £5.00	Overseas: air $15.00 (£8.35); sea $11.50 (£6.40)

Back numbers 4-8 (including p&p - overseas by air)

4/5 Individuals	UK £2.17	Overseas US $ 5.25
6/7/8	UK £0.76	Overseas US $ 2.00
4/5 Institutions	UK £4.17	Overseas US $10.50
6/7/8	UK £1.21	Overseas US $ 4.00

Subscription forms and requests for back issues should be sent to Critique of Anthropology, PO Box 178, London WC1E 6BU.

Ideology & Consciousness

Investigations in theory,
concrete analysis of current practices,
interviews, debates, polemic and correspondence
translations, expositions and reviews of key texts

NO. 3. SPRING 1978
Foucault: Politics
Rossi-Landi: Sign Systems and Social Reproduction
Women in Literature
Critique of Piaget's Psychology.

NO. 1	NO. 2
Psychology, Ideology and the Human Subject	Psychology, Prisons and Ideology
Feminism & The Language of Psychoanalysis	The Theory of Fetishism in Capital
Class, Language and Education	The Unconscious of Psychoanalysis
Vološinov on Marxism and Linguistics	Pêcheux's Theory of Discourse
	Critical Introduction to G.H. Mead

SINGLE COPIES
bookshops — £1.20 ($2.50); **by post** — inland £1.35, overseas surface £1.50 ($3.00), airmail £2.60 ($6.00).

ANNUAL SUBSCRIPTION
(3 issues) inland £3.25, overseas surface £4.00 ($9.00),
airmail £7.75 ($16.00); **student and claimant rate** (inland only) £2.25;
institutional rate £6, overseas surface £8.00 ($17.00)
airmal £11.75 ($24.00).

Payable to **Ideology & Consciousness**,
1 Woburn Mansions, Torrington Place, London W.C.1.

Social History

EDITED BY JANET BLACKMAN AND KEITH NIELD,
Department of Economic and Social History,
University of Hull

Social history has become the focus of great interest in the study of history. The purpose of this new journal is to contribute to the definition and development of social history through articles, discussions and critical reviews.

Social History seeks to be international in content, to cover all periods, and to pursue the exploration of relations with other disciplines, especially sociology, social anthropology, demography and development studies, which increasingly seek historical perspectives.

'*Social History* has without a doubt immediately established itself as enormously superior to all English-language journals in the field, with the possible exception of *Past and Present.*'

Times Educational Supplement

£1.75

Subscription Rates for 1977

Individuals (UK) £9.95 per annum
Institutions (UK) £13.50 per annum
Individuals (Overseas) £12.25 per annum
Institutions (Overseas) £16.50 per annum
Frequency: January, May and October

METHUEN, 11 New Fetter Lane, London EC4P 4EE

Radical Science Journal

No. 6 £1.00

Editorial – Science and the Labour Process
Critiques:
Les **Levidow** – A Marxist Critique of the IQ Debate
Michael **Barnett** – Technology and the Labour Process
Bob **Young** – Getting Started on the Lysenko Affair
RSJ **Subgroup** – Marxism, Psychoanalysis and Feminism
Reviews: Technology of Political Control; Sabotage/Industrial Conflict; Television/Technology and Cultural Form; Sociology of Knowledge; Essays in Self-Criticism.

No. 5 still available £1.00 136 pages

David **Triesman** – The Institute of Psychiatry Sackings: Ideology, 'Science', and the Organised Scientific Worker; Patrick **Parrinder** – The Black Wave; Science and the Social Consciousness in Modern Science Fiction; Gavin **Browning** – Notes from a Sci-Fi Freak; Bob **Young** – Science *is* Social Relations; Loup **Verlet** – La course ou la vie.

Subscription: £3.00 (individual), £9.00 (institutional) for 3 issues post paid. Individual copies: please add 20p each for postage, etc. Bulk orders: one-third reduction on 10 or more copies.

Radical Science Journal, 9 Poland Street, London W1V 3DG

Centre for Contemporary Cultural Studies   stencilled occasional papers at July 1977

1	Stuart Hall: A 'Reading' of Marx's 1857 *Introduction* to *The Grundrisse*	25p
2	Adrian Mellor: Theories of Social Satisfaction	25p
3	Richard Johnson: The Blue Books and Education, 1816–1896	25p
4	Stuart Hall: External Influences on Broadcasting	25p
5	Stuart Hall: The 'Structured Communication' of Events	25p
6	Roland Barthes: Introduction of Structural Analysis of the Narrative	25p
7	Stuart Hall: Encoding and Decoding in the TV Discourse	25p
8	Dave Morley: Industrial Conflict and Mass Media	20p
9	Dave Morley: Reconceptualising the Media Audience	25p
10	Marina Heck: The Ideological Dimension of Media Messages	20p
11	Stuart Hall: Deviancy, Politics and the Media	25p
12	Bryn Jones: The Politics of Popular Culture	20p
13	Paul Willis: Symbolism & Practice: The Social Meaning of Pop Music	25p
14	Clarke & Jefferson: Politics of Popular Culture: Cultures & subcultures	20p
16	Stuart Hall: The Hippies – an American 'Moment'	25p
17	Jefferson & Clarke: 'Down These Mean Streets' – the Meaning of Mugging	20p
18	Clarke & Jefferson: Working Class Youth Cultures	20p
19	Paul Willis: Performance and Meaning: Women in Sport	25p
20	Dick Hebdidge: The Style of the Mods	20p
21	Dick Hebdidge: The Kray Twins: Study of a System of Closure	25p
22	Tony Jefferson: The Teds: a Political Resurrection	20p
23	John Clarke: The Skinheads and the Study of Youth Culture	20p
24	Dick Hebdidge: Reggae Rastas & Rudies: Style and the Subversion of Form	25p
25	Dick Hebdidge: Sub-cultural Conflict & Criminal Performance in Fulham	25p
26	Richard Johnson: Peculiarities of the English Route	25p
27	Paul Willis: Transition from School to Work Bibliography	15p
28	Brian Roberts: Parent and Youth Cultures	20p
29	C. Critcher: Football since the War: Study in Social Change & Popular Culture	25p
30	Andrew Tolson: The Family in a 'Permissive Society'	15p
31	Butcher, Coward *et al*: Images of Women in the Media	25p
32	John Clarke: Framing the Arts: the role of the Cultural Institution	20p
33	Paul Willis: Human Experience & Material Production: Shop Floor Culture	25p
34	Stuart Hall: TV as a Medium and its Relation to Culture	25p
35	Jefferson *et al*: Mugging and Law 'n' Order	45p
37	Clarke, Critcher *et al*: Newsmaking & Crime (paper given at NACRO Conference)	25p
38	Paul Willis: The Main Reality: Transition School/Work: SSRC Report	40p
39	Critcher *et al*: Race & The Provincial Press – report to UNESCO	45p
40	Pam Taylor: Women Domestic Servants, 1919–1939	25p
41	John Clarke: The Three Rs – Repression, Rescue & Rehabilitation: Ideologies of control for working class youth	25p
42	John Clarke: Football Hooliganism and the Skinheads	25p
43	Paul Willis: How Working Class Kids get Working Class Jobs	10p
44	Fieldwork Group: Critique of Community Studies & its Role in Social Thought	20p
45	Greg McLennan: Some Problems in Marxist Historiography	25p
46	Richard Nice: Translation of Pierre Bourdieu, *The Culture Field and The Economic Field*	25p
47	Michael Green: Issues & Problems in the Decentralising of Cultural Planning	25p
48	Roy Peters: Sport in TV – 1976 Olympics	20p
49	Allon White: Exposition & Critique of Julia Kristeva	30p

CCCS pamphlet No. 1

Roger Grimshaw & Paul Lester: The Meaning of the Loch Ness Monster   40p

HQ1597 .B56 1978

WITHDRAWN
From Bertrand Library

DATE DUE			
JUN 2 3 1987			
MAY 1 9 '88			
AUG 3 1 1989			
ILL 2497322			
AUG 3 1 1993			
MAR 0 8 1994			
JUL 3 1 1996			
MAY 1 6 2000			
GAYLORD			PRINTED IN U.S.A.